Creative
LEADERSHIP

Jay,

Best of luck with
your creativity initiatives
at NJIT.

Howard

This book is dedicated to the leadership and vision of three people who continue to inspire us to lead and create:

Alex F. Osborn, who envisaged and developed the Creative Problem Solving process and whose vision to bring a more creative trend to education led the way in the development of deliberate creativity, and Sidney J. Parnes, who along with Ruth B. Noller articulated and implemented Osborn's vision with skill and passion.

We are humbled to have been the recipients of their efforts.

Creative LEADERSHIP

SKILLS THAT DRIVE CHANGE

Gerard J. Puccio
State University College at Buffalo

Mary C. Murdock
State University College at Buffalo

Marie Mance
State University College at Buffalo

SAGE Publications
Thousand Oaks ▪ London ▪ New Delhi

For information:

Sage Publications, Inc.
2455 Teller Road
Thousand Oaks, California 91320
E-mail: order@sagepub.com

Sage Publications Ltd.
1 Oliver's Yard
55 City Road
London EC1Y 1SP
United Kingdom

Sage Publications India Pvt. Ltd.
B-42, Panchsheel Enclave
Post Box 4109
New Delhi 110 017 India

Printed in the United States of America

Library of Congress Cataloging-in-Publication Data

Puccio, Gerard J.
Creative leadership: Skills that drive change / Gerard J. Puccio, Mary C. Murdock, Marie Mance.
    p. cm.
Includes bibliographical references and index.
ISBN 1-4129-1379-9 (cloth: alk. paper)
ISBN 1-4129-1380-2 (pbk.: alk. paper)
    1. Leadership. 2. Creative ability in business. I. Murdock, Mary.
II. Mance, Marie. III. Title.
HD57.7.P83 2007
658.4'092—sdc22   2006010667

This book is printed on acid-free paper.

06 07 08 09 10 10 9 8 7 6 5 4 3 2 1

Acquisitions Editor:	Al Bruckner
Editorial Assistant:	MaryAnn Vail
Production Editor:	Diane S. Foster
Copy Editor:	Diana Breti
Typesetter:	C&M Digitals (P) Ltd.
Proofreader:	Olivia Weber
Indexer:	Molly Hall
Cover Designer:	Candice Harman

Contents

Acknowledgments

M ax De Pree (1989), in *Leadership Is an Art*, noted, "The first responsibility of a leader is to define reality. The last is to say thank you. In between, the leader is a servant" (p. 9).

As we look back on the tasks involved in writing this book, there are many people who supported our vision of the importance of creativity to leadership to whom we owe a sincere thank-you.

Sarah Thurber and Justin Hall brought a sophisticated understanding of the dynamic nature of CPS and talent in graphic design to bear in bringing the Thinking Skills Model alive visually. Sarah developed the initial idea, and Justin refined it based on our feedback through *many* versions. Cory Wright used his own considerable creative skills to research and write the case studies. Meg Quinn at the Theatre of Youth and Shari Rife at Rich Products, as well as the folks at IDEO, were all gracious and cooperative in helping Cory to articulate the essence of their creativity and leadership. Both Peter Pellegrino of EDS and Tim Switalski of Darwin Associates added their special practitioner's touch by sharing their real-world experiences in elaborated examples.

Many of our current students and alumni also shared their experiences with CPS and creativity, listened to our ideas, gave us honest and useful feedback, and provided encouragement from their various professional vantage points. We are grateful for such an informed and articulate network.

Our colleagues at ICSC took our constant absorption with this book with humor, gave excellent feedback, and listened to us drone on and on long after their professional obligation to do so was over. We appreciate their unconditional support and expert comments and celebrate the creative climate in our workplace that both faculty and students contribute to so unselfishly.

We especially appreciate our reviewers, who took the time to give such detailed, thoughtful, and honest feedback on our drafts. What an amazing collegial gift. Our editor at Sage, Al Bruckner, was also supportive and patient. His encouragement and enthusiasm gave us the energy to create. MaryAnn Vail, Senior Editorial Assistant, provided us with useful information and an infinite amount of patience as we worked through this book project. At Buffalo State we had the editorial help of Janice Troutman and Cara Angie from the Office of Strategic Planning for proofing, and Debi Johnson from the Creative Studies Department compiled the reference list.

A special thanks to our families, who put up with this chaos for three years and who will be there waiting to celebrate with us when we finally get our lives back. (We will get our lives back, right?)

And finally, just a word to acknowledge the fascinating and humbling journey we had working together. We didn't get to skip a thing—ego struggles, humor, aggravation, joy, excitement, intellectual push and pull, exhaustion, discovery, stress, style differences, climate influences. And along the way, we learned all over again that creativity and leadership are our passions and that teaching and learning are our ways of being committed to change.

Gerard J. Puccio
Mary C. Murdock
Marie Mance

Introduction

C hange. Leadership. Creativity. How much thought have you given to these three words, particularly as they influence success in your life? All three have a great impact on your personal and professional success, so to what degree have you mastered change, leadership, and creativity? We imagine that most readers have a fair amount of experience when it comes to change, as we live in a fast-paced, ever-changing world. To be honest, this isn't exactly news. More than 2,000 years ago, the Greek philosopher Heraclitus observed, "There is nothing permanent except change." To understand the degree to which change plays a role in our lives, let's put his statement into context. In the 2,000 years before Heraclitus there was a grand total of ten technical and social inventions (e.g., irrigation systems, number systems, coinage) that had a major impact on history, while in the last 200 years alone there have been 25 technical and social inventions (e.g., airplanes, antibiotics, cloning, computers, credit cards, Internet) that have dramatically altered human history (Henry, 2001). It's no wonder people have made the comment that the pace of change has increased exponentially.

Leadership has also been a fairly popular topic to write about, and more recent books have even connected change and leadership under the topic of change leadership. It is natural for change and leadership to be linked because leadership efforts are often the catalyst for change, and it is effective leadership that helps teams, organizations, and communities respond to change. Leadership is obviously a critical factor when it comes to managing and inspiring change. Yet there is a missing ingredient, one that is so important that without it there would be much less change in our world. We refer to creativity, a unique human characteristic that allows us to imagine and then to create the kind of world we live and work in. Change originates in creative thought, and the ability to engage in creative thinking or foster it in others is a skill that separates those who lead from those who follow.

Effective leaders embody the spirit of creativity. As a result, they use flexible and adaptive thinking to proactively introduce change and to productively respond to external sources of change. Creative thinking is the fuel that makes leadership work. The purpose of this book is to make a deliberate connection between creativity and leadership. Toward that end, we have leveraged the more than 50 years of research and practice in the field of creativity in the service of developing effective leaders. This is not a book about creativity theory. There are many good books that explore the nature of creativity (e.g., Gardner, 1993; Stein, 1974, 1975; Sternberg, 1999). This is not a "how to be more creative" book. There are many books that offer techniques to help individuals and teams become more creative (e.g., Michalko, 1991; Nierenberg, 1996; Van Gundy, 1992; von Oech, 1998). This is not a book that attempts to describe the nature of leadership. The marketplace is full of books that describe what it takes to be an effective leader (e.g., Bass, 1990, 1998; Gardner, 1990; Goleman, Boyatzis, & McKee, 2002; Hesselbein, Goldsmith, & Beckhard, 1996; Kouzes & Posner, 1995).

Rather, this book is about creative thinking as a core leadership competence, and, as such, it contains many proven creativity strategies, principles, and approaches to develop this competence. This is a guidebook designed to help you enhance your creative talents and employ these skills as a leader—a book designed to provide a concrete set of principles and procedures based in creativity that, once internalized, will forever change how you lead. To that end, this book is based on five tenets. These premises are explicitly and implicitly woven throughout this book. Before delving into the content, we want to be clear about the assertions on which this book is founded.

1. Creativity is a process that leads to change; you don't get deliberate change without it.

2. Leaders help the individuals and organizations they influence to grow by deliberately facilitating productive change.

3. Because leaders bring about change, creativity is a core leadership competence.

4. An individual's ability to think creatively and to facilitate creative thinking in others can be enhanced.

5. As individuals develop their creative thinking and master those factors that promote creativity, they positively impact their leadership effectiveness.

❖ WHO SHOULD READ THIS BOOK?

If you are reading this book, then it is meant for you. This statement might surprise some readers. They might not believe they are creative or that they are leaders. On the contrary, everyone has the capacity to be creative in varying degrees and to imagine new possibilities. And we believe everyone has the ability to lead.

Some would say, "But I am not a leader. I'm not in a leadership position." We counter this view by pointing out that the heart of leadership is influencing others. As Mumford and his colleagues noted, "Few of us would dispute the point that leaders exercise influence, taking actions that, in one way or another, shape the behavior of others" (Mumford, Zaccaro, Harding, Jacobs, & Fleishman, 2000, p. 12). It is erroneous to assume that you must be in a formal leadership position to make a difference. To varying degrees, depending on the circumstances, everyone has the capacity to influence others through their attitudes and behaviors, no matter what their position in the organization or community. Sometimes this influence takes a positive form. Someone takes the initiative to solve a problem or to facilitate the implementation of a new idea. However, sometimes people exhibit more negative forms of influence. They impede a change initiative or their actions contribute to a negative work environment. This book is intended for those who wish to have a positive influence by bringing about productive change and responding creatively to problems.

More and more, creativity is recognized as a force that drives our economy and impacts all aspects of our lives. As Richard Florida (2002), an economist from Carnegie Mellon University, observed,

> We are embarking on an age of pervasive creativity that permeates all sectors of the economy and society—not just seeing bursts of innovation from high-tech industries. We are truly in the midst of a creative transformation with the onset of a Creative Economy. (p. 56)

Given the breadth of impact creativity has on our lives, we believe that the creativity skills described in this book are not limited to leaders found in a particular sector. Rather the principles and procedures presented in this book are applicable to all types of organizations, from private corporations to schools, from community action groups to health care agencies, from not-for-profit agencies to advertising firms, from small start-up companies to multinational corporations.

The degree to which readers will benefit from this book will vary from person to person. A critical factor that will determine the extent to which the principles and procedures in this book become internalized is *motivation*. Those who are driven to make a difference by utilizing their creative thinking to bring about change are in the best position to immediately apply the content of this book. Ask yourself, "Am I interested in changing the status quo of my team, organization, or community? Do I want to make a difference in how people think or act in any of these groups by introducing new, fresh thinking? Do I regularly encounter problems for which there are no obvious solutions? Am I directly responsible for implementing new ideas or actions? Do I have ideas and skills that would help others to implement change? Do I see ways to improve current levels of performance? Do I need to out-think my competition? Am I currently in the midst of personal or professional change and need to successfully negotiate my way through it? Have I been left to pick up the pieces of a change that was begun by someone else?" If the answer is yes to any of these questions, then you are in a good position to adopt the creativity principles and procedures contained in this book and, as a result, take your leadership skills to the next level.

❖ HOW THIS BOOK IS DIFFERENT: TAKING A CREATIVE APPROACH TO LEADERSHIP

Let us describe briefly why this book is different. At its core is a unique, and we believe useful, perspective—deliberate creativity. By **deliberate creativity** we mean *taking a proactive approach toward the production of novel and useful ideas that address a predicament or opportunity*. As creativity professionals working at the International Center for Studies in Creativity, Buffalo State College, State University of New York, we have learned much about deliberate creativity by studying it in individuals and groups, teaching creativity skills to graduate and undergraduate students, providing training in the private and public sectors, and facilitating creative problem-solving efforts within a diverse set of organizations (e.g., manufacturing, health service, government, consumer goods, telecommunications, education). From these rich experiences two specific observations emerged that led to the development of this book.

First, we work with graduate students who come from many different professional backgrounds—managers, consultants, teachers, school administrators, engineers, nurses, marketing professionals, social workers, and so on. When we teach and train them in creativity theories, models, and strategies, we find that in very clear and profound ways we are also developing their leadership skills. In a qualitative analysis of the impact of our graduate curriculum, Pinker (2002) found that leadership development was one of the key growth areas identified by our alumni. Our adult learners regularly report, and those they work with frequently observe, that they become different kinds of leaders after gaining depth and breadth in the content of creativity. Learners report the following:

- They have a greater sense of competence when dealing with change and they are more likely to introduce change into other settings.
- They are more confident in dealing with professional and personal challenges.
- They are more competent in facilitating others through a creative change process.
- They conduct meetings that engage the best thinking of all participants.
- They think more strategically.

Second, when we examined the current leadership literature through a creativity lens, we saw numerous explicit and implicit relationships between these two areas. For example, we hold that when you closely examine the qualities used to describe an effective leader, you often see characteristics and practices associated with someone who is highly creative. When you examine best practice in leadership, you see behavioral descriptors that cross over into explicit creative processes or creativity skills. The actions leaders take to foster the psychological conditions that help individuals and teams to grow and to be productive closely parallel key concepts that constitute a creative climate in the workplace.

This link between creativity and leadership became even clearer to us when we specifically examined various authors' descriptions of change leadership. We suggest that the concept of change draws an inextricable bond between leadership and creativity. For example, Karp (1996) described a change leader as

the person who wants the change to happen and is in a position to work with the group to make it happen. The role of the change leader is to provide a process that will facilitate a specific change easily and effectively. (p. 44)

Karp's description presents a change leader as someone who facilitates a process that results in something different. We would argue that such a result is a creative act; and indeed, the most popular view of creativity among researchers and writers in the field is that creativity is a process that leads to the production of original ideas that respond to a perceived problem or opportunity. As Talbot (1997) succinctly put it, creativity is "making a change that sticks (for a while)" (p. 181).

If we juxtapose change leadership with creativity, the issue of change is the essence of both. A leader often acts as a catalyst for change, while creative thinking is a process that leads to change. Further, we have found that the deliberate use of creative thinking provides a set of principles and procedures that enhances a leader's ability both to foster change and to respond to it. In short, the ability to successfully manage the creative process must be one of the core competencies of leadership.

These similarities led us to identify our creativity work with leadership. We define **leadership** as *the process of positively influencing people, contexts, and outcomes through a deliberate creative approach that is applied to open-ended, novel, and ambiguous problems—both opportunities and predicaments.* Building on this definition, and explicitly considering the kinds of creativity skills that enhance a leader's influence, we offer the following list of characteristics of an effective leader. Leaders who have mastered the core competence of creativity do the following:

- Understand the need for creative thinking in today's complex workplace and therefore seek creativity with intent
- Improve group performance through the use of a creative process that reduces friction among individuals and promotes imaginative thought
- Balance their well-developed ability to generate many diverse and original ideas with an ability to identify, refine, and implement those ideas that have the most promise
- Live and practice principles of creative thinking that enable them to respond flexibly and creatively to change
- Diagnose complex situations and design process plans that effectively respond to those various scenarios
- Create a compelling vision focused on attaining a productive opportunity and possess the foresight to identify the most significant challenges that must be addressed to achieve the vision
- Produce original ideas that are then transformed through affirmative evaluation into workable solutions

- Overcome resistance to change by creating implementation plans that proactively address barriers and enlist sources of support
- Understand the diverse ways in which people express their talents and are able to use this knowledge to more effectively draw out the creativity of others
- Foster a work climate that stimulates and draws maximum potential from every individual
- Employ creative thinking to carry out a diverse range of professional responsibilities and activities

If the skills described above appeal to you, then read on. The chapters in this book were written with these very skills in mind. In fact, it is these skills that provide the framework for this book. The chapters in Part I of this book provide the theoretical foundation for the link between creativity and leadership. While Part I is more conceptual, the chapters in Part II present practical process tools designed to assist leaders in developing their own and others' creativity skills. Part III will introduce you to concepts beyond the creative process that we believe leaders need to be aware of to facilitate creative thinking (e.g., psychological diversity, creative climate). Finally, there are case studies in the Case Studies section that illustrate applications of creativity in leadership.

Let's face it, change is here to stay. You have three choices when it comes to change: lead it, accept it, or avoid it. This book is for those who choose to lead it.

PART I

Foundational Principles
for Leaders

1

Change, Leadership, and Creativity

The Powerful Connection

Chapter at a Glance

What is the relationship between change, leadership, and creativity? How do these three concepts mutually support one another? Can you imagine a leader who is effective at introducing change but who is not creative? The purpose of this chapter is to examine more closely the three basic pillars of this book—change, leadership, and creativity. To that end, we provide some basic descriptions of these concepts and highlight the degree to which change, leadership, and creativity intertwine like the strands of a rope.

The chapter begins with a description of change, a concept we believe forms a bond between creativity and leadership. We then examine some contemporary descriptions of leadership that highlight a connection to creativity. This chapter concludes with a review of some definitions, views, and characteristics of creativity.

❖ CREATIVE CHANGE: IT'S NOT CHANGING THE BABY

To quote from Heraclitus again, "You can never step in the same river twice." In that respect, whether you are making something that wasn't there before or responding to what is already new or different, "change" is a constant process. The water looks the same, but it is different. In actuality, life and the conditions that surround it are always in motion. For example, as a natural phenomenon, your body is always changing, and this change will occur whether you want it to or not. Did you know that because the replacement of cells in your body is an ongoing process, you actually have a new liver every six weeks and a new skeleton every three months?

In its broadest sweep there are two kinds of change. First, there is change that exists naturally and is ongoing or cyclic. For example, the sun rises and sets, seasons come and go, and your body changes and grows. Second, there is change that people make either on purpose or in response to what is happening around them. Some examples of this kind of change are changing jobs, changing your mind, changing the way you do things—the order, the purpose, the method.

In the case of the former, change is a natural phenomenon. In the case of the latter, change may be equally "natural," but it has an additional human element. The kind of change that is made on purpose engages your thinking process and thus requires your thinking skills. The main difference is that you apply one more deliberately than the other. In this book, we focus on the kind of change that is introduced more deliberately—that is, intentionally engaging in creative thought to develop yourself and positively influence others.

In the Introduction we shared a definition of creativity developed by organizational psychologist Reginald Talbot (1997). He defined creativity as "making a change that sticks (for a while)" (p. 181). The words in this definition were selected with specific intent. "Making" refers to the fact that creativity is about bringing something into being. It is not enough for people to simply think that they are creative or to merely imagine new possibilities; instead, they must be able to produce both tangible and intangible products.

"Change" refers to the introduction of something new, which can fall anywhere along the continuum from continuous change (i.e., incremental improvement) to discontinuous change (e.g., paradigm breaking). Not all change is creative. It is critical to note that when we refer to change within this definition of creativity, we are not simply talking about an exchange. A change can take place when an existing item is replaced by another already established and known item, such as exchanging a broken part in your car with a functioning part. You can change a flat tire, change your mind, change your clothes, and change the baby, but these are not creative acts. When we refer to change within our definition of creativity, we refer to situations in which an explicit attempt is being made to bring an idea into being that has some degree of novelty.

Finally, the phrase "that sticks" means the creative product or idea has some staying power, which occurs as a result of its serving some need or purpose. However, the "stickiness" or value of the creative product or idea may be temporary, thus the final phrase "for a while." Creative thinking is ongoing, and at some point someone usually comes up with a better or a less expensive way of doing things—thus change is ever-present.

❖ THE LEADERSHIP-CREATIVITY LINK

Our discussion of leadership theories, models, and concepts is organized into three sections. The first section examines views that some writers have put forward to differentiate the concept of leadership from that of management. The second section focuses on conceptions of leadership that have implicit connections with creativity. The third section contains a discussion of contemporary theories of leadership that make direct and explicit statements about the centrality of creativity to leadership.

Using Creativity to Draw Apart Leadership and Management

One popular method for developing an understanding of leadership is to contrast it with the term *management*. Are managers and leaders synonymous in your mind? If not, what differentiates managers from leaders? This comparison has led a number of authors to identify the specific qualities that distinguish leadership from management (e.g., Bennis & Nanus, 1985; Gardner, 1990; Kotter, 1990; Munitz, 1988; Palus & Horth, 2002; Zaleznik, 1977, 1998). In our opinion, it is clear that one construct that distinguishes the concept of leadership from that of management is creativity. Let's take a closer look.

Bennis and Nanus (1985) interviewed 60 successful CEOs and 30 outstanding public sector leaders and found a clear contrast between management and leadership. They reported:

> There is a profound difference between management and leadership, and both are important. "To manage" means "to bring about, to accomplish, to have charge of or responsibility to conduct." "Leading" is "influencing, guiding in direction, course, action, opinion." The distinction is crucial. Managers are people who do things right and leaders are people who do the right things. (p. 21)

Bennis and Nanus summarized their findings by saying that management is driven by efficiency, a focus on mastering routine activities, whereas leadership is motivated by effectiveness. In some cases, the most effective methods for achieving important goals are not the traditional tried-and-true means, but rather new and untested approaches, in other words potentially less efficient methods. The leaders they interviewed were people who created new ideas, policies, and procedures. According to Bennis and Nanus, "they changed the basic metabolism of their organizations" (p. 23).

Zaleznik (1977), who wrote a classic essay on the difference between managers and leaders, noted that leaders are proactive. Rather than simply waiting to react to ideas, leaders are forward thinking; they initiate and shape ideas. Leaders communicate ideas that excite others, and they work with others to develop alternatives for how these future images can be made manifest. Table 1.1 provides a list of distinctions Zaleznik made between managers and leaders. The descriptions associated with the leader contain many terms commonly found in the creativity literature, for example, proactive, seek potential opportunities, seek change, tolerate chaos, avoid premature closure, develop fresh approaches, and so on.

Table 1.1   Contrasting Managers and Leaders

Managers	*Leaders*
• Focus on goals that arise from necessity	• Adopt personal attitude toward goals
• Are reactive, focus on solving problems	• Are proactive, shape ideas
• Ensure day-to-day business is carried out	• Look for potential future opportunities
• Seek order and control	• Tolerate chaos and lack of structure
• Regulate existing order of affairs	• Seek opportunities to bring about change
• Are able to tolerate mundane, practical work	• Inspire subordinates and fire up the creative process with their own energy
• Act to limit choices and coordinate opposing views in order to get solutions accepted	• Avoid premature closure, open issues to new options, and develop fresh approaches to longstanding problems
• Believe "If it ain't broke, don't fix it"	• Believe "When it ain't broke may be the only time you can fix it"

SOURCE: Zaleznik (1977, 1998).

John Kotter (1990), a business professor at Harvard University, described both leadership and management as processes. Kotter maintained that leadership is a process the function of which is to produce change, while management is a process focused on producing consistent outcomes. We would argue that creative thinking is about change. It is the introduction of new ideas and ways of doing things that serves some purpose—to overcome a problem, meet a need, or seize an opportunity. Creative thinking is a process that results in change, while leaders often act as the impetus for change.

We do not wish to create the impression that leadership is better than management or that leaders are more important than managers. To be successful, organizations require both sound management and inspiring leadership. Organizations need to be efficient at doing things right and effective at doing the right things. Fullan (2001) provided an excellent observation about the practice of contrasting leadership and management when he stated,

> I have never been fond of distinguishing between leadership and management: they overlap and you need both qualities. But here is one difference it makes sense to highlight: leadership is needed for problems that do not have easy answers. . . . For these problems there are no once-and-for-all answers. Yet we expect leaders to provide solutions. (p. 2)

In an update to his 1977 essay, Zaleznik (1998) added an addendum that drives home the idea that creativity is a core leadership competence.

> It seems to me that business leaders have much more in common with artists, scientists, and other creative thinkers than they do with managers. For business schools to exploit this commonality of dispositions and interests the curriculum should worry less about the logics of strategy and imposing the constraints of computer exercises and more about thought experiments in the play of creativity and imagination. If they are successful, they would then do a better job of preparing exceptional men and women for positions of leadership. (p. 87)

Some Contemporary Views of Leadership: Implicit Links to Creativity

The extent to which creativity plays a role in leadership is further illustrated by contemporary descriptions of leaders and leadership theories. Many of these descriptions and theories demonstrate implicit connections to creativity; the concepts contained in this work often touch on well-established concepts from the field of creativity. For example, when you scratch the surface of many contemporary descriptions of leadership, what lies underneath are traits and practices associated with creativity. Table 1.2 illustrates some of the overlap between traits commonly connected to creative people and descriptions of effective leaders. The creativity traits were drawn from Davis's (1986) summary of the research into the personalities of highly creative individuals. The first set of leadership qualities comes from a project conducted by the Drucker Foundation (Hesselbein et al., 1996). In this project, consultants, educators, and executives were asked to describe the leader of the future. The middle column summarizes some of the qualities ascribed to effective future leaders. Note the similarities between the leader of the future and past research findings on attributes of a creative person.

The extent to which creativity serves as a core leadership competence is further reinforced by the work of Kotter (1996). Kotter observed that historically, people regarded leadership as a gift granted to the rare few, but that today it is widely accepted that leadership skills can be taught and developed. Kotter went on to identify five specific skills that, when developed, enhance leadership effectiveness. These skills are found in the third column of Table 1.2. As in the Drucker

Table 1.2   Traits of the Creative Person and the Effective Leader

Qualities of Creative People	Qualities of Leaders in the Future	Leadership and Lifelong Learning
• Curious • Energetic • Experimenting • Independent • Industrious • Flexible • Open minded • Original • Playful • Perceptive • Persevering • Questioning • Risk taker • Self-aware • Sensitive	• Seek options, not plans • Look for what is possible • Must be flexible • Pursue vision with intent • Tireless, inventive, observant risk takers who are ever-hopeful builders • Challenge assumptions and paradigms • Empower the talent, intelligence, and creativity of others	• Risk taking • Humble self-reflection • Solicitation of opinions • Careful listening • Openness to new ideas
SOURCE: Davis (1986).	SOURCE: Hesselbein, Goldsmith, & Beckhard (1996).	SOURCE: Kotter (1996).

Table 1.3   Kouzes and Posner's Leadership Practices

- **Challenging the Process** – Looking for innovative ways to improve the organization
  - Search for Opportunities
  - Experiment and Take Risks
- **Inspiring a Shared Vision** – Envisioning the future, creating an ideal image of what the organization can become
  - Envision the Future
  - Enlist Others
- **Enabling Others to Act** – Building spirited teams
  - Foster Collaboration
  - Strengthen Others
- **Modeling the Way** – Establishing principles for how people will be treated and how goals will be pursued
  - Set the Example
  - Achieve Small Wins
- **Encouraging the Heart** – Making people feel like heroes
  - Recognize Contributions
  - Celebrate Accomplishments

SOURCE: Kouzes & Posner (1995).

Foundation list of leadership attributes, Kotter's five skills bear a striking similarity to qualities associated with creative people. Since Kotter suggests these skills can be developed, and because these skills relate directly to creativity, it would seem that creativity training can make a positive contribution to leadership development.

Additional evidence for the link between creativity and leadership goes beyond descriptions of personality traits. For example, Kouzes and Posner's (1995) research on what leaders do to bring about extraordinary results bears a resemblance to known process practices that bring about creative acts. Specifically, when Kouzes and Posner analyzed their data, they found that leaders who were able to facilitate extraordinary accomplishments among their followers tended to engage in five specific behaviors. Kouzes and Posner's five leadership practices are found in Table 1.3. Each leadership practice is followed by two sample strategies.

It is our opinion that the behaviors described by Kouzes and Posner (1995) align with the activities people engage in when involved in the creative process. For example, highly creative people challenge the status quo, take risks, experiment with new approaches, and examine alternative ways of solving problems (i.e., Challenge the Process) (Davis, 1986; MacKinnon, 1978; Torrance, 1979). Highly creative people also focus on future possibilities, daydream about potential outcomes, think in terms of "what if" or "what might be," and are adept at getting others to buy into their ideas (Sternberg & Lubart, 1992; Torrance, 1979). These would appear to be related to Kouzes and Posner's Inspiring a Shared Vision. With respect to Modeling the Way, research in the field of creativity has shown that highly creative individuals had mentors who guided them or paragons who influenced their work (Simonton, 1987). Furthermore, creative acts are more likely to come about when people are highly motivated, particularly when they are passionate about their ideas or have great internal drive (Amabile, 1987). This relates to the practice of Encouraging the Heart. So, once again, there are direct relationships between the fields of leadership and creativity. However, in this case rather than finding similar traits between those who lead and those who create, the kinds of practices leaders engage in to bring about great success correspond with the kinds of practices people engage in when they are being highly creative or inspiring creativity in others.

We are not suggesting that creative people and effective leaders are one and the same. Though the ideas or products developed by successful creative people may ultimately influence others, creative people do not always engage in creative acts that involve others or intentionally seek leadership roles through which they may inspire change. Rather, what we hope to highlight is the fact that in today's complex work and social environments, creativity plays a crucial role in helping leaders to be more effective at facilitating change.

Further evidence for the crucial role creativity now plays in leadership can be found among current leadership theories. Early leadership studies focused on the identification of innate traits associated with individuals who achieved great leadership status. This approach is commonly referred to as "great man" theories of leadership. The underlying assumption was that leaders were born, and as such the key to the identification of successful leaders was to find a stable set of traits that could predict greatness. This line of research did not yield a definitive set of traits; instead, it was found that individuals with certain traits might be successful leaders in one situation but not in other situations (Stogdill, 1948). The failure to find a set of leadership traits led to a shift from a personality-based conception of leadership to a more process-oriented approach—that is, views of leadership began to focus more on the dynamic interplay between the leader and his or her followers.

This transition from a trait to a process approach parallels work in the field of creativity, which began by studying the qualities of eminent creators (Cattell, 1906; Cox, 1926; Ellis, 1904; Galton, 1869) and later broadened to include more process-based descriptions of the creative act (Osborn, 1953; Wallas, 1926). The adoption of more process-oriented views of creativity and leadership represents another conceptual convergence between the two fields. For instance, Northouse's (2004) summary of the main characteristics found across contemporary views of leadership reflects close conceptual links between leadership and creativity. Northouse identified four basic components of leadership: "(a) leadership is a process, (b) leadership involves influence, (c) leadership occurs within a group context, and (d) leadership involves goal attainment" (p. 3). Each of these four elements can be applied readily to creativity. Creativity is commonly described as a process, a process aimed at achieving some goal that as a consequence has a positive influence on the situation. And often the context in which the creative process is carried out is in groups. Given these parallels, it would seem the strategies and tools drawn from the creative process can do much to enhance a leader's ability to guide a group toward a goal.

An example of a leadership approach with implicit connections to creativity is transformational leadership. Though the term originated in the early 1970s (Downton, 1973), there is recent elaboration from a variety of sources (see Avolio, 1999; Bass, 1985, 1998; Tichy & DeVanna, 1990; Yammarino, 1993). Transformational leaders focus on developing others to their fullest potential. Their goal is to change and transform others in a positive way. Transformational leadership enables others to achieve beyond what is expected. Northouse's (2004) description of one of the main characteristics of transformational leadership—intellectual stimulation—provides a direct link to creativity:

It includes leadership that stimulates followers to be creative and innovative, and to challenge their own beliefs and values as well as those of the leader and the organization. This type of leadership supports followers as they try new approaches and develop innovative ways of dealing with organizational issues. It promotes followers' thinking things out on their own and engaging in careful problem solving. (p. 177)

Northouse's comment captures why creativity is central in organizations and how leadership encourages creative thinking.

Changes in organizational structures further support the need for creativity in organizations and for creative leadership. As models of organizations are transformed from the dominant mechanistic view in which management is needed to control by authority, there is a greater call for leadership to emerge (Handy, 1993). Wheatley (1999) observed that the former twentieth-century organizational structures narrowly defined workers and treated them as "replaceable cogs in the machinery of production" (p. 14). Given this view of organizations, tight management was necessary to avoid chaos and inefficiency. Employees did not need to think or to be creative. They simply needed to carry out their tasks as assigned. To survive in today's competitive environment, organizations must find ways to grow through the creative potential found in their workforce. This competitive environment also exists outside of the realm of business. Not-for-profit organizations compete for limited funding; colleges and universities compete for students; professional and community organizations compete for members and volunteers who have little discretionary time to give. Thus, organizations need leaders—such as those described in transformational leadership theories—who can draw on and facilitate the creative talents of others and who, in their own right, embody the spirit of creativity. This applies equally to those individuals in assigned leadership roles as well as to individuals who emerge to take the lead on a particular task or issue.

Direct Connections: Conceptions of Leadership That Place Creativity at the Core

The previous two sections refer to aspects of creativity but do not formally position it as a core construct of effective leadership. Recently, some authors have been more explicit about the centrality of creativity in leadership (Csikszentmihalyi, 2001; Goertz, 2000; Mumford et al., 2000; Sternberg, 2002; Sternberg, Kaufmann, & Pretz, 2004). Indeed, Sternberg and his colleagues use the term "creative leadership" (Sternberg et al., 2004).

Sternberg (2002) began his exploration of creative leadership by describing the specific role intelligence plays in determining successful leadership. The traditional view has been that effective leadership depends on an individual's level of analytic intelligence—an ability to analyze and evaluate existing ideas and systems. Sternberg, however, suggested that effective leadership relies on successful intelligence. He provided the following description of successful intelligence: "People achieve success by recognizing and capitalizing on their strengths and by recognizing and either correcting or compensating for their weaknesses" (p. 10). Though analytic intelligence serves to support successful intelligence, Sternberg has added two further abilities, which have been largely ignored with respect to leadership effectiveness: practical and creative intelligence. Practical intelligence allows people to successfully shape their environments to suit themselves. Creative intelligence allows leaders to form a vision, to decide where they wish to lead others. At the core of creative intelligence is the ability to gain support from others by convincing them that your unpopular ideas have merit.

Sternberg (2002) went on to identify specific kinds of creative leadership. According to Sternberg et al. (2004), creative leadership is about propelling others "from wherever they are to wherever the leader wishes them to go" (p. 146). They suggested three fundamental ways in which creative leadership propels others forward. One type of creative leadership accepts current paradigms but finds ways to extend them. A second type rejects current paradigms and tries to replace them. The third form of creative leadership integrates existing paradigms to create a new one.

These three fundamental forms of creative leadership can be further broken down into eight types of creativity. Table 1.4 summarizes the eight types of creativity described by Sternberg et al. (2004). These authors note that different circumstances call for different forms of creative leadership. For instance, Replication is most appropriate when an organization is successful and the goal is to maintain current status, whereas Forward Incrementation is appropriate when the goal is to achieve progress through continuity.

Where Sternberg and his colleagues described different styles of creative leadership, Mumford et al. (2000) proposed a leadership model that articulates the specific attributes that enable a leader to be successful. Mumford and his colleagues' model is directly related to the major proposition of this book: Creativity is a core competence of leadership and creative problem-solving skills enhance leadership effectiveness. You will discover later that a good portion of this book is dedicated to principles and procedures that are extracted from the Creative Problem Solving process. Indeed, Mumford et al. (2000) argued that creative problem-solving skills are critically important to leadership performance. You will learn more about the Creative Problem Solving process in later chapters. For now, we will close this section by describing Mumford and his colleagues' model.

In contrasting their approach to past theories that attempted to understand leaders through their behaviors (e.g., transformational leadership, theories of behavioral style, leader-member exchange), Mumford et al. (2000) suggested that, "Leadership can be framed not in terms of specific behaviors, but instead in terms of the capabilities, knowledge,

Table 1.4   Sternberg and Colleagues' Forms of Creative Leadership

Eight Types of Creative Leadership	Brief Definition	Example
Accepts Current Paradigm and Attempts to Extend It		
1. Replication	Leadership that attempts to show the field or organization that it is in the right place at the right time	Luthiers who try to reproduce a past musical instrument, such as a Stradivarius
2. Redefinition	Leadership that focuses on showing that a field or organization is in the right place, but not for the reasons that others think it is	Redefining aspirin for its value in preventing heart attacks
3. Forward Incrementation	Leadership that attempts to lead an organization or field forward in the direction it is already going	The introduction of product extension, such as Cheerios with mixed berries
4. Advance Forward Incrementation	Leadership that focuses on moving an organization or field forward, but beyond where others are ready for it to go	Fax machines, which were slow to catch on, at least at first
Rejects Current Paradigm and Attempts to Replace It		
5. Redirection	Leadership that attempts to redirect an organization, field, or product line from where it is heading toward a different direction	The electric razor— the basic cutting mechanisms are the same as a manual razor, but it was taken in a new direction that resulted in quite a different product
6. Reconstruction/ Redirection	Leadership that moves a field, organization, or product line back to where it once was so	American Airlines adding leg room in coach seating, products that represent a return

Eight Types of Creative Leadership	Brief Definition	Example
	that it might move onward from that point, but in a direction different from the one it took from that point onward	to the past (e.g., Bromo-Seltzer or Brill Cream)
7. Re-initiation	Leadership that endeavors to move a field, organization, or product line to a different, as yet unreached starting point and then to move from that point	The first spaceships in comparison to airplanes; products that meet the same need, but in a different way
Integrates Existing Paradigms to Create a New One		
8. Synthesis	Leadership that integrates two ideas that previously were seen as unrelated or even opposed	Seaplanes that combine features from boats and airplanes into one product

SOURCE: Sternberg et al. (2004).

and skills that make effective leadership possible" (p. 12). From this central premise, they developed a theory which holds that leadership performance is directly related to the ability to solve problems.

Figure 1.1 provides our summary of the logical structure of arguments that guided Mumford et al. (2000) from their original contention that leadership can be thought of in terms of capacities to the conclusion that a core leadership capacity is problem solving. These authors are quick to note that the kinds of problems leaders contend with are not of the routine sort. Rather, they are characterized by complexity (e.g., ill-defined problems with no single solution path), novelty (e.g., new or changing situations), and ambiguity (e.g., gaps in information). Thus, Mumford et al. suggested that complex, novel, ambiguous problems cannot be solved through routine solutions, but rather require individuals to reshape and reform their prior knowledge. In short, the problem solving required to be an effective leader must involve creative thinking. These authors concluded, "The skills involved in creative problem solving influence leader performance" (p. 17).

Figure 1.1   Conceptual Underpinnings to the Mumford et al. (2000) Leadership Capacity Model

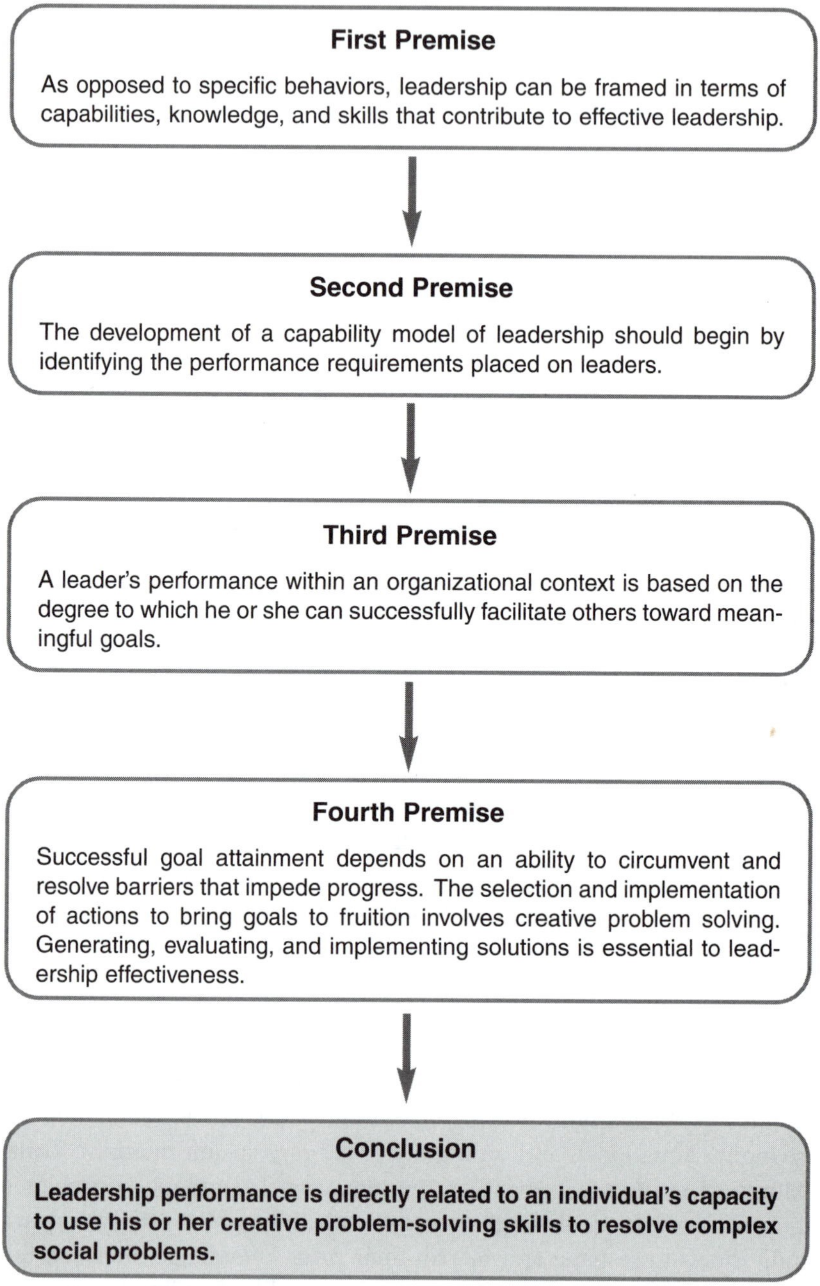

First Premise

As opposed to specific behaviors, leadership can be framed in terms of capabilities, knowledge, and skills that contribute to effective leadership.

Second Premise

The development of a capability model of leadership should begin by identifying the performance requirements placed on leaders.

Third Premise

A leader's performance within an organizational context is based on the degree to which he or she can successfully facilitate others toward meaningful goals.

Fourth Premise

Successful goal attainment depends on an ability to circumvent and resolve barriers that impede progress. The selection and implementation of actions to bring goals to fruition involves creative problem solving. Generating, evaluating, and implementing solutions is essential to leadership effectiveness.

Conclusion

Leadership performance is directly related to an individual's capacity to use his or her creative problem-solving skills to resolve complex social problems.

SOURCE: Mumford et al. (2000).

Figure 1.2   Mumford and Colleagues' Leadership Capacity Model

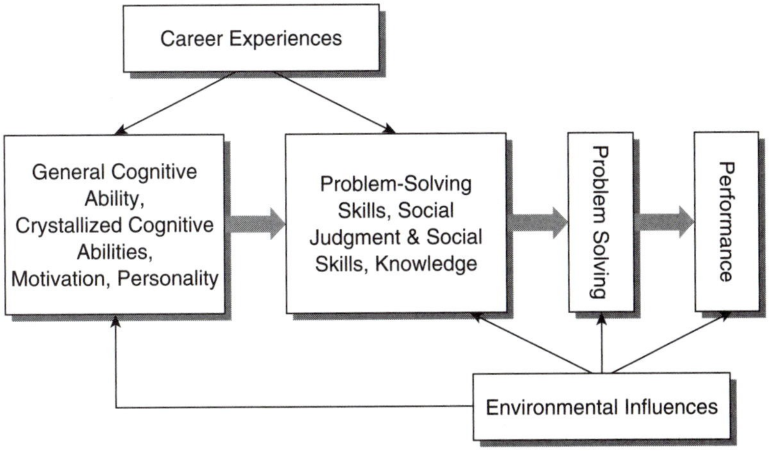

SOURCE: Mumford et al. (2000). Reprinted with permission.

Figure 1.2 presents Mumford and his colleagues' (2000) model. This model is designed to illustrate how specific leadership characteristics determine leadership performance. As already noted, problem solving is predicted to have a direct impact on performance (see right side of the graphic). Again, recall that problem solving in this model refers to an ability to employ creativity to effectively address complex social problems. Three factors contribute to individuals' problem-solving abilities: (1) their problem-solving skills, (2) social judgment and social skills, and (3) knowledge. At the far left of the model are a number of basic attributes that in turn influence an individual's ability to acquire complex problem-solving skills. These attributes are: (a) **general cognitive ability** (*innate abilities, such as intelligence*), (b) **crystallized cognitive abilities** (*abilities that can be developed, such as fluency, speed of closure, divergent thinking*), (c) **motivation** (*willingness to take on complex problems*), and (d) **personality** (*openness, tolerance for ambiguity, curiosity, risk taking, adaptability, etc.*). Although the main thrust of the model focuses on the direct impact personal capabilities have on problem solving and, ultimately, leadership performance, Mumford et al. (2000) do acknowledge the direct and indirect influence of external forces. Thus, Career Experiences and Environmental Influences surround the main facets of the model because they have the potential to affect these person-based components and, in the case of the immediate environment, potentially have a direct effect on leadership performance. People's past career experiences can have a dramatic effect on crystallized cognitive abilities, motivation, knowledge, and problem-solving skills. Finally, opportunities and constraints in the environment can have a direct effect, positive or negative, on all aspects of this model, from the development of the individual attributes found in the left side of the model to leadership performance on the right.

The purpose of this section on leadership was to provide support for the conceptual link between creativity and leadership. We now turn our attention to the concept of creativity.

❖ CREATIVITY: THE NECESSARY FUEL FOR CHANGE

Because our major premise is that what we know about creativity can assist in developing leaders, we will examine what we mean by creativity, including some basic definitions, views, and characteristics of creativity.

Changing Views of Creativity:
From Fringe to Essential Workplace Skill

As creativity professionals, we have noticed that people's views of creativity have changed over the last decade or so. In the early 1990s, when we asked participants in our workshops to describe creativity, it was not uncommon for us to hear comments like: "You have to be eccentric to be creative." "You can't enhance someone's creativity." "Some people have it and some don't." "That's for artists and scientists." "Creativity is unpredictable." "You can't measure it." "It's bizarre." "That's what happens in research and development." "Children are creative." "I'm not creative." To a certain degree, there was a perception that creativity was strange, weird, and uncontrollable.

These past reactions to creativity did not surprise us. As Sternberg and Lubart (1999) put it, notions of creativity have been steeped in mystical beliefs. To the Greeks, the muse or some other external force allowed individuals to create. Davis (1986) indicated that some people believe creativity is a "mysterious mental happening"; ideas seem to come from nowhere and cannot be controlled, and if the creative process is too closely scrutinized there is a risk of damaging it (pp. 50–52).

Today our audiences give us more productive descriptions of creativity. When asked to list words or phrases they associate with creativity, we typically receive responses like "imagination," "problem solving," "risk taking," "challenging the status quo," "being innovative," "necessary for survival," "being adaptable," "creating change," "thinking outside of the box," "being original," "fun," "energizing," "nonlinear thinking," "dynamic," "thinking of possibilities," "invention," and "growth." It is clear to us that there is a greater appreciation of the importance of creativity in all aspects of life. This observation is further supported by the work of Florida (2002), who provided the following explanation of the force behind the accelerated pace of change that has occurred over the last half century:

> The driving force is the rise of human creativity as the key factor in our economy and society. Both at work and in other spheres of our lives, we value creativity more highly than ever, and cultivate it more intensely. The creative impulse—the attribute that distinguishes us, as humans, from other species—is now being let loose on an unprecedented scale. (p. 4)

About the time we began to see a change in how people responded to the word "creativity," there was a study conducted by the American Society of Training and Development (ASTD) that revealed a positive view of creativity. ATSD wanted to find out what skills employers believed were most important in the workplace. Carnevale, Gainer, and Meltzer (1990) conducted an extensive 30-month investigation within organizations across the United States. Their data were gathered from a wide variety of organizations that included health care, manufacturing, service, education, and government. They found that "increasingly, employers have been discovering that their work forces need skills that seem to be in short supply, skills over and above the basic academic triumvirate of reading, writing, and computation" (p. xiii). Analysis of their data generated a list of skill sets believed to be essential in today's workplace. Two of these basic skill sets were creative thinking and problem solving. The full set of workplace skills is found in Table 1.5. In addition to creativity, you will see that leadership is also a skill featured in this list.

The research sponsored by ASTD highlights the perception that creativity is not simply about the arts, but that it is an important skill in the workplace, whether it be government or industry, public or private, for profit or not-for-profit. Furthermore, creativity is a skill that is valuable at all levels of the organization and in all functions. Creativity is not limited to the R&D (research and development) function anymore. Opportunities to solve problems and to engage in breakthrough thinking can and should happen throughout the organization (Henry, 2001; Kuhn, 1988; Van Gundy, 1987; West, 1997).

Table 1.5   Workplace Basics

• The Foundation Knowing how to learn
• Competence Reading, writing, and computation
• Communication Listening and oral communication
• Adaptability Creative thinking and problem solving
• Personal Management Self-esteem, goal setting, motivation, personal and career development
• Group Effectiveness Interpersonal skills, negotiation, teamwork
• Influence Organizational effectiveness and leadership

SOURCE: Carnevale, Gainer, and Meltzer (1990).

Further support for the importance of creativity and related skills is found in the *Wall Street Journal's* recent assessment of business schools. In 2001 the *Wall Street Journal* began to publish the results of recruiters' evaluation of business programs (Alsop, 2001). The survey recruiters used to critique business schools resulted from a year-long consultative process with business school representatives, corporate recruiters, students, search firms, independent consultants, and members of relevant associations. According to Alsop (2001), "the goal was to identify school and student characteristics that recruiters consider most important when they make decisions about which schools to recruit from and which students to recruit" (p. R4). Among the 13 student attributes, four appeared to be directly related to creativity: original and visionary thinking; analytical and problem-solving skills; strategic thinking; and adaptability, which included the ability to deal with ambiguity. The same business school evaluation was conducted in 2002 and 2003 and produced similar results. More recently, the August 1, 2005 issue of *Business Week* featured a special report on creativity (Nussbaum, Berner, & Brady, 2005). One of the main points in this report was that organizations can no longer compete just on cost or quality. In the future, the core competency that will separate successful organizations from those that fail will be creativity.

Defining Creativity: Novelty Made Useful

Thus far we have described how views of creativity have changed over the last decade, but we have not fully delved into what is meant by creativity. Perhaps the most common definition of creativity offered by those in the field of creativity is the production of original ideas that serve some purpose. What is important to note about this definition is that creativity is not synonymous with pure novelty or being different. Being original and being creative are not the same. Rather, creativity is clearly about doing something in an original way that is at the same time useful. Using these two primary features of a creative act—novelty and usefulness—Figure 1.3 presents a simple two-by-two matrix that helps to show what distinguishes creative products from other products or ideas. In this matrix, the upper right quadrant is reserved for those products that have some element of newness and that clearly meet some purpose in a satisfactory way, such as the recent success associated with the Apple iPod. When we say products, we do not limit this to tangible products, but mean to include intangible items such as services, music, ideas, and theories. This is the intent of deliberate creativity: to introduce something that is both new and useful—a creative change.

When something is not new, has no element of originality, yet is highly useful, such as the standard No. 2 pencil, we refer to this as a utilitarian product. In other words, we use it because it does what it was

Figure 1.3   What Makes a Product Creative?

	Low Usefulness	High Usefulness
High Novelty	**Fads** (product disappears when novelty wears off)	**Creative Products** (original and meets a need)
Low Novelty	**Repeating Past Mistakes** (unproductive traditions or habits)	**Utilitarian Products** (product that stands the test of time)

made to do. When we go to the store to purchase a standard No. 2 pencil there is no shock or surprise by what we find. The product hasn't changed in decades. We use it because it continues to serve its purpose well.

In the upper left quadrant of Figure 1.3 are fads. These are products and ideas that have great novelty but low usefulness. A product or idea whose primary appeal is its novelty, such as the 1970s pet rock and the fashion trend of platform shoes for men, will soon fade away when people realize it has little practical value. In some cases, fads get recycled by the next generation. This is often the case in fashion and hairstyles. This happens because what is old hat for one generation might be novel for another.

Finally, in the lower left quadrant of Figure 1.3 we have ideas and products that are not new and have little usefulness. We call it repeating past mistakes because thoughts and actions in this quadrant have been tried before, thus they are not novel, and they either met with successful results initially, but not now, or weren't useful from the very start. Outdated laws that are still on the books provide excellent examples of this quadrant. A law in Austin, Texas, for example, states it is illegal to carry wire cutters in your pocket (Powell & Koon, n.d.). Why? This law was enacted in the days of the Wild West when cowboys would cut barbed wire fences of property owners to allow their cattle through.

Customs and traditions also provide excellent examples of this quadrant. By definition customs and traditions cannot be new, and sometimes they are not very useful. In organizational life you may run into useless traditions, such as policies and procedures that appear to have lived well beyond their usefulness. Have you ever earnestly questioned an organizational practice only to get the response, "But that's the way we've always done it" or "That's our policy"? Statements like this are clear indicators that you are bumping into something that is definitely not new and may no longer be satisfactorily fulfilling its intended purpose.

Another behavior we associate with this quadrant is doing something over and over again and expecting a different result. Have you ever hit an illuminated elevator call button numerous times expecting your repeated efforts to bring the elevator car faster? Have your ever tried to solve a computer problem by repeating the same commands, hoping that just once it might work? These are simple examples. More serious examples include repeating the same sales strategies that produced modest outcomes and expecting a dramatic gain in sales, leaders who want to change their relationship with their followers but who do not change the nature of their interactions, or teachers who expect students to show significant gains in skill level but who find it impossible to adopt new teaching strategies.

A Systems Model for Creative Change

The novelty-usefulness definition of creativity tells us what is and is not creative, but it does not tell us how creativity operates. To do this we turn to a systems model of creativity. Many scholars agree that creativity is made up of four distinct facets (MacKinnon, 1978; Rhodes, 1961; Stein, 1968). The four main elements of creativity are person(s), process, environment, and product. Although these facets have their own discrete attributes, they do influence one another and therefore create a system for how creativity works.

In Figure 1.4, the Creative Change Model, we depict how these facets interact to yield creative products and eventually produce creative change (again, we say "creative" change because we are talking about the deliberate introduction of something that is new). Creativity begins with an individual or a team of individuals. The **person(s)** facet in this system *considers individual skills, knowledge, personality, experiences, and motivation that all have an influence on the amount and kind of creativity an individual or team is likely to produce.* The **process** facet refers to *the stages of thinking individuals and teams go through as they develop creative ideas in response to predicaments and opportunities.* As in the case of the person facet, the quality of the process often has a direct impact on the quality of the product produced. These two facets are not completely independent; in fact, we suggest that they interact. In Chapter 12 we describe how people possess different preferences for certain aspects or stages of the creative process.

Creative thinking does not happen in a vacuum. It takes place in particular settings. In some cases these settings may stimulate creative thinking, and in other cases they may inhibit creative thought. This facet is referred to as the **environment**, *the ways in which the psychological and*

Figure 1.4   Creative Change Model: A Systems Approach

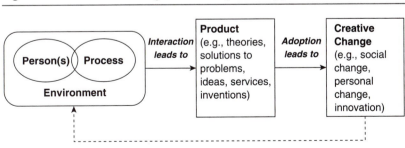

physical workplace climates, or the cultures in which you live, influence the expression of creative behavior. You cannot take someone who has all the right personality characteristics and thinking skills to be creative and simply put him or her in any situation and expect great things. Recent research by Teresa Amabile (Amabile, Burnside, & Gryskiewicz, 1999) of the Harvard Business School has identified the kinds of characteristics of the workplace that tend to facilitate or undermine creative performance.

The three facets of person, process, and environment interact to yield particular outcomes. In other words, the quality of the creative product depends on people working through certain processes in particular kinds of environments. People with the right skills, knowledge, and personal traits who work through an effective process in an environment that is conducive to creative thought are more likely to produce creative **products**—*tangible and intangible outcomes that are new and useful.*

Creative change does not automatically occur because an individual, team, or organization has developed a new product. We define a **creative change** as *the adoption of a creative product that can come in many forms.* If the product is intended for use only by the individual creator, such as a new plan for reducing stress, then creative change occurs when this person has implemented the idea. By contrast, innovation occurs when an organization has successfully commercialized a new product or implemented a new program or service. The creative product is the starting point for business innovation, and according to Janszen (2000), "innovation is generally accepted as being the golden route to building a growing and prosperous company" (p. 7). Soo, Devinney, Midgley, and Deering (2002) showed that organizations that were rated in the top 20% for innovation enjoyed more than 35% more market share than those organizations in the bottom 20%. So if innovation is critical to the long-term success of an organization, and the creative product is the impetus to innovation, then it will be critical for organizations to create the right interaction between the person, process, and environment. If organizational leaders do not nurture the basic elements that support creative behavior, it is unlikely that their organizations will bring about creative change, whether that is an innovative product, social change, educational reform, enhanced level of human service, and so on.

The process has an iterative aspect to it; that is, once a creative change has been successfully adopted, it is highly likely that this new idea, product, service, or practice will have a transformative effect on people, their processes, and their environments. Although this model focuses on the successful adoption of creative change, it is possible that when a proposed change is rejected, this failure has the potential to have some measurable effect on people, processes, and environments as well.

This systems view of creativity illustrates why creativity is difficult to bring about in organizations. Like the ingredients in a recipe, although all have their own unique flavor, it is the combination of the ingredients that results in a complete dish. Figure 1.4 shows how these basic creativity elements interact with one another. For example, we know that training in creative thinking (i.e., process) improves the work climate (i.e., environment) of teams (Firestien, 1996). Individual personalities (i.e., persons) influence the nature of the work environment (Ekvall, 1991). Formal training in creativity techniques and principles (i.e., process) significantly enhances individuals' thinking skills (i.e., persons) (Parnes, 1987). Returning to the recipe metaphor, organizational creativity is achieved only when the right ingredients are combined. Assuming that an organization will be creative, for example, because it has hired highly creative people is like assuming that the only ingredient necessary to make a good chicken soup is the chicken itself.

Leaders who wish to foster creative thinking and change must recognize the importance of all the facets of creativity. They must understand their own and others' creative abilities. They must master the creative process and be able to facilitate this process in others. They must find ways to build work environments that encourage creative thought. Given the importance for leaders to understand these elements of creativity, we have used person, process, and environment as a basic framework for much of this book. Chapters 5 through 11 focus on mastering the creative process, specifically the Creative Problem Solving (CPS) process. Chapter 12 focuses on people and how individuals express preferences for different aspects of the creative process. Understanding how different personalities engage in creative thinking is invaluable for understanding how to improve a team's ability to move through the creative process and introduce change. Chapter 13 describes the kind of work environment leaders should create to stimulate creativity and change. The final chapter discusses how the creativity principles and procedures presented in this book can become internalized so that individuals can begin the process of developing into creative leaders.

❖ APPLYING WHAT YOU'VE LEARNED

The intent of this chapter was to underscore the critical link between leadership and creativity—change—thereby positioning creative thinking as a core competence of leaders who bring about positive change. The close relationship between creativity and leadership was captured well when Simonton (1984) observed that "when the most famous creators and leaders are under scrutiny, the distinction between creativity and leadership vanishes because creativity becomes a variety of leadership" (p. 181). The following activities will help you deepen your understanding of this important connection.

- What is your personal definition of creativity? How do you define leadership? Examine these definitions and identify ways in which they relate. What are the conceptual connections?
- Identify a leader in your life who had a profoundly positive impact on you. List the qualities that you believe made this person an effective leader. Inspect this list of qualities and identify items that are closely related to creativity. Ask yourself to what degree do you possess these same qualities. Consider what you might do to develop some of the qualities you believe are most important.
- Identify a leader who was successful in drawing out the creative thinking of others. What did he or she do, and what was the consequence of this ability to promote creative thinking in others? Now consider a leader who undermined creative thinking. What did he or she do that had a negative influence on creativity? What was the consequence of his or her behavior?

2

Creative Problem Solving

Background and Introduction to the Thinking Skills Model

Chapter at a Glance

This chapter focuses on how Creative Problem Solving (CPS) provides a system and process steps that help leaders be more deliberate about how they think and act. The chapter begins with an introduction to the CPS process, its history and purpose, followed by a description of reactive and proactive approaches to problems as a rationale for CPS use. We've also included key definitions and features of CPS and a specific description of its structure. Finally, we'll take a look at the hallmark feature of CPS—the balance of the generation of many options against the winnowing down and evaluation of these options.

❖ GETTING TO KNOW CREATIVE PROBLEM SOLVING: GOING FOR THE GOLD

Suppose you had a treasure map that would lead you to gold no matter where or when you used it—all you had to do was set a few goals, figure out the general direction, and know how to effectively use the map under a variety of conditions. Oh, and did we mention that this map is a bit like the paintings at Hogwarts in the Harry Potter books where the characters are dynamic and move about interacting with each other? The CPS is a thinking and doing map that will get you the gold—the nuggets of ideas and the glimmer and shine of implementation. Many people have mined for CPS gold over the years. It has a rich history, and variations of its conceptual model have been widely adopted to deliberately foster creative thought. Box 2.1 gives a brief overview of CPS history.

Box 2.1   Historical Note

Creative Problem Solving: A Brief History

Our center—The International Center for Studies in Creativity—was founded on the pioneering work of three individuals. Alex Osborn, an advertising executive who developed the creative thinking tool brainstorming, was the originator of the Creative Problem Solving (CPS) process and model. Osborn began his work on deliberate creativity in the 1940s. In the 1950s he teamed with a college professor, Sidney Parnes, to further develop and research CPS. The early studies carried out by Parnes demonstrated that training in the CPS process enhanced individuals' creative thinking skills (Meadow & Parnes, 1959; Meadow, Parnes, & Reese, 1959; Parnes & Meadow, 1959, 1960). Parnes, in turn, teamed with Ruth Noller, originally a professor of mathematics, to design, deliver, and test the groundbreaking college curriculum in creativity at Buffalo State College (Noller & Parnes, 1972; Parnes & Noller, 1972a, 1972b, 1973; Reese, Parnes, Treffinger, & Kaltsounis, 1976). At the same time that research into the impact of CPS training was occurring, the model itself was being modified. Lessons learned through research and application guided the evolution of the CPS model. Although the original seven-step model introduced by Osborn in 1953 (i.e., Orientation, Preparation, Analysis, Hypothesis, Incubation, Synthesis, and Verification) has changed through the years, current versions of the process still retain many of the hallmark features found in the early work. For a review of the evolution of CPS see Puccio et al. (2005) and Isaksen and Treffinger (2004).

Since Osborn first developed CPS, the process has undergone continuous development and research, keeping it dynamic and fresh. The reason the CPS process has stood the test of time is that "It works!" What makes the CPS process work so well?

1. The CPS process parallels people's natural creative thinking processes by efficiently organizing what happens when they work with problems. This means that CPS has an intuitive base that is easy to tap into in more explicit ways.

2. Through the alternating phases of divergent (generating options) and convergent thinking (evaluating options) and the use of tools that support them, CPS provides a way to manage that most ferocious opponent of creative thinking—premature or inappropriate judgment.

3. CPS combines thinking with doing, which helps people accomplish concrete actions and get results from their initial ideas.

4. Finally, CPS provides a flexible format that is capable of taking in many creativity tools and approaches.

❖ CREATIVE PROBLEM SOLVING: SOME BASIC TERMS

What do we mean when we talk about Creative Problem Solving? **Creative Problem Solving** is a comprehensive cognitive and affective system built on our natural creative processes that deliberately ignites creative thinking and, as a result, generates creative solutions and change. The CPS process has a dual function: thinking AND doing. As human beings we are not strangers to thinking and doing or we would not have survived and thrived this long, but we are less familiar and often less comfortable with being deliberate about the processes we use. To be clear, a **process** is defined as *a particular method of doing something, generally involving a number of steps or operations.* CPS as a deliberate creative process takes intuitive responses to open-ended problems and moves them from trial and error to targeted strategies. In accomplishing this, CPS (a) influences how people think about themselves and the world around them in relation to change, and (b) improves individual and team performance for problems that appear to have no immediate solution.

Does this sound like a natural partner for leadership? We think so—especially since leaders *have* to think differently. Because novelty is inherent in creative change, leaders often confront novel situations that have no set procedure or single "right" pathway forward. Under such conditions, leaders have to help their intuition along a bit—there is a need for deliberate creative thinking and this is the job of CPS. It's the map that can lead you to the gold. Again, when we say **Creative** we mean *the production of ideas or options that are both new and useful*, and this is the outcome leaders are searching for when they are challenged by novel situations. Discovering new ways to improve customer service, finding the next product idea to stay ahead of the competition, identifying energizing ways to engage learners, or revitalizing a city are examples of the kinds of novel and complex situations in which leaders must search for creative solutions.

We will now turn to the second word in the CPS acronym, problem. We look at **Problem** in its broadest sense to describe *what exists when there is a gap between what you have and what you want*. This gap creates dissatisfaction, and dissatisfaction, in turn, creates interest in finding some means for closing the gap. Mumford et al. (2000) indicated that leadership problems are quite different in their nature from managerial problems. They defined the types of problems leaders face as being **ill-defined** (i.e., *no single solution path*), **novel** (i.e., *the situation is either changing or new*), and **complex** (i.e., *information is missing or it is difficult to determine what is relevant*). Their definition captures the kinds of problems CPS is designed to address.

Finally, by **Solving** we mean *taking action in some way*—it's the implementation part of the CPS process. Here solving implies finding an answer or resolution to situations, but it also encompasses everything involved in looking for or refining those answers. Creativity isn't complete by just thinking about something new or useful—it is the direct result of someone taking action and bringing a new idea to fruition. CPS as a process is about transforming creative ideas into creative solutions for complex problems, thereby leading to productive change.

Since its introduction more than 50 years ago, CPS is one of the most widely used creative process models in both education and industry. Given its popularity, CPS has been the subject of many research studies. These studies have empirically evaluated the effectiveness of CPS training. If you are interested in the research that supports the impact of CPS, see Box 2.2.

Box 2.2   Research Note

Does Creative Problem Solving Work?

In the late 1960s and early 1970s, Parnes and Noller carried out a comprehensive examination of the impact of CPS training. The Creative Studies Project is reported in a number of sources (see Parnes, 1987; Parnes & Noller, 1972a, 1972b, 1973; Reese et al., 1976). Parnes and Noller studied the effects of four semester-long creativity courses on undergraduate students. The main creativity model featured in this educational program was CPS. Students entering the freshman class at Buffalo State College were invited to participate in the research study. Volunteers were randomly assigned to either an experimental group, who were enrolled in the four creativity courses taught over a two-year period, or to a control group, who were not enrolled in the creativity courses.

Pre- and post-test paper-and-pencil measures were administered to all students in the study. Many of these measures were drawn from Guilford's Structure of the Intellect model (Guilford, 1977). These comparisons revealed that the experimental group had statistically significant gains after the training in comparison to the students in the control group. The students who participated in the creativity courses showed significant differences on measures of divergent production, convergent production, and cognition.

A number of other researchers have conducted studies in which various creativity programs have been compared in regard to their effectiveness (Rose & Lin, 1984; Scott, Leritz, & Mumford, 2004a, 2004b; Torrance, 1972; Torrance & Presbury, 1984). Such studies supported the positive effects of CPS training. Torrance (1972), who studied the effectiveness of nine different kinds of creativity programs, found that CPS achieved the highest percentage of success (i.e., 20 of the 22 studies yielded significant results). Rose and Lin (1984) conducted a meta-analytic evaluation of creativity programs. To provide a basis for their evaluation of different creativity programs, Rose and Lin evaluated research studies that used the *Torrance Tests of Creative Thinking* as a measure of the impact of training. In examining the effect training had on Torrance's measure of creative thinking skills, these authors concluded that the substantial impact of CPS on verbal creativity provided clear evidence of its effectiveness. A more recent comparative analysis by Scott et al. (2004b) found that cognitively oriented creative process programs, such as CPS, proved to have positive effects on participants.

Many of the studies involved in these comparative reviews were carried out in educational contexts, but what about the impact of CPS

(Continued)

(Continued)

training in organizational settings? A number of studies have empirically evaluated CPS training with professionals, perhaps most notably the program of research carried out by Basadur and his colleagues. Basadur, Graen, and Green (1982) demonstrated that employees trained in CPS outperformed control and placebo groups. For example, employees trained in CPS were more fluent in generating new product ideas, produced better ideas for new products, and were more effective at problem finding. Basadur, Graen, and Scandura (1986) reported that CPS training significantly enhanced engineers' attitudes toward divergent thinking. Basadur went on to demonstrate that similar results could be achieved with managers in Japan (Basadur, Wakabayashi, & Takai, 1992) and South America (Basadur, Pringle, & Kirkland, 2002). He also reported the positive effects of CPS training on union-management negotiations. According to Basadur, Pringle, Speranzini, and Bacot (2000), CPS training improved trust between negotiating parties and resulted in new solutions. Positive results of CPS training in the workplace have been reported by Kabanoff and Bottger (1991); Fontenot (1993); Wang, Wu, and Horng (1999); Wang and Horng (2002); and Wang, Horng, Hung, and Huang (2004). See Puccio, Firestien, Coyle, and Masucci (2006) and Puccio et al. (2005) for a review of additional CPS impact studies in organizations.

As a result of a recent quantitative analysis of creativity programs, Scott et al. (2004a) concluded that creativity training does work. Specifically, training has been shown to significantly impact divergent thinking, problem solving, performance, attitudes, and behaviors. These authors cited CPS as one of the more successful creativity programs. This success was attributed to this program's description of "the key cognitive processes underlying creative thought" (p. 383) in combination with strategies for applying these processes.

❖   USING CREATIVE PROBLEM
     SOLVING: HOW TO, WHEN TO

Not all situations require creative thinking. Figure 2.1 illustrates the kinds of problems that might benefit from CPS. The matrix is based on analyzing the nature of the problem and the approach to that problem. The horizontal axis is divided between **reactive** and **proactive** approaches to problems. A reactive approach occurs when there is a change within an existing system, situation, or process. This change results in declining performance or the potential for negative outcomes. For example, a machine goes down on the manufacturing line; a cook is missing a key ingredient for the recipe; a child's sleeping pattern changes and the old bedtime routine no longer works; crime is up, sales are down, friction in the team is causing tension; or people are no longer paying attention to an advertising campaign.

Figure 2.1   Types of Problems

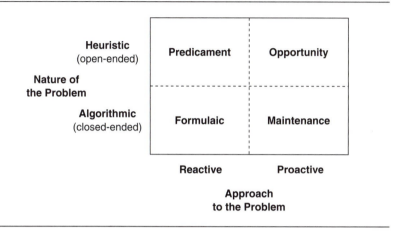

SOURCE: © 2005 Puccio, Murdock, and Mance. Reprinted with permission.

In other situations you may need to take a proactive approach and seek forward thinking. A proactive approach to problem solving is about seizing a new opportunity or finding ways to continually improve existing circumstances. Proactive problem solving has much more to do with pursuing a vision or establishing goals. For example, a business pursues a new market; an inventor creates something that makes life easier; an organization introduces a variation of its old product line to increase sales; a care provider introduces new services to the delight of its members; and a family seeks a different kind of vacation experience. In all of these cases, creative thinking has been used as a means to support forward thinking rather than as a response to a threat.

The vertical axis of Figure 2.1 refers to the nature of the problem, which can be either closed- or open-ended. In closed-ended problems, the method for resolving the situation is known and there is usually a single correct solution or a limited range of options. These kinds of problems are **algorithmic** problems because *they always lead to a single correct answer;* therefore, creative thinking is not required. In contrast, a **heuristic** problem is open-ended. *There is no set method to follow or* *obvious solution.* Because creative thinking is required for heuristic problems, a deliberate approach like CPS is best employed for situations in the upper portion of the matrix. Deliberate creative thinking is not required when the method and solution are known, no matter whether the problem is reactive or proactive (i.e., the bottom portion of the matrix).

When the two types of approaches to problems are crossed with the two kinds of problems, four different kinds of problem scenarios emerge. In the lower left quadrant you have the **formulaic** scenario. *This is a situation in which something changes or breaks down, and by simply following a process or formula, you can correct the situation.* When you anticipate a future change that will negatively impact performance and you know what needs to be done to avoid any negative consequences associated with this change, you are operating in the lower right quadrant in a **maintenance** scenario. For example, people regularly change the oil in engines because they anticipate negative consequences if they do not. You need very little creative thinking to carry out routine maintenance.

Creative thinking is required, however, when the nature of the problem is heuristic. When something goes wrong in an existing situation and you are unsure about how to correct the problem, you need creative thinking. You also need creative thinking when you perceive an external threat that will change current levels of success, such as the entry of a new competitor to the marketplace or an anticipated change to regulatory policies. These are examples of problems that we refer to as a **predicament** (see the upper left quadrant). A predicament is *a difficult, complicated, or perplexing situation.* You have a predicament when something threatens current levels of performance and you need to discover or invent the best way to respond. When you find yourself in the upper right quadrant you are presented with an **opportunity**, *a favorable juncture of circumstances.* These are situations in which you decide to actively pursue some desirable possibility—for example, you believe there are unmet consumer needs in your market; you use an accidental discovery to create a new industry; or you believe there are new ways to structure schools. CPS is useful in dealing with predicaments and opportunities because in both scenarios the solution is unknown and needs to be discovered through the deliberate application of the creative process. Furthermore, we suggest that individuals who decide to exert their leadership to bring about change will need to resolve predicaments and pursue opportunities. Again, Mumford et al. (2000) based their leadership model on the premise that successful leaders are adept at resolving complex problems through creative problem solving.

❖ CREATIVE PROBLEM SOLVING: INTRODUCING THE THINKING SKILLS MODEL—A PROCESS MAP FOR FINDING YOUR WAY TO THE GOLD

So what is CPS and how does it work? In this section we present our current view of the CPS process along with a graphic model that depicts how the process operates. As we noted earlier, the CPS process has been refined through the years, and what we present is an extension of this work. Also, it should be noted that given the extent to which CPS has been diffused, there are alternative conceptions of this deliberate creative process in use (see Basadur, 1994; Isaksen, Dorval, & Treffinger, 1994, 2000; Miller, Vehar, & Firestien, 2001; Parnes, 2004). Figure 2.2 presents our view of CPS—an approach that we think works for developing the thinking skills related to creativity that help leaders effectively respond to predicaments and take advantage of perceived opportunities. Since this version of CPS is the first to specifically articulate the thinking skills associated with each step of the process, we refer to it as *Creative Problem Solving: The Thinking Skills Model*. Chapter 3 reviews the specific thinking skills associated with each step of the model.

Model Structure

The structure of CPS, working from the outside inward, comprises three conceptual stages, six explicit process steps with six repetitions of divergence and convergence within each, and one executive step at the heart of the model to guide them all. The three conceptual stages— **Clarification, Transformation,** and **Implementation**—are related to your natural creative process. These are general terms that identify the beginning, middle, and end of the creative process. People implicitly move through them in a natural progression whether they are consciously aware of it or not. For instance, to get started with any process, you must understand *what needs be resolved* **(Clarification Stage)**. Next, you need to *identify potential ideas and craft them into workable solutions* **(Transformation Stage)**. Finally, you need to *refine the solutions and put together a plan for taking effective action* **(Implementation Stage)**.

In fact, Mintzberg, Duru, and Theoret's (1976) examination of real-life problem solving yielded three major phases labeled "identification" (understanding the problem), "development" (creating potential solutions), and "selection" (deciding among the solutions). Various researchers have identified similar three-stage descriptions of problem solving (Johnson & Jennings, 1963; Simon 1965, 1977). After reviewing

Figure 2.2   Creative Problem Solving: The Thinking Skills Model

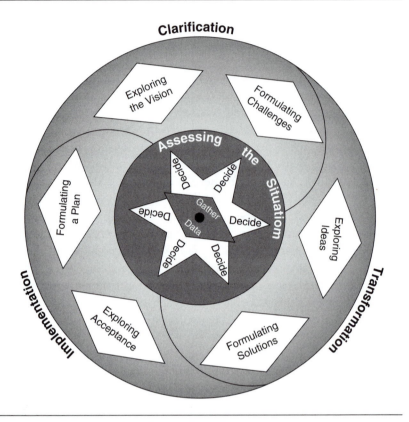

SOURCE: © 2006 Puccio, Murdock, and Mance. Reprinted with permission.

the problem-solving research, cognitive psychologist Geir Kaufmann (1988) concluded, "There is a striking agreement in the literature describing the phases of a problem solving event. Normally, three major phases are identified" (p. 98). We believe these three phases are reflected in CPS.

Although the basic stages of the problem-solving process have been shown to be empirically distinguishable, researchers have found that people will naturally move forward, backward, and across these elements (Mintzberg et al., 1976). So, although the three stages of CPS represent the natural progression individuals go through when faced with an open-ended problem, this flow will not always occur in a sequential manner. Sometimes it may seem like you have skipped stages, but in reality your mind is working so quickly that you may not be aware of your stages of thought, or the issue may be relatively simple and require less time to process.

Understanding the basic structure of CPS can help when you get lost in non-systematic, explicit use of the creative process. For example, have you ever been in a meeting where things got so complicated that you lost track of where you or others were in the conversation? Or have you ever heard people say things like "Where are we going with this?" "What are we supposed to be doing?" "It feels like we are going in circles." If you find yourself wondering, "Aren't we just spinning our wheels here?" then you probably are! Think of the CPS model as a cognitive map and the three stages as major regions within this map. When you find yourself lost while addressing a predicament or pursuing an opportunity, use the CPS cognitive map to guide yourself out of the woods. Ask questions related to the CPS framework to help locate yourself within the process. "Do I/we need to further clarify this situation?" "Have I/we explored a sufficient number of ideas to identify a potential solution to this situation?" "Am I or are we committed to a solution to be implemented?" Such questions can help get a derailed process back on course.

The formal application of CPS involves six explicit process steps. These six steps are designed to help enhance people's effectiveness by linking their natural process to a systematic and explicit series of operations. The six formal steps of CPS are *Exploring the Vision, Formulating Challenges, Exploring Ideas, Formulating Solutions, Exploring Acceptance,* and *Formulating a Plan.* In each natural process stage there are two steps: The first explicit step begins with the word "Exploring" and the second step begins with "Formulating" because the first is more general or abstract than the second. In this manner, the movement from the first step in each stage to the second should represent a transition from the exploration of broader concepts to the formalization of more concrete outcomes. Clarification begins with the broad examination of a vision (Exploring the Vision) and concludes with the identification of specific challenges that must be addressed in order to achieve the vision (Formulating Challenges). Transformation begins with the broad search for potential ideas to address the previously identified challenges (Exploring Ideas) and ends with the best ideas being developed into concrete solutions (Formulating Solutions). Finally, Implementation starts with a review of the factors that will help or hinder the successful advancement of the solution (Exploring Acceptance), which are then used to create a detailed plan of action (Formulating a Plan).

Each of the six steps is represented by a diamond-shaped figure that shows the internal phases of divergent thinking (i.e., generating options) and convergent thinking (i.e., selecting or evaluating options) within each step. This repeating function continually separates and then applies the use of judgment in a balanced way, giving change and novelty a better chance at surviving the powerful censors that people often place on something new. This balance between divergent and convergent thinking has been the hallmark of the CPS process and, as such, is described in further detail in the section to follow.

The six explicit steps have no required order for use, although they are presented here in the natural flow of the conceptual stages. You can begin with any step that you need or want to; you can go back if you realize you forgot something or just think it's a better place to be at the time. You can skip over any of them if you have what you need. Effectively using CPS is like going to the checkout line when you have finished your shopping—it's not the number of items that you have in your cart that indicates you are finished, but that you have all you came for, that your purpose was accomplished.

There is one more step to the CPS process, the executive step, called Assessing the Situation. We refer to Assessing the Situation as the executive step because it helps you to stand above the other steps to determine where to go in the process and how to progress through it. Assessing the Situation involves the use of metacognitive thought. Based on Flavell's (1976) work, we define **metacognition** as *an individual's ability to monitor and control his or her own cognitive processes.* Simply put, metacognition means thinking about your own thinking. When Assessing the Situation, you gather data and use this data to make decisions about how to proceed. As such, the higher-order function of this step becomes the gateway to the six explicit steps—sources of data in the form of facts, intuition, feelings, or answers to questions will enable you to determine which of the six CPS steps will be most useful in addressing a predicament or opportunity. Since there is no predetermined second step in CPS, the diagnosis of information from Assessing the Situation determines where you should go next. Use of the rest of the model is based on what the situation dictates: Do you need to explore or formulate, and if so, how—by clarifying, transforming, or implementing? CPS is a thinking person's process. You can't switch on autopilot and switch off thinking. You don't simply take every situation, no matter what its qualities, and force it through the whole model, although if you need all the steps, you can certainly use them. The flexible nature of CPS is a characteristic that has made it useful and enduring, and that flexibility makes it appropriate to manage change effectively.

Box 2.3   Key Vocabulary

Key Phrases Describing the Creative Problem Solving Model Structure

For a quick at-a-glance version, here are the key phrases that describe the concepts of CPS: The Thinking Skills Model.

The Three Conceptual Stages of Natural Process: If you get lost in your thinking or action, find where you are by asking yourself, Do I need to **Clarify? Transform? Implement?**

The Explicit Process Steps: Exploring the Vision, Formulating Challenges, Exploring Ideas, Formulating Solutions, Exploring Acceptance, and Formulating a Plan.

The Executive Step: The Engine That Drives Decisions: Assessing the Situation to see what you want or need to do and then going to the appropriate step(s).

Dynamically Balanced Phases: Diverge (generate) and Converge (select).

❖ DYNAMIC BALANCE: THE HEART OF
   THE CREATIVE PROBLEM SOLVING PROCESS

The balanced application of divergent and convergent thinking that runs throughout the process is represented in CPS by the diamond structure (see Figure 2.3). Where the diamond opens up illustrates **divergent thinking,** *a broad search for many diverse and novel alternatives.* By stretching your mind, you avoid the risk of limiting yourself to what is already familiar to you. You deliberately extend your thinking in a way that allows you to make new discoveries. Where the diamond closes down represents convergent thinking. Here you select or synthesize the most promising options generated during the divergent phase. **Convergent thinking** is *a focused and affirmative evaluation of alternatives.* In CPS we intentionally separate these two forms of thinking into a "dynamic balance" of first one and then the other. This balance is core to effective thinking. Ruggiero (1998) noted,

> for decades psychologists of thinking stressed that the mind has two distinctive phases—the production phase and the judgment phase—that complement each other during thinking. They stressed further that proficiency in thinking requires the mastery of all approaches appropriate to each phase and skill in moving back and forth between them. (p. 5)

Figure 2.3   Dynamic Balance: The Core of the CPS Process

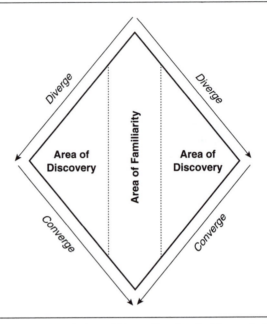

Using the concept of dynamic balance is one way to make your own thinking or the problem-solving efforts of a team immediately more effective. Why? Often when you have an idea, the very next thought that comes to mind is a negative judgment regarding that idea, a reason not to go forward with it. "I'll be laughed at." "It will never work." "So-and-so will never buy it." "The resources don't exist to make it happen." As a result, ideas are often scrapped, and the search for a new idea begins all over again. This kind of start-and-stop thinking mixes divergent and convergent thinking. An alternative is generated and then quickly judged. This is not an efficient way of thinking, especially when you need to use creative thinking. Mixing convergent thinking with divergent thinking is one sure way to see that unique thoughts will be tossed aside. Also, you run the risk of simply stopping at the first alternative that appears to be satisfactory, which may be far from the best alternative—much like hastily ordering vanilla ice cream in a plain cone only to discover afterward that if you had looked further down the menu, you could have had your favorite ice cream treat, chocolate chip cookie dough in a homemade waffle cone.

You often see the inefficiency of start-and-stop thinking in meetings. Someone—a committee chair, team leader, project manager, administrator—asks whether anyone has ideas for a problem. Another person offers an idea, which is immediately met with criticism. All the reasons it will not work are quickly identified. Since the initial idea was shot down, the team members now go back to the mental drawing board to consider other possibilities. However, their thinking is influenced by the exchange that just occurred. People may become overly concerned about how their ideas will be received. There is an awkward silence—ideas are scrutinized internally to the point that they are never shared publicly. This is unfortunate because many worthwhile ideas may never make it to the table.

In the CPS process, you eliminate start-and-stop thinking by separating divergent and convergent thinking in every step. This repetition, contrary to people's first reaction to it, is a more efficient way of thinking. We would suggest that it is more efficient to first lay out all of your options, then take the time to deliberately review and evaluate a full range of alternatives to find the best course of action, than to make a snap decision that does not fully satisfy the needs of the situation. Swartz (1987) suggested that the complementary nature of first using creativity to generate options and then employing critical thinking to make choices among alternatives is necessary for good thinking.

Bob Hope, a great American entertainer, employed the dynamic balance between divergent and convergent thinking to develop his comedy monologues. Hope had a staff of writers who would produce his material. They called themselves the "Double Cross and Circle Club." The writing team would generate between 200 and 500 jokes for a monologue. Hope would read all of them and place an "X" next to the ones he liked. Then he would reread those jokes he liked and make a double cross on those he still liked. He would make a final pass through the list of jokes, focusing only on those with a double "X," and would circle those that would be performed in front of an audience.

In their study of organizations that have stood the test of time, Collins and Porras (1994) found that successful organizations also find ways to balance divergent and convergent thinking. Their description of the work at Johnson & Johnson provides an example of how dynamic balance works in successful companies:

> To this day, Johnson & Johnson consciously encourages branching and pruning. It tries lots of new things, keeps those that work, and quickly discards those that don't. It stimulates variation by fostering a highly decentralized environment and encourages individual initiative and allows people to experiment with new ideas. At the same time, J&J imposes rigorous selection criteria. Only those experiments that prove to be profitable and that fit with J&J's core ideology get to remain in the company's portfolio of business. (p. 147)

This balance between divergent and convergent thinking is so central to CPS that we have devoted a chapter to the principles that allow individuals to more successfully manage this dynamic balance in thought. Chapter 4 provides a description of specific guidelines individuals and teams can use to enhance both their divergent and convergent thinking skills. However, before leaving this chapter we wish to specifically explore the kinds of skills that are associated with divergent and convergent thinking.

❖ DIVERGENT THINKING SKILLS: FLUENCY, FLEXIBILITY, ELABORATION, AND ORIGINALITY

Psychologist and early proponent of creativity J. P. Guilford was among the first to describe the characteristics of divergent thinking. Guilford (1977) identified four basic characteristics within the operation of divergent thinking that are the generally accepted skill areas in creative thinking today: **fluency** (*getting a large number of ideas or responses*), **flexibility** (*getting variety in kinds or categories of ideas or responses*), **elaboration** (*adding to or developing existing ideas or responses*), and **originality** (*getting new, novel, or different ideas or responses*).

The main aim of CPS is to produce novel approaches to problems. Fluency, flexibility, and elaboration improve your ability to think in original ways, which is often needed to get the breakthrough necessary to handle an open-ended problem. Someone who is highly fluent is able to come up with many options when faced with an open-ended problem, and the more thoughts you have, the more likely you are to have an original thought. The value associated with the ability to be a fluent thinker was captured well by the famous Irish playwright George Bernard Shaw when he said, "Few people think more than two or three times a year; I have made an international reputation for myself by thinking once or twice a week." Flexibility ensures that your mind covers the situation from as many different perspectives as possible, which again encourages novel views. Elaboration allows you to find new applications within existing systems, such as the creation of product extensions (e.g., going from individual crackers, to putting two crackers together with a cheese filling, to peanut butter filling). This kind of extended thinking allows you to add new wrinkles to existing ideas.

Are these skills important to success? E. P. Torrance, a pioneering researcher in the field of creativity, conducted a longitudinal study to examine the value of these divergent thinking skills. Torrance assessed the divergent thinking abilities of school-age children and 22 years later examined their achievement levels as adults; he found that divergent thinking abilities were significantly correlated with creative achievement (Torrance, 2004).

Are divergent thinking skills important for leaders? A study by Zaccaro, Mumford, Connelly, Marks, and Gilbert (2000) showed that the divergent thinking abilities of 1,800 military officers had the largest positive correlation, among all other variables tested, with complex problem-solving skills. Practically speaking, the ability to generate more diverse options to challenges and opportunities increases your power (Karp, 1996). When you come up with only one pathway forward to a situation, this does not allow for any choices, and without choices, your power is limited—you are forced to accept your lot. When you are able to generate two options, you create a choice, but often these choices are black and white or good and bad. Having two options is not much better than having one. You are forced to pursue one or the other. You enhance your power through the generation of many diverse and original options. Leaders who possess excellent divergent thinking skills empower themselves and others because the greater number of choices they have, the more likely they are to be successful.

❖ CONVERGENT THINKING SKILLS: ENVISION AND EVALUATE

Convergent thinking is a focused search (Guilford, 1977). In the dynamic balance that occurs within CPS, convergent thinking follows divergent thinking. Therefore, its function is to help you focus on identifying the most promising options. If divergent thinking is done well, there should be many diverse and novel options to be considered during the convergent phase. If the ultimate goal is to find a creative pathway forward in the face of a predicament or an opportunity, then convergent thinking should be applied in a way that marries novelty with usefulness.

There are several skills associated with effective convergent thinking that can be sorted into two sets. To effectively work with many options you need specific selection skills. The following three skills will enable you to better manage a large number of options: **screening** (*filtering—keeping some and discarding others for a particular reason*), **sorting** (*categorizing or grouping by some implicit or explicit schema*), and **prioritizing** (*determining the rank order among options*). In describing effective decision making, Swartz (2001) identified similar skills. Swartz suggested that deciding which option is best depends on such skills as ranking/prioritizing, valuing, comparing, and contrasting.

These basic skills will help you manage the large amount of options you get from divergence, but what about the novelty? Here, in our experience, another subset of convergent skills is needed: **supporting** *(examining for positive attributes, identifying and putting them forward to be considered further)* and **developing** *(strengthening, improving, fleshing out the overall option so that it appears doable)*. The skill of supporting requires that you put your affective feelings about the potential of your options to work in concrete ways. What are the strengths of the choices—both the obvious and the overlooked? What works about the option under consideration? What might work with a little extra effort? This affirmative approach to evaluation allows you to remain open, to not prematurely jump to conclusions or simply go after the low-hanging fruit. In particular, it ensures that you allow your mind to stay open to new thoughts and ideas, options that at first might be dismissed simply because they are unfamiliar to you. The skill of developing then takes over and enables you to take an idea that seems to hold some promise and to perfect it, to transform it from a rough concept to a clear pathway forward. This is a particularly valuable skill when you are blazing a new way forward.

❖ APPLYING WHAT YOU'VE LEARNED

In this chapter, we introduced the CPS model and described the importance of balancing divergent and convergent thinking. We also described some of the skills associated with divergent and convergent thought. By explicitly identifying the skills that make up CPS, individuals are in a better position to focus on developing these skills. Below are a few exercises to help your development.

- Identify a problem you successfully solved. Think back to the process steps you went through in solving this problem. Record these steps and then compare them to the CPS process described in this chapter. How is what you did similar to CPS? How is it different? In what ways might an explicit creative process, such as CPS, help improve your effectiveness? What aspects of CPS do you feel come most naturally to you? What aspects of CPS do you think will be most beneficial for you to learn? Why?
- Think about your personal strengths. Make a list of those strengths (i.e., abilities, skills, positive qualities, etc.) that come to mind immediately. When you can't think of any more, stop and count

the number of items in your list. Now challenge yourself to triple that number. For example, if you generated 5 strengths, come up with 10 more for a total of 15, or if you came up with 9, challenge yourself to generate 18 additional strengths. Use the divergent skills of fluency, flexibility, and originality to add to your list of strengths. Once you have your full list, review it and select five strengths that you believe are most important or valuable. How many of these options came during your second round of generation? In what ways did divergent thinking help you?

- The next time you are in a meeting, make observations to yourself about the balance between divergent and convergent thinking. Note how often an idea is shared that is then immediately met by judgment. What were the outcomes or consequences of this start-and-stop thinking?

3

Identifying Complex Thinking Skills Associated With the Creative Problem Solving Model

Chapter at a Glance

In Chapter 2 we introduced the Creative Problem Solving (CPS) model. The purpose of this chapter is to provide an overview of some basic thinking skills that support the CPS process and to examine why leaders need them. Because thinking is influenced by emotions, we will also examine some related affective skills that support the thinking skills. The chapters that immediately follow (Chapters 5 through 11) contain elaborated procedures associated with each of the seven Thinking Skills Model steps and the leadership connections to each.

❖ CREATIVE THINKING SKILLS FOR LEADERS

In Chapter 1 we argued that leadership effectiveness hinges on a person's ability to use creative problem-solving skills to resolve ill-defined, novel, complex problems. What, then, are these creative problem-solving skills? Because problem solving is a mental process, one could reasonably conclude that leaders must possess certain thinking skills to be effective, and especially thinking skills that foster creativity. We have described *Creative Problem Solving: The Thinking Skills Model* as a cognitive model because its function is to improve people's thought processes so that they are better able to resolve predicaments or pursue opportunities that bring about productive change. We suggest that using CPS in the context of leadership can enhance the kinds of thinking skills leaders need to resolve complex problems.

❖ COMPLEX THINKING FOR COMPLEX PROBLEMS: THE CREATIVE PROBLEM SOLVING MODEL AS A MACRO PROCESS

Before we describe the thinking skills associated with CPS, let's take a look at a general definition of thinking. According to Ruggiero (1998), **thinking** is *"any mental activity that helps formulate or solve a problem, make a decision, or fulfill a desire to understand. It is a searching for answers, or reaching for meaning"* (p. 2). Ruggiero also noted that thinking is a purposeful mental activity over which we exert control. He suggested that we engage in thinking when we actively direct the movements of our mind.

Much has been written about the specific kinds of skills that constitute thinking; there seems to be agreement that the skills associated with thinking can be organized according to their complexity. Bloom's taxonomy was one of the first structured models for sorting thinking skills (Bloom, Englehart, Furst, Hill, & Krathwohl, 1956). Others have grouped thinking skills into two sets: basic and complex thinking processes. According to Presseisen (2001), the main distinction between basic and complex thinking processes is the transition from "simple to more complex operations, from observable to abstract dimensions, and from an emphasis on working with known materials toward an emphasis on creating or inventing new, previously unknown approaches or materials" (p. 48). People who intend to lead creative change clearly engage in such complex thinking processes.

The relationship between complex thinking processes and the complex problems that leaders frequently face is further reinforced when one examines specific complex thinking processes. Cohen (1971) and Presseisen (2001) described four specific complex thinking processes: **problem solving** (*resolve a known difficulty*), **decision making** (*choose the best alternative*), **critical thinking** (*understand particular meaning*), and **creative thinking** (*create novel or aesthetic ideas or products*). Leadership requires all four of these processes. Although CPS focuses on nurturing creative thinking in problem solving, it also involves decision making and critical thinking. Thus, we make the case that CPS operates as a macro process for thinking. We suggest that as a macro process, specific thinking skills can be sufficiently identified within the framework of the CPS model to provide rubrics that guide people in knowing and choosing kinds of thinking that will help them operate more effectively. In operational terms, there are a number of discrete thinking skills people use when they engage in the CPS process, and these thinking skills vary from one step of the process to another. The nature, purpose, and operation of each of the seven steps in CPS are fundamentally different. Therefore, there are different basic thinking skills in each step, although, as noted earlier, divergent and convergent thinking are used across all steps.

Compare this to how a computer operates. It is designed so that many functions can be directed and carried out. The software programs stored on your computer are used to carry out different operations. Some software is used for word processing, some for analyzing numerical data, others for searching for information, and so on. The nature and purpose of the software programs vary, but they all run on the same operating system. Similarly, the CPS framework is a macro system that organizes complex thinking to carry out different operations. When these steps are put together into their natural sequence, CPS can support your thinking from an analysis of the current conditions **(Assessing the Situation)** to the development of an action plan designed to introduce change **(Formulating a Plan)**.

Table 3.1 presents some basic thinking skills associated with the seven steps of the CPS process that were identified when we examined the nature and purpose of each of the CPS steps (Puccio et al., 2005). Barbero-Switalski (2003) tested the proposed thinking skills through an analysis of the literature and feedback received via a focus group of CPS experts. She used this information to modify the set of thinking skills and their definitions. The final definitions were based on a number of literature sources (i.e., Costa, 2001; González, 2002; Isaksen, Dorval, & Treffinger, 1994; Marzano et al., 1988; Morrisey, 1996; Sternberg, 1985). For other thinking skills related to creativity and CPS, see Puccio and Murdock (2001).

Table 3.1 Some Key Thinking Skills Associated With CPS

Step	Assessing the Situation (executive step)	Exploring the Vision	Formulating Challenges	Exploring Ideas	Formulating Solutions	Exploring Acceptance	Formulating a Plan
Purpose	1. To describe and identify relevant data 2. To determine next process step	To develop a vision of a desired outcome	To identify the gaps that must be closed to achieve the desired outcome	To generate novel ideas that address important challenges	To move from ideas to solutions	To increase the likelihood of success	To develop an implementation plan
	Diagnostic Thinking	*Visionary Thinking*	*Strategic Thinking*	*Ideational Thinking*	*Evaluative Thinking*	*Contextual Thinking*	*Tactical Thinking*
	Making a careful examination of a situation, describing the nature of a problem, and making decisions about appropriate process steps to be taken	Articulating a vivid image of what you desire to create	Identifying the critical issues that must be addressed and pathways needed to move toward the desired future	Producing original mental images and thoughts that respond to important challenges	Assessing the reasonableness and quality of ideas in order to develop workable solutions	Understanding the interrelated conditions and circumstances that will support or hinder success	Devising a plan that includes specific and measurable steps for attaining a desired end and methods for monitoring its effectiveness

SOURCE: Puccio, Murdock, and Mance (2005). Reprinted with permission.

Goleman (1998) has maintained that "the act of innovation is both cognitive and emotional. Coming up with a creative insight is a cognitive act—but realizing its value, nurturing it and following through calls on emotional competencies such as self-confidence, initiative, persistence, and the ability to persuade" (p. 100). Creativity, or the production of change, is a result of both thinking and emotion; it is a matter of both the head and the heart. To create positive change, you must marry clear thinking with such emotional states as courage, risk taking, and tolerance for ambiguity. Although CPS may be perceived as primarily a cognitive process, deliberate creativity does not result exclusively from a thought process. To do this ignores the direct effect that affective states, such as motivation and passion, have on your ability to create (Amabile, 1987; Torrance, 1983). Recent research supports the importance of emotions in learning (Goleman et al., 2002).

Consider how strong emotions, such as anxiety, love, hate, and anger, influence thinking—in both positive and negative ways. Therefore, just as we described the thinking skills associated with each step of the CPS process, we are also presenting some affective skills in Table 3.2 that support the main thinking skill associated with each step.

By **affective** we mean the ways *"in which we deal with attitudinal and emotional aspects of learning, including feelings, appreciation, enthusiasm, motivations, attitudes, and values"* (Butler, 2002, p. 3). Examples of behaviors that are observable when people engage affectively are found in Krathwol, Bloom, and Masia's (1964) descriptors of **receiving** *(being aware, willing to hear, selectively attentive)*, **responding** *(actively participating, attending to the topic)*, **valuing** *(the worth of something as evidenced by a person's acceptance and commitment)*, **organizing values** *(comparing, relating, synthesizing the worth of things to resolve discrepancies and create a unique value system)*, and **internalizing values** *(exhibiting a value system that controls behavior in a pervasive, consistent, characteristic manner)*. We use the word "skills" to refer to both thinking and affect because they are necessary for effective performance within each step and can be developed through practice. We are not making a case here that these skills are discrete to each step with no overlap—there are many cognitive and affective skills involved even in small tasks. We are instead making the case that some categories of thinking skills are more basic to the function of some CPS steps than to others, and that these thinking skills are enhanced through some specific affective dispositions.

In addition to affective skills that are commensurate with the function of each step, there are several that are essential to effective functioning across the entire CPS process. Without the attitudes of **openness to novelty** *(being able to entertain ideas that may at first seem outlandish or*

Table 3.2 Some Key Affective Skills that Support CPS

Step	Assessing the Situation (executive step)	Exploring the Vision	Formulating Challenges	Exploring Ideas	Formulating Solutions	Exploring Acceptance	Formulating a Plan
Purpose	1. To describe and identify relevant data 2. To determine next process step	To develop a vision of a desired outcome	To identify the gaps that must be closed to achieve the desired outcome	To generate novel ideas that address important challenges	To move from ideas to solutions	To increase the likelihood of success	To develop an implementation plan
Affective Skills	*Curiosity* A desire to learn or know; inquisitive	*Dreaming* To imagine as possible your desires and hopes	*Sensing Gaps* To become consciously aware of discrepancies between what currently exists and is desired or required	*Playfulness* Freely toying with ideas	*Avoiding Premature Closure* Resisting the urge to push for a decision	*Sensitivity to Environment* The degree to which people are aware of their physical and psychological surroundings	*Tolerance for Risks* Not allowing yourself to be shaken or unnerved by the possibility of failure or setbacks
Affective Skills That Underlie All Steps of CPS							

Openness to Novelty: Ability to entertain ideas that at first seem outlandish and risky.

Tolerance for Ambiguity: To be able to deal with uncertainty and to avoid leaping to conclusions.

Tolerance for Complexity: Ability to stay open and persevere without being overwhelmed by large amounts of information, interrelated and complex issues, and competing perspectives.

SOURCE: Puccio, Murdock, and Mance (2005). Reprinted with permission.

risky), **tolerance for ambiguity** *(being able to deal with uncertainty and to avoid leaping to conclusions)*, and **tolerance for complexity** *(being able to stay open and persevere without being overwhelmed by large amounts of information, interrelated and complex issues, and competing perspectives)*, you will not be successful in using the CPS process. Perhaps you recognize the impact of these three attitudes on creative thinking in such phrases as "This will never work"; "What a silly idea"; "Keep it simple—if you can't put it on one page, don't bother me"; and "I want the answer, and I want it NOW!" Getting beyond this initial negative level of reaction is critical because it influences your readiness to engage in the CPS process.

❖ A CLOSER LOOK AT THE COGNITIVE AND
   AFFECTIVE SKILLS IN CREATIVE PROBLEM SOLVING

Let's take a quick look at the steps in the Thinking Skills Model of CPS to see how the cognitive and affective skills operate within each step.

Assessing the Situation: Diagnostic Thinking

The heart of the CPS process, and the step that initiates it, is **Assessing the Situation**. Assessing the Situation is called the executive step because it requires an ability to stand above the process to determine whether CPS is appropriate given the circumstances, and if so, where to begin in the process. This requires metacognition—the ability to think about your thinking. An ability to stand above process allows you to observe and direct it. This view from the top is critical in CPS because it is directed by the needs of the task, not by a lock-step approach in which steps must be sequentially followed.

Just as a doctor diagnoses a patient before prescribing treatment, so a user of CPS must first determine what is going on and what process actions are needed. As a friend of ours likes to say, "Prescription without diagnosis is malpractice." The same is true of effective use of CPS. Often people fall into the trap of thinking that the best response to every situation to is to generate ideas, to employ brainstorming or other idea production techniques. This wastes time if you already have what you need to move on. When using CPS, you start by considering both the content of the challenge and the process steps that might best fit the situation. Thus, you always begin by gathering data and then determining the next step in the CPS process from which you can most benefit.

The basic cognitive skill that underlies **Assessing the Situation** is an ability to use **Diagnostic Thinking**. In CPS this is a twofold skill. The first part involves *making a careful examination of a situation, describing the nature of the problem.* You might ask yourself, "Why do I want to work on this? Who is involved? How soon do I need to act on the situation? What have I tried before? What's stopping me from taking action?" This extensive understanding of the situation then leads to the second aspect of Diagnostic Thinking, which is *the ability to use this information to make decisions about appropriate process steps to be taken.*

A key affective skill underlying Diagnostic Thinking is **curiosity**—*a desire to learn or know or inquisitiveness.* A curious attitude is an affective skill that motivates people to look deeper into situations for underlying causes or to identify hidden opportunities. Without the interest that curiosity stimulates, it is unlikely that you will be motivated to put energy into deliberate thinking, and yet this first step of engagement is essential to tackling problems. Do you like puzzles—crossword puzzles, jigsaw puzzles, or manipulative games? Do you look at machines or electronic devices and wonder what makes them work? Do you look at people and wonder what makes them "tick"—why do they think and act as they do? Then your curiosity is at work and your readiness to problem solve is just waiting to be tapped.

Exploring the Vision: Visionary Thinking

Having a vision—looking at how things might be instead of how they currently are, or seeing things in different ways—often is identified as a key aspect of leadership (Bennis & Nanus, 1985; Goleman et al., 2002; Kotter, 1996; Kouzes & Posner, 1995). Because it is concerned with establishing a direction for the future, the step of Exploring the Vision in CPS requires the cognitive skill **Visionary Thinking**—*articulating a vivid image of what you desire to create.*

The basic question that this step addresses is "Where do I want to go?" In CPS, Visionary Thinking helps you imagine these future possibilities and then describe a lively and concrete picture of what direction you want to take to make them happen. The more clearly you can think through what you want your vision to contain, the easier it is to keep it in mind over time and to move toward it with energy. There is an old saying, "If you don't know where you are going, any road will take you there." Exploring the Vision in CPS is about getting more specific about what you want so that you can focus energy on achieving that outcome rather than waste time by going down blind alleys. As Kouzes and Posner (1995) stated, "All enterprises or projects, big or small, begin in the mind's eye; they begin with imagination and with the belief that what's merely an image can one day be made real" (p. 93). The goal that you identify during this step might be years away, such as introducing a new product successfully to market, or more immediate, such as increasing the performance of a team. Whatever the timeline is for the goal, the formulation of how you see the end result guides all thinking that is to follow.

A key affective skill that supports Visionary Thinking is **dreaming**. By dreaming we mean *the ability to imagine as possible your desires and hopes.* Dreaming helps you to be unconstrained in constructing your future. As Henry David Thoreau noted, "If one advances confidently in the direction of his dreams, and endeavors to live the life which he has imaged, he will meet with success unexpected in common hours." To imagine, to wish, and to envision that which does not exist in a current, concrete form heightens your awareness of favorable circumstances that you might be able to create in the future. As a result of dreaming, you expand your horizon of possibilities and enlarge your reality well beyond what you might normally consider.

Formulating Challenges: Strategic Thinking

An important basic cognitive thinking skill that makes Formulating Challenges in CPS work is **Strategic Thinking**—*identifying the critical issues that must be addressed and pathways that are needed to move toward the desired future.* Engaging in this step answers the key question, "What do I need to consider to get to my goal?"

In CPS, strategic thinking involves the generation and selection of challenges that require creative thought—those for which there are no predetermined solutions—and the formulation of these challenges into statements that invite imaginative thought. As a result of strategic thinking, you open up more directions and consider a broader range of choices. As a leader, you use Strategic Thinking in CPS to deliberately identify the challenges that stand between you and your goal and then to frame them into challenge statements that become springboards for idea generation.

An important affective skill that supports Strategic Thinking is awareness of the barriers that separate you from your goal. We refer to this as **sensing a gap**—*becoming consciously aware of discrepancies between what currently exists and what is desired or required.* This skill is about how you receive and process tacit information. Goleman et al. (2002) discuss tacit knowing that relies on intuition as being "the smart guess." They comment that "the smart guess matters now more than ever to leaders because they face such a deluge of data—often with no clear map of what the future portends" (p. 42). They cite Richard Fairbank, CEO of CapitalOne, who said,

> Finding a visionary strategy you believe as a leader is a very intuitive thing. There are things a leader can't predict using data. How do you know what you will need to have in three years? You've got to start developing now or you won't have it when you need it. (p. 42)

One way to develop your ability to sense gaps is to become more aware of your intuition, your hunches, and your "gut feelings." For example, do you recall the last time you had one of those "nagging feelings" that something was just not right about a decision you or someone else made? Or the last time that you tacitly "knew" you were on the right track, even though there was no immediate, concrete evidence to support it? What did you do about these feelings? Ignore them? Sleep on them and look at them again? Act on your hunch? How did you recognize this feeling? Regardless of what you did, you needed first to recognize that "something" was missing or "something" positive was there that was not apparent at first. Developing awareness of gaps helps you uncover possible obstacles that could impede progress or blindside you later; it helps you uncover the unknown rather than focus on the obvious. People who are not sensitive to gaps or discrepancies will find themselves tripping over unexpected hurdles as they move toward their goals.

Exploring Ideas: Ideational Thinking

The purpose of **Exploring Ideas** in CPS is to identify tentative solutions for the challenges that inhibit progress towards the vision. If the main question for the previous step was "What do I need to consider to get to my goal?" then for this step it is "What are my options?" In Exploring Ideas you use imaginative thought to address the most significant challenges before you. Your hope is that ideas with potential can be transformed into solutions that will close the gap between your present situation and the desired vision. The main thinking skill employed in this step is **Ideational Thinking,** which is *the ability to produce original mental images and thoughts that respond to important challenges.* A person who is adept at Ideational Thinking can easily generate many original and varied ideas.

A key affective skill that complements Ideational Thinking is **playfulness**. By playfulness we mean *freely toying with ideas*. Do you have anything on your desk to "toy" with while you talk or work? A playful attitude releases inhibitions and allows you the freedom to explore new or different ideas or angles. Games, toys, and interesting manipulative objects are not just for kids, and neither is a playful attitude. These kinds of things promote divergence in thought and allow you to look at a situation with a fresh and unique perspective. For example, employees at the design firm IDEO are well-known for their freewheeling and playful activities at work, including lots of brainstorming and the generation of wild ideas that are waiting to be tamed into sellable products. (To learn more about IDEO, see the Case Studies.)

Formulating Solutions: Evaluative Thinking

Alfred North Whitehead, an English mathematician, pointed out that "we think in generalities; we live in detail." He could just as easily have been describing what happens in **Formulating Solutions,** the purpose of which is to transform the potential idea or ideas into workable solutions that resolve the challenge(s) identified earlier. The question that is answered through this step is "Which options will work best?" The main thinking skill that enables you to determine this is **Evaluative Thinking.** When you use Evaluative Thinking in CPS, you closely *scrutinize the merits of an idea, and those ideas that seem most feasible are refined into solutions.* Strengths and weaknesses of the broad ideas are examined, weaknesses are overcome, and ideas are developed into solutions that have greater depth.

The research and development function within organizations provides an analogy to the relationship between the Exploring Ideas and Formulating the Solution steps. Research is the activity that often generates new product concepts; development efforts transform these initial concepts into marketable products and services. Good Evaluative Thinking prevents ideas that are not well-formed or are half-baked from going public.

A key affective skill that supports Evaluative Thinking is to **avoid premature closure**—*resisting the urge to push for a decision.* In CPS, you intentionally entertain novel approaches to problems, which requires you to consider ideas that at first seem outlandish and risky. Often people reject ideas simply because they have not heard them before. By resisting closure for a time, you give wild ideas a chance to survive and, perhaps after closer inspection, an opportunity to be refined into a solution that becomes revolutionary. Think of all the "wild" things that are now taken for granted that would not have come into existence if premature closure had been able to snuff them out completely—give up your cell phones, take off your digital watch, forget e-mail, and don't even think about flying anywhere, let alone to the moon.

Exploring Acceptance: Contextual Thinking

If you already know what you want to do, you will need to turn attention toward how to ensure success in the larger social context. The purpose of the **Exploring Acceptance** step in CPS is to examine factors that will help or hinder successful implementation of a change you have identified. The main question you want to answer here is "What are the things around me that will help or hinder how this solution is understood and accepted?" Many inventions that exist today were initially resisted—airplanes, automobiles, and talking movies were not immediately embraced with welcoming arms. As George Seldes, an American journalist, noted, "All great ideas are controversial, or have been at one time."

Effective work in the Exploring Acceptance step is dependent, in part, on your ability to engage in **Contextual Thinking,** which is *an understanding of the interrelated conditions and circumstances that will support or hinder success.* It is here, in particular, in the CPS process that leadership begins to "go public." You are no longer working inside your head—visioning, strategizing, ideating. Now you need to think about the impact of your solutions on a world where other people's ideas, opinions, and understanding of the situation may be very different from your own. Contextual thinking requires careful and deliberate consideration of your surroundings. For example, have you ever gone to a sports event and sat in an area where you were surrounded by fans of your opponent? Under those circumstances, would it be a good idea to boo the referee loudly if a call went against your team? If you are thinking contextually, you might decide this was a bad idea. In Contextual Thinking, you want to notice who, what, when, where, why, and how pockets of assistance and resistance can be identified and used.

Contextual Thinking is enhanced by the affective skill of **sensitivity to one's environment**. Sensitivity to one's environment means *the degree to which people are aware of their physical and psychological surroundings.* Contextual thinking begins with this affective skill, and sometimes your awareness of what is around you is all there is between you and a disaster. Sensitivity to your environment will help you to both hear and be heard by others so that you can identify areas of assistance and resistance and put them forward for a final examination before you have to implement. Is the timing good or bad to introduce a solution on Friday afternoon at 5 o'clock or as your boss is on her way out the door to go to a meeting? Is the solution complex or simple—how much time will you need to help others understand? Are there policies or cultural norms that might help or hinder the way your solution is presented? From whom should you get support first? Who is on your side? Who has the most to gain by your solution? The most to lose? Your ability to understand your interactions with others and to leverage the impact you have on them will be crucial in actually getting your solutions adopted.

Formulating a Plan: Tactical Thinking

In the final CPS process step, **Formulating a Plan,** you identify specific actions that you will take to ensure successful implementation of your solution. The main question to ask yourself here is "What concrete things do I have to do to make this happen?" These actions are then organized into an implementation plan by both time (short, intermediate, and long-term) and person (who is responsible for doing what by when?).

Because Formulating a Plan is the most concrete of all the process steps, the overarching cognitive thinking skill that makes this step successful is **Tactical Thinking**. By Tactical Thinking we mean *devising a plan that includes specific and measurable steps for attaining a desired end and methods for monitoring its effectiveness.*

A key affective skill influencing how successful you are in implementing your plan is **tolerance for risks.** Tolerance for risks means *not allowing yourself to be shaken or unnerved by the possibility of failure or setbacks.* Increasing your tolerance for risk is about (a) giving yourself permission to fail; and (b) managing your emotions when you do. When you reach the implementation step, you will be testing your commitment to the solution because it will be subjected to the views, opinions, and values of others, some of whom may not see its value in the same ways that you do.

Creativity researcher E. Paul Torrance (1971) commented, "You need courage to be creative. Just as soon as you have a new idea, you are in a minority of one. And being in a minority of one is uncomfortable—it takes courage" (p. 8). Developing this skill gives people the fortitude to pursue new ideas, which are often full of risks. One way to do this is to build up your emotional stamina for withstanding criticism by starting with small, low-risk actions. Deliberately decide on something simple that is a risk for you and just do it—eat a new food, go up to a stranger and say hello, say what is on your mind in a kind way instead of avoiding the issue. Afterwards monitor how you felt when you took the risk and what it would take to stretch a bit more next time. In classes and training, we often introduce the idea of giving yourself and others a mistake quota—a set number of, say, 20 a day. The idea of the activity is that to be successful at risk taking, you must meet your quota. If, when the day ends, you are under quota, then keep trying—you need to make a few more mistakes to successfully reach your goal. If you are over the quota before the day is over, then celebrate your success and raise your quota by another 10 mistakes.

❖ APPLYING WHAT YOU'VE LEARNED

Winston Churchill once said, "Empires of the future are empires of the mind." In this chapter, we have proposed that creative thinking is a building block for developing this unique empire, and CPS can be an organizing system for the deliberate use and practice of many of the thinking skills that can enhance leadership abilities. Try the activities below to further understand and practice the concepts in this chapter. You will have additional opportunities to develop these skills in depth in Chapters 5 through 11.

- Think of a leadership task you successfully completed. What were some of the skills you needed? List them. What were some of the skills you wish you had possessed but didn't? Relate these skills to those discussed in this chapter.
- Identify a current personal or professional situation for which you might use Diagnostic Thinking, Visionary Thinking, Strategic Thinking, Ideational Thinking, Evaluative Thinking, Contextual Thinking, or Tactical Thinking.
- For three days, observe and monitor how effectively you use the affective skills listed in this chapter. Which are your strong ones? Which could you improve?
- When watching your favorite TV show or movie, see if you can identify the kinds of thinking that are used to solve problems.

4

Transforming
Your Thinking

*Principles for Divergence
and Convergence*

Chapter at a Glance

Did you ever tackle a tough problem and wish you could come up with a few more options to help you achieve a breakthrough? Have you ever been overwhelmed with too many options, unsure of the best way to proceed? The purpose of this chapter is to go more deeply into divergent and convergent thinking. Specifically, we will describe a number of principles that guide effective divergent and convergent thought. Once internalized, these principles can do much to improve your ability to resolve predicaments and seize opportunities. In groups, these principles can be used as guidelines to keep individuals focused and to make meetings more efficient.

❖ DIVERGE AND CONVERGE: IT'S ABOUT THINKING AND BEHAVING

The divergent and convergent phases of CPS are unique in their function and purpose, and effective use of them will either make CPS stop or go. Like breathing in and out, these two alternating phases provide a natural movement across all steps of the CPS process that helps you manage your judgment and decision making to (a) get novelty and (b) keep it alive in your thinking and acting. The phases of diverging and converging are set up to do this by first requiring that you defer decisions to try to get something new or different and then by guiding how you actually *do* make decisions about the unique results to keep the creative elements alive. Because people are not accustomed to separating generating and judging, perhaps because of past training or experiences, we will present a set of principles that with practice can enhance your ability to think in divergent and convergent ways.

Over the years the many developers of CPS have devised and refined a set of principles to help people improve their ability to engage in divergent and convergent thinking (Isaksen & Treffinger, 1985; Miller et al., 2001; Osborn, 1963). Building on this work, Table 4.1 provides a summary of our current list of divergent and convergent principles along with one "wild card" principle. It is these principles that make CPS work. For individuals, these principles have the power to change thinking and thus, behavior. Once internalized, these same principles help to transform an individual into an active creative thinker.

These principles can also be productively employed in a group meeting. They can be presented as guidelines to help group members

Table 4.1   Divergent and Convergent Principles

To diverge . . .	To converge . . .
• Defer Judgment	• Apply Affirmative Judgment
• Go for Quantity	• Keep Novelty Alive
• Make Connections	• Check Your Objectives
• Seek Novelty	• Stay Focused
Wild card principle:	
• Allow for Incubation	

SOURCE: Based on Isaksen and Treffinger (1985); Miller, Vehar, and Firestien (2001); Osborn (1963).

engage in a discussion that reflects the thinking required at that time on a particular problem-solving task. When a group needs options, use the divergent principles as guidelines for the generation of alternatives. When decision making is required, use the convergent thinking principles. By using the principles as meeting guidelines, you can go a long way in preventing the start-and-stop thinking that grinds group problem-solving efforts to a halt.

❖ PRINCIPLES FOR DIVERGENT THINKING

There are four key principles that make divergent thinking work in CPS: (1) **Defer Judgment,** (2) **Go for Quantity,** (3) **Make Connections,** and (4) **Seek Novelty.** When you learn to use these principles, your thinking will focus with ease on new possibilities and your behavior will demonstrate to others that you are open to new ideas. Following these principles has been shown to dramatically improve divergent thinking skills for both individuals (e.g., Kabanoff & Bottger, 1991; Meadow & Parnes, 1959; Rose & Lin, 1984; Torrance, 1972) and teams (e.g., Basadur et al., 1982; Firestien & McCowan, 1988; Fontenot, 1993).

Defer Judgment

Have you ever prematurely discarded or criticized an idea only to find out after looking closer that the idea had merit? The purpose of the Defer Judgment principle is to help you avoid this tendency in your thinking. To defer judgment means to hold evaluation until a later time. In CPS, deferring judgment requires the ability to suspend disbelief and to entertain the potential value of each and every alternative you might generate.

The benefits of deferring judgment are:

- Increasing your awareness of and respect for possibilities
- Replacing a "can't" mentality with a "can-do" mindset to make you more open and receptive to new things
- Expanding your array of usable choices
- Helping you get a different idea or new way of looking at things, rather than working with "more of the same"

The Defer Judgment principle is crucial in divergent thinking because when judgment starts, divergent thinking stops. To be able to successfully diverge and generate many diverse and novel alternatives, you must switch off your judicial faculties. Judgment gets turned on again only after a considerable number of alternatives have been produced.

We are not saying that judgment is not important to the creative process. Judgment has its place in CPS, and its greatest value comes during the convergent phases of the process. When evaluative thought enters into the divergent phases, it severely limits your ability to produce many diverse and original options; it puts blinders on your ability to see alternatives, some of which may be quite useful.

The value of the Defer Judgment principle was one of the very first aspects of CPS to be experimentally tested. In an early study, Parnes and Meadow (1959) had research participants solve a problem alone. Some were asked to generate ideas by following the Defer Judgment principle. Individuals in this group were to record every idea that came to mind. The second group of participants was instructed to evaluate ideas as they were generated. These participants also worked alone; however, they were asked to record only their good ideas. Analysis of the ideas generated by the two groups showed that individuals who followed the Defer Judgment principle generated almost twice as many good ideas as those who simultaneously generated and evaluated their ideas.

Go for Quantity

You are at great risk when you have a critical problem to solve and only one idea in mind. The Go for Quantity principle is primarily aimed at building fluency in thought, which depends on an ability to generate many possibilities. The power of Go for Quantity was captured well by Nobel Laureate Linus Pauling when he simply said, "The best way to have a good idea is to have a lot of ideas."

Going for quantity and producing many ideas has at least four practical benefits.

- It increases the likelihood that one of your ideas will become a breakthrough idea.
- The more you produce, the more you learn. Every idea generated provides an opportunity to learn what will and will not work.
- Research has shown that the most original ideas come after a period of extended idea generation. When a list of ideas is evaluated for originality, the final third of the list typically reflects the most original thinking (Parnes, 1961).
- It prevents groups from making the mistake of jumping on the first idea that sounds like it might work—which has **often** been

the case for teams in the reality show "The Apprentice"—or a project leader from becoming enamored with his or her own idea rather than considering it just one among many ideas.

Dean Simonton, a current creativity researcher, found support for quantity promoting quality in his longitudinal research of individuals who were socially recognized for their creativity (Simonton, 1977, 1985, 1997). Simonton (1998) concluded that "the number of successful products that emerge during a given career has been shown to be a positive linear function of the total number of works generated" (p. 155). This implies that the more ideas you play with, the more products you are likely to create. Box 4.1 provides examples of how some highly creative people pursued quantity.

There is similar support for the Go for Quantity principle in organizations. To get one idea to market, people in organizations must first generate and test hundreds, if not thousands, of ideas. For example, CapitalOne tested 45,000 ideas for new credit cards in 2000. Most of the ideas failed, but having so many ideas to test and refine is one major reason why this company holds more than 30 million credit card accounts (Sutton, 2002). In his book *Weird Ideas That Work,* Sutton (2002) gives several examples of the value of going for quantity. He cites the careful records kept at a small toy design studio at IDEO as illustrative of how many ideas it takes to eventually arrive at a handful that are believed to have any market value. In 1998, the IDEO design group generated 4,000 ideas for new toys, 230 of which were deemed promising enough to develop drawings and prototypes. Of the 230 ideas that were elaborated, 12 were eventually sold to clients. This isn't true just for toys. A cross-industry study showed it took an average of 3,000 initial ideas to get to one successful market innovation (Stevens & Burley, 1997).

The Go for Quantity principle has had such an influence on group behavior that many organizations have even systematized it in the workplace. For example, in the late 1990s, to ensure an idea-rich work environment, 3M adopted a management practice that encouraged all employees to develop creative ideas (Sorensen, 1997). In technical areas, employees were allowed to use up to 15% of their time to explore and develop ideas of their own choosing. Many organizations also have suggestion systems or idea banks. These idea management systems were created to draw out a large number of ideas from employees across the entire organization, in the hope that a smaller number will emerge that will significantly reduce costs, increase profit, or improve performance.

Box 4.1   Real-World Example

Go for Quantity: Some Well-Known People and Results

Many people who are socially recognized for their creativity have followed the Go for Quantity principle. They generated many ideas and products from which the truly best emerged. Well-known artists, such as O'Keeffe, Picasso, Cezanne, and Dali did not simply create a small number of paintings that became masterpieces; rather, they created a large number of paintings from which their greatest works emerged. Inventors like Thomas Edison, Alexander Graham Bell, and George Washington Carver pursued many invention ideas from which a smaller number revolutionized the world. William Shakespeare wrote 154 sonnets and 37 plays. Not surprisingly, an assessment of Shakespeare's sonnets reveals that although many are recognized as exemplary works, others are of lesser quality (Simonton, 1999). The experiences of these highly creative individuals underscore Alex Osborn's position that quality comes through quantity.

Make Connections

Have you ever found that one thought immediately triggers another, or perhaps you've been involved in a conversation where a person shares something that sparks an idea in your own mind? This third principle for divergent thinking, Make Connections, takes advantage of the fact that the human mind readily makes these kinds of associations. This principle is a great friend to novelty because if you don't get something unusual from your initial fluency, then you have yet another chance to create it by "piggy-backing" off other ideas or comments. The benefits of the Make Connections principle are:

- It increases the likelihood of obtaining unusual responses and solutions.
- It encourages flexible thinking.
- It helps to elaborate on or extend initial ideas.
- It provides cross-fertilization of ideas and results.

You can use other people's ideas or information from other fields to either extend or elaborate on your own thinking or to introduce a new train of thought. For example, Shakespeare used the poem *Romeo and Juliet* by Arthur Brooke and transformed it into a play (Davis, 1986). Alexander Graham Bell demonstrated this kind of thinking when he used the human ear as a model to develop the telephone. Salvador Dali's painting *The Persistence of Memory* (also known as *Soft Watches*), in which a number of clock faces appear to be melting, was in fact inspired by a dream about runny camembert cheese. The famous dome that dominates St. Paul's Cathedral in London owes its design, in part, to the microscope. Robert Hooke, the engineer, who wrestled with the technical challenges associated with architect Sir Christopher Wren's ambitious vision for the dome, had perfected the microscope and, in fact, Hooke had written a book on microscopy called *Micrographia*. Like a microscope, the great dome of St. Paul's has a smaller oculus at the top and a larger oculus in the middle, which creates the illusion of great light (Jardine, 1999).

From these examples you can see how making connections enhances creative thought, but since they are about famous people, you might wonder whether this principle is applicable in everyday life or to organizational problems. With approximately 50% of sales coming from the drive-through business, McDonald's wanted to find a way to speed up this service (Cambou & Hill, 2000). Analysis revealed that the bottleneck in the process was the time required for cash transactions. Efficiency experts and think tank gurus set on the problem, but no satisfactory solution emerged. That is, until a McDonald's owner/operator, Patti Widdicombe, made a connection. Returning from a meeting in which this had been discussed, she entered a toll road and noticed that the transponder in her car eliminated the need to stop at the tollbooth. The proverbial light bulb then went on. Why not use transponders to eliminate cash transactions? You give your order and pick up your food, then bypass the pay window because a transponder in your car charges your credit card. This system, called FasTrac, is now being tested in limited locations.

We don't know whether the FasTrac system will take off for McDonald's, but we do know that a number of very successful products resulted from the Make Connections principle. Synectics™ (Gordon, 1961), a creative process methodology based on the use of metaphors, has been applied to a variety of real business challenges. When engineers were faced with the challenge of finding better fasteners for space suits, burrs (those round prickly brown balls that stick to your pants when walking through tall grass) led to the creation of Velcro. When a business wanted a better way to package and ship potato chips so they would not break, noticing the way wet leaves can be compactly packed into garbage bags because they conform to one another led to the development of Pringles Potato Chips (Gordon, 1980).

A recent book by Johansson (2004), *The Medici Effect: Breakthrough Insights at the Intersection of Ideas, Concepts, and Cultures,* makes a strong case for the value of making connections, what Johansson refers to as the Intersection. He argued, "For most of us, the best chance to innovate lies at the Intersection. Not only do we have a greater chance of finding remarkable idea combinations there, we will also find many more of them" (p. 20). Johansson's book provides numerous real-life examples of the cross-fertilization of ideas, as well as advice and strategies to enhance this skill.

Seek Novelty

There is a saying that "those who believe the sky is the limit have a limited imagination." The purpose of divergent thinking is not to only entertain all possibilities, no matter how outlandish they may appear at first glance, but to actively go after them. The Seek Novelty principle encourages you to really stretch your thinking—to get your mind "out of the box." This principle challenges you to look at a situation and find a new opportunity that has never been considered, come up with a new view of an old problem, or generate an idea that is paradigm breaking.

The divergent principle of Seek Novelty specifically focuses on the need to introduce originality into the divergent phases of the process. Some of the benefits associated with the Seek Novelty principle are:

- It leads to breakthrough ideas.
- It stimulates other ideas that may be practical.
- It fosters a playful and creative atmosphere in groups.

Certainly, the other three principles help to facilitate the production of original thought, but they may not be sufficient to ensure it. It is not difficult to imagine someone generating a long list of options among which there is great flexibility but little originality. For example, take a moment to create a list of all the birds that come to mind (International LearningWorks, 1996). You can either write it down or do it in your mind. When you are finished, read on.

The list you generated is probably fairly long and might contain different categories of birds, such as waterfowl, birds of prey, and so on. However, does your list include more unusual alternatives? Does your list include birds that few others would identify? For example, does your list include the ex-professional basketball player Larry Bird, Robert C. Byrd, the Senator from West Virginia, the shuttlecock used to play badminton, or the name of an airplane such as the Boeing 747? Many people would not think of these more unusual perspectives on the word "bird," unless they were instructed to do so. That deliberateness is the reason why Seek Novelty is a principle for divergent thinking.

The development of Post-it Notes™ is the direct result of a scientist who intentionally sought novelty. Although 3M at the time was interested in producing ever-stronger adhesives, their scientist Spencer Silver created an adhesive that didn't stick very well to other objects. As Sorensen (1997) retells the story, "Spencer Silver tested a new monomer by overloading a reaction mixture far beyond textbook standards, just to see what would happen. He discovered a novel substance that clung to its own molecules better than to other molecules" (p. 29). Silver's approach epitomizes the principle of seeking novelty because he intentionally tried something new just to see what might come of it. As is often the case with novel concepts, it took many years to gain acceptance; however, this highly unusual thought created an entirely new industry.

In some cases, a wild idea might stimulate a practical one. Linemen who worked for Pacific Power and Light were faced with a difficult and dangerous responsibility each fall and spring (Camper, 1993). The ice storms that occur in the Pacific Northwest during these seasons led to serious ice accumulation on the power transmission lines. After such storms, linemen were sent out to remove the ice build-up by climbing the icy poles and then using long poles to shake the power lines. There were a number of injuries. Brainstorming sessions were held to come up with a solution. In one session, the idea of training bears to climb the poles to shake the ice loose was suggested. This met with laughter. This was soon followed by a comment that although it would be difficult to train bears, perhaps a pot of honey might be placed on top of the pole to coax the bears up. More laughter. One participant sarcastically quipped, "Why don't we use one of the corporate helicopters to place the honey pots on the poles?" Following this period of laughter a secretary spoke up. She had been a nurse's aide in Vietnam and saw many injured soldiers arrive by helicopter. She wondered out loud whether the down wash from the rotating helicopter blades might be powerful enough to clear the power lines. Silence. Soon after this meeting, Pacific Power and Light began using helicopters to fly over power lines after ice storms.

Even if novel ideas do not themselves lead to breakthroughs, the experience of allowing for novelty still provides some benefits, especially in groups. When highly unusual alternatives are generated they are often met with laughter. This laughter encourages playfulness and creates a relaxed atmosphere, which helps to facilitate further divergent thoughts.

We have now completed our description of the principles that can enhance your ability to think divergently and, as a result, improve your effectiveness as a leader. In Box 4.2 we provide a description of research conducted by Sutton and Hargadon (1996) that gives some insights into the organizational benefits of applying many of the principles just described. These researchers were curious about how the design firm IDEO could remain so innovative through the years. What they concluded was that the principles of divergent thinking had much to do with IDEO's success.

Box 4.2   Research Note

Creativity Principles Drive Innovation at Product Design Firm

Sutton and Hargadon (1996) conducted a year-long, ethnographic study within IDEO, the largest product design firm in the United States, to understand why this organization has been so consistently successful in developing innovative products. These researchers began their study with the broad question "How does IDEO innovate routinely?" Early in their research they discovered a major variable that appeared to be critical to IDEO's success, namely brainstorming. At IDEO, brainstorming, which is based on Osborn's original work, follows five guidelines: defer judgment, build on the ideas of others, have one conversation at a time, stay focused on the topic, and encourage wild ideas.

Sutton and Hargadon discovered that the guidelines used to conduct formal brainstorming sessions were not confined solely to these idea-generation meetings, but permeated the entire organization.

> Designers conveyed this with statements like "brainstorming is a way of life here" and "we have a brainstorming culture." IDEO is a place in which people, in doing much of their work, try to avoid criticizing others, build on others' ideas, have one conversation at a time, and generate a lot of ideas. These aspirations and actions are often easier to observe in brainstorming sessions than in informal conversations or e-mail exchanges, but there often isn't much difference between the way the designers act inside and outside of these sessions. (pp. 714–715)

From this observation it would seem that IDEO has created a work ethos based largely on the creative process principles outlined in this chapter. Furthermore, as noted in this chapter, these meeting guidelines have been internalized to such a degree at IDEO that they have become principles that guide individuals' behavior in the workplace. Through their analysis, Sutton and Hargadon attributed six powerful organizational benefits to the application of these creativity principles.

First, the research team concluded that these principles supported organizational memory of design solutions. Both the formal brainstorming meetings and the interactions that occurred outside such meetings provided opportunities to add new design ideas to IDEO's organizational memory. This storehouse of solutions was often drawn upon and applied in new ways to solve current design challenges. Second, brainstorms within IDEO promoted the acquisition of skill variety among designers. Brainstorming sessions allowed designers to learn about new products and industries, to blend old ideas in new ways, to work with others' ideas, and to create rough prototypes. Third, the use of brainstorms and the brainstorming principles supported the attitude of wisdom. Because designers recognize the limits of their knowledge, they readily seek the advice of others, listen to others' ideas, examine all sides of the issue, and are not afraid to admit making mistakes—all attributes of wisdom. Fourth, brainstorms and the related principles contributed to a business environment in which status is achieved, in part, through technical skills and idea production prowess. Fifth, the positive, creative, and fun working climate in brainstorming meetings often made such an impression on clients that even if the resultant prototypes were themselves not impressive, the clients would sign on for long-term projects with IDEO. Finally, the brainstorming sessions, for a variety of reasons, were a useful source of income.

This is only a brief review of Sutton and Hargadon's research on benefits of brainstorming in the broader organizational context. For greater detail, we suggest readers examine the original report. See Chapter 8 for further information on brainstorming. To learn more about IDEO go to the case study section in the back of this book. Also see Kelley and Littman's (2001) book *The Art of Innovation: Lessons in Creativity from IDEO, America's Leading Design Firm*.

❖ PRINCIPLES FOR CONVERGENT THINKING

In CPS, divergent and convergent thinking are a package deal—they function together in a dynamically balanced way first to engender novelty and then to protect it until it has a chance to be developed and used. When the principles for divergent thinking are used accurately, the result will be a menu of alternatives that is large in number, varied, and unusual. In convergence, you turn your energy away from generating alternatives and focus on examining what has been created and on making decisions about how it will be used. Alternatives must be evaluated and perhaps strengthened or developed. The goal of the convergent phase in each step of the CPS process is to arrive at a short list of alternatives that stand head and shoulders above the rest.

There are four principles that guide the convergent phases within CPS: (1) **Apply Affirmative Judgment**, (2) **Keep Novelty Alive**, (3) **Check Your Objectives**, and (4) **Stay Focused**. These principles support the functions of convergent thinking for individuals and become guidelines for team decision making when applied effectively in groups.

Apply Affirmative Judgment

To converge effectively you must learn to work with your judgment. In contrast to the suspension of judgment while thinking divergently, the key principle in convergent thinking is to Apply Affirmative Judgment. **Affirmative Judgment** is about *using effective critical thinking as opposed to faultfinding*, which is a habitual or excessive emphasis on identifying shortcomings. When you judge an option in an affirmative manner, you carefully consider both the positives and the negatives. The effective use of affirmative judgment sets the tone for convergent thinking. With it, the momentum of the creative process can be sustained; without it, the spark of creativity may be snuffed out.

When we say judgment enters the CPS process during its convergent phases, we are not referring to a slash-and-burn approach to evaluation—"OK, now that we are finished with divergent thinking, let's go in and get rid of all the bad ideas." Such an approach to evaluation focuses exclusively on shortcomings and limitations, and, as a consequence, any alternative that is even remotely unusual is likely to be eliminated. This negative approach tears down ideas rather than building them up. The net result of screening alternatives based on finding what is wrong leads to the premature elimination of options that might be improved with modifications.

When presented with a new idea, often the first thing people notice is why it won't work. This is not unexpected because people have been trained to be critical, to find gaps and flaws. People seek order and consistency, and they develop habits. Experience has taught what works and what does not work. Being an effective critical thinker, developing habits, and creating structure and order are not bad things. They help make people more efficient. However, these same things can undermine creative thinking. Divergent thinking intentionally opens up new possibilities. It challenges paradigms and creates new knowledge.

When these new insights come they are usually imperfect and not fully formed. Thus, a natural reaction to a divergent thought is to reject it, to find the flaws. You may have experienced this yourself. Have you ever shared an idea only to be immediately met with all the reasons why it won't work? People typically react to such criticism in two ways. They either become defensive about the idea or they withdraw it. Both scenarios are unproductive and derail positive exchanges in regard to ideas. See Box 4.3 for a historical lesson related to an inability to affirmatively judge an idea.

Box 4.3   Real-World Example

**The Visionary Leadership of Billy Mitchell:
How a Lack of Affirmative Judgment
Grounded the American Air Force**

Aviation recently celebrated the 100th anniversary of controlled powered flight. Although the benefits of commercial and military flight are without question today, this has not always been the case. In fact, in the early days of military aviation there were staunch opponents, primarily military leaders of the established branches (e.g., Navy and Army) who believed airplanes contributed no real advantage.

One visionary, Billy Mitchell, the first American to fly over enemy positions during World War I, recognized how the stalemate and tremendous bloodshed associated with trench warfare could be eradicated through airpower. At that time, Colonel Mitchell envisioned how airplanes could strike at the strategic nerve center of the enemy, and thus, in his estimation, reduce the tremendous loss of human life associated with traditional methods of warfare.

Upon returning to the United States after World War I with the rank of General, Mitchell began to speak out about the centrality of airplanes in the future of warfare. General Mitchell described with great eloquence how future wars would be defined as much by what occurred in the air as by what happened on land and sea. This visionary leader, as is often the case, was viewed as a heretic. He was perceived as a threat by the military establishment. Where current military leaders could see only two dimensions to war, land and sea, Mitchell was describing a third dimension—air.

His superiors ordered Mitchell to tone down his message. In response, Mitchell redoubled his efforts to share his vision. Things came to a head in July 1921, when Mitchell was invited to put his ideas of airpower to the test against a captured German battleship, the *Ostfriesland*, a massive ship

(Continued)

(Continued)

believed to be unsinkable. With some 300 military, governmental, and public leaders present, a fleet of Martin bombers, tiny specks in contrast to the behemoth battleship, took off at 12:19 p.m. Some 20 minutes later they released their bombs and at 12:40 the unsinkable battleship disappeared below the surface. Despite the obvious success of this test, most military leaders still claimed to see no merit in the idea of airplanes as main instruments of warfare. In fact, General John Pershing, General of the Armies, released a report concluding that battleships were still the backbone of the Navy.

Despite intense criticism of his ideas, Mitchell continued to share his vision of the future with audiences across the United States. In response, the military sent Mitchell on an extended inspection tour of Hawaii, the Philippines, China, India, and Japan. His hiatus from the United States did not dampen his enthusiasm for military aircraft. Conversely, his observations overseas further convinced him that it would be imperative to control the skies in future wars. In the mid-1920s, Mitchell predicted impending war with Japan and hypothesized that the Japanese would use a surprise attack from the air to initiate a war with the United States.

On February 19, 1936, at the age of 57, Billy Mitchell passed away. Approximately six years later Japan attacked Pearl Harbor from the air. During the onset of World War II, President Roosevelt was faced with numerous momentous decisions. One of his first decisions changed the nature of military conflict. Remembering the vision of Billy Mitchell, Roosevelt overturned his advisors' suggestions to build up the traditional modes of warfare. Instead, he diverted money to military aircraft. Prior to Roosevelt's request, the United States had produced just 800 planes in a two-year period. Now Roosevelt demanded that 4,000 military planes be turned out per year.

The story of Billy Mitchell, and the critical response to his ideas, illustrates how others with entrenched thinking are often unwittingly incapable of taking an affirmative view of new ideas.

SOURCE: Bradley (2003).

Keep Novelty Alive

The principle of Keep Novelty Alive is directly related to the need to protect and sustain the novelty that came during the divergent phase. Where the Affirmative Judgment principle helps to modify how people react to and evaluate ideas in general, the Keep Novelty Alive principle specifically challenges you to entertain highly original ideas. Imagine you are the CEO of a soap manufacturing company and your marketing team is presenting their latest marketing strategy to you.

Here's their new exciting idea—drum roll please—they wish to give away a solid oak desk with the purchase of a case of soap. They wait for your reaction and you say. . . . So what would you say to that idea? How would you react to an idea of giving away a solid oak desk with a purchase of 100 bars of soap? Our experience is that most people quickly say that the idea is crazy. It will never work.

Well, guess what? In the late 1800s–early 1900s, the Larkin Soap Company of Buffalo, New York really did offer a free solid oak desk with the purchase of a case of soap, and the venture was a huge success (Larkin, 1998). The soap manufacturer gave away a variety of premium items, such as piano lamps and oak chairs. But the most popular premium gift was the oak Chautauqua desk. Initially the Larkin Soap Company bought the premium gifts wholesale from the manufacturer, but soon they learned it was more profitable to produce their own. This led the company into such subsidiary activities as furniture production and pottery making. In fact, today's Buffalo China company is a descendant of Buffalo Pottery, started by the Larkin Soap Company in 1901.

So why was the idea so successful? There were a number of reasons. First, the profit margin was substantial. The Larkin Company would sell a case containing 100 bars of soap for $10. The soap cost pennies to produce, and the Chautauqua desk cost $4. Thus, on this very popular premium package (in one day alone in February 1900, they sold 2,036 cases of soap) the company netted a 50% profit on each sale. One of the principle reasons why the company grew into a $30 million business (roughly $24 billion in today's dollars) was its very successful marketing strategy of giving away premium gifts, such as the solid oak desk. After all, if you just received a beautiful desk with your purchase of a case of soap, wouldn't you tell your friends about it?

To Keep Novelty Alive not only means that you should entertain original concepts that have been previously generated, but also suggests that it is important to be open to the unexpected. Sometimes, when in pursuit of a creative solution to one problem, people accidentally discover something quite unexpected. The Keep Novelty Alive principle advises not to simply discard the unexpected outcome as a mistake, but to be open to benefits associated with the new discovery. The microwave oven originated this way. The magnetron was invented during World War II in England. A magnetron tube, which emits microwaves, was installed in radar systems to help spot German warplanes on their way to bomb England. A few years later, while working with microwaves, a scientist named Percy LeBaron found a melted chocolate bar in his pocket. Rather than ignoring this unusual incident,

LeBaron became curious and deduced that microwaves were the cause. With a little more investigation it was discovered that microwaves could cook many foods faster than conventional ovens (The Great Idea Finder, n.d.).

The story of Viagra provides another example of how remaining open to novelty can lead to positive outcomes. Viagra's developer, the multinational pharmaceutical company Pfizer, did not start out searching for a drug to address penile dysfunction, but thanks to some sharp-eyed clinicians that is what they found. Viagra—originally known as compound UK-92,480—was created in 1989 as an antihypertensive drug, but shortly thereafter was targeted as a potential treatment for angina. During clinical trials as a remedy for angina, a curious side effect occurred. A clinician, in reporting the results of a recent clinical trial to the project manager, mentioned as an afterthought an unexpected side effect—penile erection. In light of this novel piece of information, and despite the common belief that penile dysfunction was a psychological disorder, the project team took up this line of research, which eventually lead to Viagra, an oral drug for penile dysfunction.

In summary, the purpose of the Keep Novelty Alive principle is twofold. First, it is designed to prevent people from eliminating novel ideas too quickly. The second purpose of this principle is to encourage an open-minded curiosity about unexpected outcomes.

Check Your Objectives

The divergent thinking principles are designed to rid your thinking of possible constraints. The goal is to allow your mind to freewheel. During the convergent thinking phases of the process, it is important to carefully consider the reality of the situation. You need to be aware of the standards that must be met to ensure success. The clearer the criteria for success, the easier it is to make decisions about which alternatives are most useful. This principle is referred to as Check Your Objectives.

To some readers, it may seem paradoxical to have one principle for convergent thinking that focuses on maintaining novelty, while another, Check Your Objectives, focuses on what is realistic. We do not believe that these two principles negate one another. Rather, their juxtaposition highlights the balance in thinking that is required to eventually arrive at a creative change. Recall that the most common definition of creativity is the production of novel associations that are useful. This delicate balance between novelty and usefulness was captured well in Oldach's (1995) advice to graphic designers: "You must embrace both realism and creativity throughout the evaluation process. Being too creative can cause you to lose sight of the communication objectives for the project. Being too realistic can blind you to risky, innovative solutions" (p. 88). Constraints do not necessarily eliminate creative thought; rather, the constraints define the framework within which an original concept will have its greatest impact.

Creativity is not about producing something that is novel for novelty's sake; the true creative genius finds a way to produce something that is original and successfully meets a need. A creative product can be original either by extending the current paradigm or by creating a new paradigm. In both cases, however, to eventually be considered creative these products must be useful. Placing a second door on the driver's side of the minivan is an example of the former. The creation of Post-it Notes™, which produced an entire new market, is an example of the latter. Ultimately, both products had to meet certain constraints to be considered useful—they had to meet consumers' needs. Thus, the alternatives generated via divergent thinking must meet the objectives associated with the people whose needs are being addressed, such as the consumer, client, the student, or yourself.

Stay Focused

Convergent thinking requires a thoughtful and measured approach. Where more dynamic energy is employed during divergent thinking, convergent thinking is more reflective and purposeful. There should be at least as much time invested in evaluating and selecting the best options as there is time used to produce the divergent list of alternatives. We have seen far too many meetings in which the 80–20 rule is more descriptive of the balance between divergent and convergent thinking. In such meetings, we have witnessed teams invest about 80% of their time in generating alternatives and then use the remainder of their scheduled time together to cull through the alternatives to arrive at a decision. Team members lose track of themselves as they explore what might be done and suddenly recognize that only a short amount of time remains to come to a decision. The risk in such cases is that the pressure to reach a decision may result in the most expedient alternative being selected, which may not be the best. Thus, the final principle for convergent thinking is to Stay Focused, to invest the necessary thought and energy to ensure that the best alternatives are being selected and then developed.

When we say Stay Focused, we are not trying to negate the "Aha" phenomenon, those situations in which an elegant idea suddenly presents itself. We have seen individuals and teams strike upon a breakthrough in the midst of a divergent thinking phase. When such a breakthrough is so compelling, it is appropriate to shift immediately from divergent thinking to convergent thinking. Although it is exciting and energizing to be able to fix so quickly on one standout alternative, which eliminates the time required to closely weigh a larger set of options, it is still important to closely examine and test the breakthrough thought before running with it. As the old carpenter's adage goes, "measure twice, cut once." It is also wise to have backup alternatives waiting in the wings.

There are numerous examples of how extraordinary creative people have used a deliberate convergent thinking process to develop creative products that are widely recognized by society. In fact, it could be argued that if it had not been for an ability to deliberately and systematically refine one's thinking, to stay focused, some of these great creators might not be recognized today for their obvious creative talent. Analysis of William Wordsworth's poetry revealed that his work did not simply emerge as a first and final draft; rather, he invested a great deal of time in revising and reworking the lines. In fact, Wordsworth spent 40 years revising and rewriting a piece called *The Prelude.* Wordsworth was known for his ability to beautifully describe the natural environment. In assessing this skill, Jeffrey (1989) observed, "This naturalism was not achieved by simple spontaneity. It required a great deal of deliberate, knowing self-criticism and revision. In the course of writing his poetry, Wordsworth sometimes noted the need for revision." (p. 71). Box 4.4 describes how Pablo Picasso displayed this ability to stay focused.

Box 4.4   Real-World Example

How Pablo Picasso Stayed Focused

Few artists have had a greater impact on modern art than Pablo Picasso. Picasso was a child prodigy whose works as an adolescent quickly surpassed that of the local master artists, including his father. Although Picasso was clearly a prodigy, it was not simple artistic talent that enabled him to define modern art. Picasso's creative products were born out of great labor. Radiographic studies revealed that Picasso continuously refined his paintings. Below the surface of the painting might be many other images and figures that Picasso decided not to include in the final product. Harvard professor Howard Gardner noted that although Picasso produced numerous works each year of his life, there was a smaller number in which Picasso saw greatness. Of these works, Gardner (1993) commented, "the canvas would be bigger, the preparation would take longer, there would be many drafts and sketches" (p. 152). In some cases it would take a decade to produce a final product. Ultimately it was these works that became most famous. For instance, before Picasso produced *Les demoiselles d'Avignon*, one of the most important paintings of the 20th century, he refined the ideas for this piece in at least eight full notebooks.

Staying focused while converging means balancing intuition with critical analysis. Intuition helps you determine which alternatives are most promising to pursue, while critical analysis helps you to objectively test and refine your subjective insights. Palus and Horth (2002) refer to this as the analytic sandwich. They recommend that leaders use critical analysis to counterbalance the ambiguity associated with intuitive decision making and use intuition and feelings to unlock the analysis paralysis that can arise from strict objective decision making. In a study on the effectiveness in selecting candidates for senior management positions, Guzzo and Palmer (1998) found that participants made the best decisions when intuition and deliberate analysis were combined in the deliberation process. Specifically, they found the most effective combination to be the use of intuition and personal preference in the early stages of the selection process, followed by more deliberate analysis. To summarize, intuition is like the metal detector: it helps us to zero in on the possibilities. Critical analysis is like the digging technique used to eventually unearth the hidden treasure. It is the combination of intuition and critical analysis that epitomizes what we mean by staying focused during the convergent phases of the creative process.

We have now described the main principles associated with divergent and convergent thinking. The next section describes our wildcard principle, Allow for Incubation.

❖ ALLOW FOR INCUBATION: THE WILDCARD PRINCIPLE

In this chapter we have offered principles for both divergence and convergence. In closing, we would like to suggest one more principle, which we refer to as a wildcard because it supports both divergent and convergent thought. That principle is Allow for Incubation. The classic description of the creative process by Graham Wallas (1926) featured four stages of thought, Preparation, Incubation, Illumination, and

Verification. Preparation refers to the stage in which a problem is consciously and systematically investigated. During Incubation, however, the problem is not consciously worked on. Incubation provides a break from the active pursuit of a solution to the problem. The term Incubation comes from a description of the development of a chick within the egg. The chick is invisible to the observer, and it is sometimes the case that your ideas develop without your full awareness. Often, after a period of incubation, a solution suddenly comes to mind; the light bulb goes on. Wallas referred to this stage as Illumination. In the final stage, Verification, the solution is tested for its soundness.

Although it is counterintuitive to believe that an idle period could be valuable when you are trying to solve an important problem, there are many examples in history that underscore the value of allowing your mind to move away from the problem (Smith & Dodds, 1999). German physicist Herman von Helmholtz claimed that his best ideas never came while at his desk, but rather when he was in a relaxed state such as enjoying a walk in the sun. French mathematician Henri Poincaré reported that two of his greatest discoveries came to him while he was not consciously engaged in mathematical problem solving. One insight came while serving as a military reservist, the other while on a journey (Wallas, 1926). The vision of the condenser that eventually allowed James Watt, the Scottish inventor, to maximize steam power came to him while he was in bed (Carnegie, 1905). Kary Mullis, a biochemist preoccupied with the problem of the replication of DNA molecules, experienced his breakthrough idea while driving in the California hills. Shortly afterward, Mullis received the Nobel Prize, due in part to the revolutionary insight that came to him in his car (Smith & Dodds, 1999).

Undoubtedly you have your own personal examples of incubation at work. Have you ever noticed how some of your best work-related ideas came to you while not at work? Perhaps you were driving your car, engaged in physical exercise, shaving, or daydreaming when suddenly you had a breakthrough for a workplace challenge. Beyond anecdotal evidence of the benefits of incubation from our own experiences and the reported experiences of individuals recognized for their creative genius, scientific research has underscored the benefits of incubation time. Smith and Dodds (1999) reviewed a number of studies that demonstrated that research participants who were given incubation time outperformed participants in the control group on a variety of tasks, such as designing experiments, solving insight problems, and memory recall.

A number of theories attempt to explain how incubation works (Smith & Dodds, 1999). One view holds that incubation time allows the mind to refresh. Thinking takes physical energy, and by temporarily suspending your conscious efforts to solve some problem, you recharge your mental batteries. Some have argued that during an incubation break you are exposed to stimuli and experiences that are incorporated into your thoughts about the problem that may eventually lead to a breakthrough (e.g., recall the story of Sir Isaac Newton and the falling apple). Another theory about incubation holds that time away from the active search for solutions allows you to forget the incorrect solutions. By forgetting, you stop focusing on unproductive solutions and clear a path for the best solution to emerge. These theories, and others, were developed to explain how incubation works. As of yet, scientific research has not conclusively pinpointed which theory is most accurate.

Although researchers have not arrived at a strict conclusion about how incubation works, there appears to be some consensus regarding the role knowledge plays in leading to creative breakthroughs (Kaufmann, 1988; Weisberg, 1999). You can incubate all you wish, but if you do not possess the requisite background knowledge for a particular problem, it is highly unlikely that you will have a creative idea in that domain. As Kaufmann (1988) noted,

> We may now expect that high-level creativity is crucially dependent on a large amount of well-organized domain-specific knowledge. Before the fruits of creativity can be reaped, then, we may expect that a long history of building up domain specific knowledge and skills must precede. (p. 114)

Even though there is no single best description of how incubation works, we do believe that the results produced through incubated thought are often quite beneficial to both divergent and convergent thinking. With respect to divergent thinking, time to incubate helps you to generate further options, perhaps leading to a true breakthrough. When active methods of divergent thinking fail to produce a satisfactory option, it may be useful to intentionally inject an incubation period. Take a break, go on to some other project, engage in some physical activity, but be prepared to capture any incubated thoughts that come to mind.

Incubation can also help when evaluating a promising alternative. For example, the expression "I need to sleep on it" is a way of saying that you need to allow information to soak in. Ruminating on an alternative before leaping to action gives you a greater understanding of its strengths, weaknesses, and possible implications. The pressure of some work schedules does not promote incubation, but whenever possible, it may be a wise investment of time.

One final thought on incubation. Since it occurs naturally, whether you explicitly allow for it or not, it is wise to be prepared to capture your incubated thoughts. Leonardo da Vinci and Charles Darwin had their journals. Pablo Picasso had his notebooks. Michael Faraday had an idea book. Ideas can come at any time, and if they are not captured, they are easily forgotten. We recommend creating a system for capturing your ideas. Idea systems can be used to capture fresh ideas and elaborated thoughts from previous ideas, questions, observations, and daydreams.

❖ APPLYING WHAT YOU'VE LEARNED

It has been said that leadership is about action, not position. Individuals who learn to embody the principles shared in this chapter will engage in actions that clearly demonstrate their ability to engage in creative thinking. They will stand out as people who are flexible-minded innovators able to uplift themselves and others by developing novel solutions to open-ended challenges and opportunities. Below are some activities designed to assist you in internalizing the principles described in this chapter.

- Over the course of several days or a week, keep a journal and record observations about how you and other people have responded to ideas. Describe how you and others have judged ideas. What was the impact of such judgments? Commit to practicing affirmative judgment in response to new ideas that get presented to you. For several days or a week, keep a journal on how this goes. What were the consequences associated with your affirmative responses to ideas? How easy or difficult was it to stay positive?
- Think of a problem you are currently facing for which you are uncertain about how to proceed. Record what you have already thought of or tried in regard to this situation. Actively practice the principle of Strive for Quantity and generate a list of at least 50 new ways of dealing with the situation; be sure to include some novel ideas. In what ways was it beneficial to stretch for more options? What new insights did this provide you?

- When faced with a dilemma, decision, or creative problem in the past, how have you used incubation time? In what ways was this useful or beneficial? What do you currently do to make sure you have time to reflect? How do you record or keep track of your incubated thoughts? How might you increase your incubation time? Over the next several weeks, commit to keeping an idea journal—a book in which you keep track of your ideas, thoughts about projects, problems you've identified, possible future direction or opportunities, and so on. After some allotted time period, look back over your idea journal and identify new and useful insights or entries that you might carry forward. Reflect on the process of keeping an idea journal; how is it useful?
- Identify an unusual, highly novel idea, perhaps one that you have been introduced to or one that you might generate on your own. Really stretch—the idea should appear outlandish. Once the idea has been identified, force yourself to list all the positive points associated with that idea. What are its strengths? After you have made a list of positive features, move to what you consider its shortcomings. Make a list of the weaknesses of the idea. Review the shortcomings; can you find ways to overcome any of these limitations? How might the original idea be modified to make it more acceptable? In what ways was it useful to be open to novelty and not to reject an unusual idea at first glance?

PART II

Thinking Tools
for Leaders

5

Assessing the Situation

Tools for Diagnostic Thinking

Chapter at a Glance

Have you ever felt at a loss for what action to take because you had either too much information or not enough? Effective diagnosis is at the heart of good problem solving and information is at the heart of diagnosis. In this chapter we will first discuss the importance of data and their relationship to the cognitive skill of Diagnostic Thinking. We will then examine the dual content and process functions of the data-based CPS step of Assessing the Situation and how the step and Diagnostic Thinking work together to obtain and manage novel information. Finally, we will describe four divergent and convergent thinking tools (Five W's and an H, Why/Why Diagram, Hits, and Highlighting) for gathering data and introduce three Metacognitive Tools (the 4 I's, Key Word Search, and If-Then Analysis) for making decisions about how to manage the CPS process. Together these tools help leaders effectively diagnose situations that relate to overcoming predicaments and recognizing opportunities.

❖ DIAGNOSTIC THINKING IN LEADERSHIP: GATHERING
   AND USING DATA TO MAKE INFORMED DECISIONS

Leadership is about influencing others. To know the answer to a critical
question, or to know where or how to find the answer, is to have the
opportunity to influence how people think and behave. The development of such technological advances as the World Wide Web and instan-
taneous satellite transmission combine speed and volume to bring us
large amounts of immediate information on almost any topic imagin-
able. But how to manage that amount of information and how to make
decisions using large amounts of information are other issues entirely.

Do a quick mental inventory and make a guess about how
much information you will encounter today. Consider some of your everyday sources of information—other people, reading, TV, radio, Internet
searches and news, e-mail, phone calls, and so on. How many pieces
of information would you guess—one hundred? One thousand? Ten
thousand? The sheer volume of information at a leader's disposal is
overwhelming. We believe how you manage information and use it to
make informed decisions is a key leadership issue. As Conner (1992)
noted in his book *Managing at the Speed of Change,*

> We move at a variable rate that fluctuates according to our capac-
> ity for assimilating new information and influences. How well we
> absorb the implications of change dramatically affects the rate at
> which we successfully manage the challenges we face, both indi-
> vidually and collectively. (p. 11)

Box 5.1   Key Vocabulary

Some Key Concepts for Assessing the Situation

Assessing the Situation: The meta-step in CPS the dual purpose of which is to
(1) describe and identify relevant data and (2) determine the next process step.

Data: Information gathered from the five senses such as observations, facts,
information, descriptions, sounds, even tastes or smells or from more intuitive sources such as *hunches, guesses, hypotheses, emotions, incongruities,
nags, gaps in information.*

Diagnostic Thinking: Making a careful examination of a situation, describing the nature of a problem and making decisions about appropriate process
steps to be taken.

> **Metacognition:** An ability to monitor your thinking processes and to direct your thinking in a way that achieves cognitive objectives, that is, to be able to think about your thinking and to direct your cognitive processes.
>
> **Metacognitive Tool:** A structured strategy that focuses, organizes, and guides an individual or group's thinking about how to engage and interact with CPS or other processes.
>
> **Thinking Tool:** A structured strategy that focuses, organizes, and guides an individual or group's thinking.

As we mentioned in Chapter 3, in CPS a basic kind of thinking that is called for when we examine and use data is **Diagnostic Thinking,** which we define as *making a careful examination of a situation, describing the nature of a problem, and making decisions about appropriate process steps to be taken.* Just as a doctor tries to determine the cause of an illness, to work effectively in a leadership role you need to determine *what* needs to be done, *who* can help or hinder you, *why* you should (or shouldn't) do it, and *how* it should be done. In Diagnostic Thinking, you take in data, examine the situation, analyze your choices, make a decision, and then determine what process steps you need to take. Clearly this is an overarching skill that links to many others and, indeed, its executive function is a leadership blueprint for handling data and decisions throughout the CPS process.

Diagnostic Thinking is at the very heart of effective leadership not only because of the power of information itself, but also because leaders need to monitor and direct their thinking in decision making. This function mirrors the executive thinking leaders use to navigate through complex initiatives. Those who find themselves in formal leadership positions are typically expected to direct groups through complex situations that result in positive outcomes. Consider how government officials, football coaches, event planners, symphony conductors, theatrical directors, project managers, school principals, plant managers, college presidents, and others in formal leadership positions must constantly monitor situations so that they can direct activity toward desired results. There is no room for leaders to set their minds on autopilot, lest they run the risk of allowing complex situations to get out of their control and influence.

Because of their unique impact on the very fabric of society, leaders involved in social change must be particularly adept at gathering data and using it to monitor the effectiveness of situations and actions.

Consider, for example, the social change initiated by the women's suffrage movement in the U.S. In 1848, a small group of reformers gathered to draw attention to the social, civil, and religious conditions and rights of women at a convention in Seneca Falls, New York. This convention was a catalyst for leadership activity that lasted over 70 years, culminating with the passage of the Nineteenth Amendment in 1920 that gave women the right to vote. The women involved at the outset of this movement, such as Elizabeth Cady Stanton, Lucretia Mott, and Susan B. Anthony, were not appointed by some group or body to lead it. Indeed, it was the lack of opportunity to take leadership positions in American society of the mid-1800s that compelled these women and others to assume leadership roles and pursue social change. At that time, women were not allowed to speak in public, hold office, attend college, or earn a living other than as a teacher, seamstress, or mill worker.

Activities of this scope show the need for continual assessment of data in combination with ongoing monitoring of progress and pitfalls because leadership initiatives are often not quick and easy fixes based on one or two decisions and a few follow-up actions. We suggest that among other skills, Diagnostic Thinking aided these leaders because they were able to (a) observe and draw from other women's movements in Europe and on other continents, (b) build on the worldwide anti-slavery movements, (c) use the Declaration of Independence as a foundation for women's rights, and (d) orchestrate activities that eventually led to reform.

Elizabeth Cady Stanton, one of the principle leaders in the women's rights movement, exemplified an ability to monitor and learn from other situations. Her early work in the temperance movement, which focused on the abuse of women and children, provided Stanton with her first reform experience. Later she joined the anti-slavery movement and used lessons learned from this work to further her argument for women's rights. Stanton's own words provide a testimonial to the importance of Diagnostic Thinking for leaders; she observed, "The older I get, the greater power I seem to have to help the world; I am like a snowball—the further I am rolled the more I gain."

Block (1987) described leadership as "the process of translating intentions into reality" (p. 98). We suggest that Diagnostic Thinking, an ability to assess a situation and to identify the appropriate process steps, enhances the probability that leaders, like those involved in the women's suffrage movement, will be able to successfully transform their aspirations into reality.

Table 5.1   Key Reasons Why Leaders Need to Be Skilled at Assessing
the Situation

- Because leaders are in a position to influence and to be influenced, they need an accurate understanding of data that they give and receive.

- Because change is a constant condition in people's lives, leaders need to move quickly in response to new ideas and situations.

- Leaders need to continually monitor situations to make adjustments and respond appropriately to evolving circumstances and change.

- Leaders are gatekeepers of the flow of information; they must recognize what information needs to be shared with what people at any given time.

- Leaders are constantly inundated with information—some of which is important and some of which is not; skill in Assessing the Situation helps leaders sort through information and find the salient points quickly.

- A leader's job is not just to make decisions, but to make good or wise decisions; thus, they need to actively seek out data and base their decisions on a full range of information.

- Leaders need a wide net to capture data so that opportunities are not missed.

- In order to know what direction to take, leaders need to understand the context of their current reality; the richer the information, the more likely they are to identify creative, effective pathways to change.

- Leaders must not only gather data, but must also interpret data and explore its meaning.

- To guide and advise others, leaders must be cognizant of what is happening in process as well as in content and be able to help others locate themselves in process at any point in time.

© 2005 Puccio, Murdock, & Mance. Reprinted with permission.

❖ THE NATURE AND PURPOSE
OF ASSESSING THE SITUATION

Imagine yourself on the bridge of the starship *Enterprise*. Picture the technology, the action, the information, the decisions. . . . The bridge of the *Enterprise* is Command Central—the heart of a complex information system and the place where decisions are made. In CPS, this Command Central function is performed when you (a) examine data pertinent to a challenge and (b) determine whether and how you might proceed if you think your situation would benefit from CPS. The higher the stakes, the more you need accurate data to guide your choices and decisions and the more careful your thinking needs to be.

Figure 5.1   Assessing the Situation in the Creative Problem Solving
Thinking Skills Model

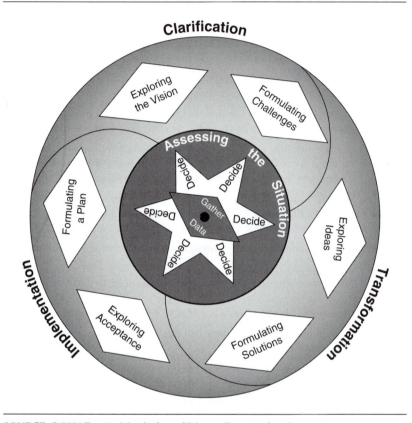

Assessing the Situation is a unique step within the CPS process
(see Figure 5.1). It is the step that kick-starts the CPS process. To engage
effectively in addressing a problem, whether it is a predicament or
opportunity, you have to first take stock of your needs and the nature
of the problem; therefore, engagement in CPS always begins in some
way with Assessing the Situation. This step is not only about identifying information that is relevant to the content of your problem, it is
about getting information that will help you decide what process step
will be the most effective to begin your problem-solving efforts.

Just like efficient traveling anywhere, how far you are going and
how long the trip will take depends on where you start. In the case of
using CPS, you may need to make the whole trip from the beginning
of the line to the end of it (Exploring the Vision, Formulating Challenges,

Exploring Ideas, Formulating Solutions, Exploring Acceptance, and Formulating a Plan) or you may only need to take a short hop. For example, if you want to strengthen solutions and then gain acceptance from others along the way, you can make a quick hop from Exploring Solutions to Formulating a Plan as needed. The good news about the flexibility of CPS is that you have lots of choices—you are in control of CPS Command Central. The bad news about this flexibility is that you have lots of choices—you are responsible for the process decisions and the content outcomes that are made in CPS Command Central.

Let's take a closer look at these dual content and process functions. To engage in Assessing the Situation, you begin by gathering data to understand what exactly is going on. Remember not to limit data collection to just observable facts. Consider the character of Mr. Data in the TV series *Star Trek: The Next Generation*. One of the reasons he is such a useful team member is that unless he has a major malfunction in his circuitry, the captain and crew can always count on him to give them loads of information on any topic. His one flaw on the information side is that he can only deal with "facts" and the logical hypotheses that stem from linear thinking. When it comes to anything beyond that, Mr. Data is out of his league. This is not the case with our use of data in CPS. The term data as we use it in Assessing the Situation can be gathered from our five senses—**observations, facts, information, descriptions, sounds, even tastes or smells**. But data that are pertinent to CPS can also come from more intuitive sources—**hunches, guesses, hypotheses, emotions, incongruities, nags, gaps in information** (Isaksen & Treffinger, 1985). We use "data" here to include a range of inputs and sources that provide a more divergent basis on which to base choices, decisions, and actions.

Once you have an informed understanding of the situation or the content on which you want to work—who is involved, what are the important aspects of it, what have you tried before, when does it take place, where does it take place, why is it important to do this, and so on—it is time to decide where to go next in using the CPS process. This preparation is analogous to a medical doctor who uses his or her diagnosis of the symptoms of an illness to recommend an appropriate treatment. In some cases there is a need to gather more information. For example, you are sent to a specialist for further tests and once this information is analyzed, then the course of treatment is prescribed. The point is that you determine the most appropriate next step after a careful examination of what you need and what each step can provide. Fortunately, CPS is much more forgiving than making an error in judgment about medical treatment; it is a flexible process. If you find that the next step you initially decided on in Assessing the Situation is not working for you, reassess and move to another, more appropriate step. For example, we have seen numerous occasions where people believed they knew the exact nature of the problem and therefore moved quickly into Exploring Ideas, only to discover after a few ideas had been generated that they were actually not working on the right problem. In such cases, this false start generally causes people to reassess the situation and move back to the Formulating Challenges step to recheck their data and to redefine the challenge.

In an earlier chapter we commented that CPS is a thinking person's process. This is particularly evident in Assessing the Situation. Using CPS is not really difficult, but learning to navigate the steps requires some basic understanding of function and structure of the model and the ability to think about your thinking—that is, not only to work your problem through the process, but to be able to stand above the process to ensure that you are taking the most productive path through it. In this sense, you never really leave Assessing the Situation behind. As you move around in CPS, you will be involved in ongoing checking, monitoring, and deciding about the meaning and usefulness of your information. "Am I in the right step of the process?" "Is this step working for me?" "Do I already have what I need for this step and can I move forward to another step?" "Have I sufficiently diverged and can I now move to the convergent phase of this step?" These questions represent the kinds of continuous Diagnostic Thinking that occurs when you use CPS. Like the driver of a car, you cannot fall asleep at the wheel, but must remain alert throughout the journey in order to arrive successfully at your final destination.

❖ EXECUTING EACH STEP OF THE CREATIVE PROBLEM SOLVING PROCESS: A WORD ABOUT TOOLS

In the previous section we described the nature and purpose of Assessing the Situation. Our goal was to help you understand the dual function of this step. To successfully execute a step in the CPS process, it is not sufficient to merely know its function. That would be like describing the function of a kitchen to someone without giving him or her the tools necessary to actually prepare meals. Just as a chef has tools to carry out particular tasks in the kitchen, so CPS provides tools that enable you to carry out the various steps of the process.

The general definition of a **tool** that we are using here is *something that serves as a means to carry out a task*. In CPS, we use **Thinking Tools** to carry out the steps of the CPS process. It is these tools that explicitly enable individuals, whether working alone or as a group, to achieve the intended function of each step. For the purposes of CPS we define a **Thinking Tool** as *a structured strategy to focus, organize, and guide an individual or group's thinking.* Therefore, in each of the chapters on the process steps (Chapters 5 through 11), we will present tools that are useful to, though not limited to, that particular step. If you are familiar with other tools that work well in Diagnostic, Visionary, Strategic, Ideational, Evaluative, Contextual, and Tactical Thinking, by all means use those as well within the CPS framework.

As noted in Chapter 2, each step of the CPS process has a divergent (i.e., generating options) and convergent (i.e., screening, selecting, and supporting options) phase. Most tools can be further sorted as to whether they are designed to promote either divergent or convergent thinking. With one exception—the Formulating Solutions step—the tools in each subsequent chapter are categorized as either divergent or convergent tools. The tools associated with Formulating Solutions tend to be more integrative and thus encompass both the divergent and convergent phases in the service of Evaluative Thinking.

We now turn to some basic Diagnostic Thinking Tools that will help you to engage in Assessing the Situation, followed by some key Metacognitive Tools for Assessing the Situation in the CPS process. These two sets of tools reflect the dual function of Assessing the Situation—describe and identify data and determine the next process step.

❖ DIVERGENT THINKING TOOLS FOR ASSESSING THE SITUATION

All of the divergent tools presented here will help you to think broadly about the content of any situation you face, that is, to cast a very wide net as you gather data—the first function of the Assessing the Situation step. The tools presented in Table 5.2, and the elaborated descriptions that follow, use divergent thinking to explore situations from as many angles as possible.

Five W's and an H

Diagnostic tools are all about questions, and the most familiar ones have been around since journalists first tried to give us the basics in a short amount of time or space. The "5 W's and an H"—Who, What, When, Where, Why, and How—provide fundamental questions for data identification and management (Isaksen & Treffinger, 1985; Noller,

Table 5.2   Assessing the Situation: Divergent Tool Overview

Tool Name	What the Tool Does	What You Do
5 W's and an H Sources: Isaksen & Treffinger (1985); Noller, Parnes & Biondi (1976).	Provides a basic overview of the data by asking "who, what, when, where, why, and how." Through the use of these categories, an individual or group can explore data associated with an opportunity or predicament.	Gather data, ask and record answers to the general questions "who, what, when, where, why, and how." Add "else" to get more of each. If you keep the divergent guidelines in mind for each category, you will get even more stretch, including original perspectives that you might have otherwise overlooked.
Why/Why Diagram Sources: Higgins (1994); Majaro (1991).	By asking a series of "Why?" questions you are able to uncover what is behind a situation.	Identify a situation that requires creative thinking. Pose the question "Why?" in regard to this situation. For example, "Why is this happening?" "Why is it a problem?" or "Why is this important?" Ask "Why?" a multitude of times. Once initial responses are recorded, conduct a second round of "Why?" questions, but this time on the answers yielded by the first round.

Parnes, & Biondi, 1976). But here's a divergent tip that will help you get even more mileage out of these basic diagnostic questions—add the word "else" to each word and you will get even more information in the same category—who/who else? what/what else? It's a simple semantic technique—ask targeted questions and your mind will seek appropriate answers; add "else" and your mind will go on a search for even more data for you to choose from in the same category. To apply Five W's and an H,

1. **Follow the principles for divergent thinking.** Commit to using the divergent thinking principles either individually or within a group.

2. **Identify a situation and apply Five W's and an H.** Find a situation for which you need to develop a better understanding. List each of the Five W's and an H on separate sheets of paper, or divide one sheet into parts with one question in each part. Taking each category separately, generate responses to each question and write them under the appropriate question. To get you started, see the list of questions below for examples within each category; generate further questions to allow yourself to examine more data relative to each category. Don't worry if your responses overlap. An overlap in data is much better than a gap. Finally, if a question does not apply, skip over it.

> **Who:** Who is involved? Who is the primary decision maker? Who are all the people affected by this situation?
>
> **What:** What is the history behind this situation? What is the ideal outcome? What has already been tried?
>
> **When:** When did this start? When would you like to take action? When would you like to have this resolved?
>
> **Where:** Where is this taking place? Describe the physical and psychological factors that surround this situation. Where has this situation been successfully managed? How has it been managed? Where are there situations similar to this? How are they similar?
>
> **Why:** Why is this important? Why is this occurring? Why are you, or others, concerned about this situation?

3. **Use the tag "else" to stretch for more data.** Note that no one question is necessarily better than another, nor is any particular order significant. If some questions don't stimulate much information, ask "Who/what/when/where/why/how else" and then move on to another question if information isn't flowing. Remember to go for quantity, make connections, be wild, and add incubated data later if needed.

4. **Check your data.** Scan your data for quantity and variety: if you are satisfied, move on to convergence; if not, generate more or different things in as many categories as you need.

Why/Why Diagram

The Why/Why Diagram is based, in part, on the Japanese quality technique called the "Five Whys." The purpose of the Why/Why Diagram is to get to the heart of a problem in a systematic way and to relate the results to the overall problem. Asking why forces your mind to search for reasons, and continuing to ask why of the same data perpetuates more abstract answers as well as restatements of the problem. To complete this tool,

1. **Recall the principles of divergent thinking.** Review the principles for divergent thinking and use them to guide your application of this tool.

2. **Identify a situation and apply "Why?" questions.** Identify a situation you feel needs to be clarified. Give the situation a title and write it midway down on the left side of a sheet of paper. As an individual or as a group, pose the question "Why?" to this situation. Use "Why?" questions that help you to dig more deeply into the situation. "Why is this happening?" "Why is it a problem?" Think of as many "Why?" questions as you can. Your responses to these questions should be listed in a column to the right of the situation.

3. **Ask "Why?" again to broaden your view.** Create a second column of responses by asking "Why?" of the list of answers you just generated. Challenge yourself to look at the situation more deeply by generating multiple responses to this second round of "Why?" questions. When you have finished, the responses will fan out from the title you gave the situation on the left side of the paper.

4. **Extend each strand.** Continue to fan out by asking "Why?" along each chain of responses. Continue until you have explored the possible causes and whys thoroughly. When you are satisfied that you have carried each strand out to its logical conclusion, shift to a convergent tool to identify the most critically important views of the situation.

Using the divergent tools above, or others that might be familiar to you, will generate many different pieces of data. Now that you have stretched to examine the situation from as many angles as possible, what comes next? In each step of the CPS process, divergent thinking is balanced with convergent thinking. In order to make the diverged data more manageable, you need to converge on data that are most important. The next section describes some Thinking Tools that help to narrow down a large set of data.

❖ CONVERGENT THINKING TOOLS
FOR ASSESSING THE SITUATION

Have you ever heard someone use the expression "Too much information"? This phrase is typically used when someone feels overwhelmed by information or learns something he or she did not want to know. You might feel this way as you look at the large amount of data generated through the divergent tools in Assessing the Situation. In CPS, it is critical to identify the salient pieces of data to move forward. There are convergent Thinking Tools that we can apply in Assessing the Situation to avoid this feeling and to identify the most relevant pieces of data.

Table 5.3 provides a summary of some convergent Thinking Tools that can help you identify the most pertinent data in your situation.

Table 5.3   Assessing the Situation: Convergent Tool Overview

Tool Name	What the Tool Does	What You Do
Hits Source: Treffinger, Isaksen, and Firestien (1982).	Uses an intuitive approach to identify the most pertinent data within a large set. Reduces individual data points to a more manageable number.	Review your list of data. As you look over your data, mark those items that jump out at you or seem most relevant to the situation.
Highlighting Source: Treffinger, Isaksen, and Firestien (1982).	Identifies the most relevant individual pieces of data and then organizes individual data points into clusters.	There are three basic steps to Highlighting. First, identify the Hits among your data. Second, group only those data that have been selected into categories. Third, name each category.

© 2005 Puccio, Murdock, & Mance. Reprinted with permission.

Hits

Hits is a convergent tool that is used extensively with all kinds of thinking because of its simple but effective convergent function—selecting. Believe it or not, sometimes decision making is just that—simple—and once you select, you can move on to a variety of actions that may or may not require CPS. Hits is a straightforward tool. Scan the array of data that has been generated and put an asterisk, check mark, or some identifying mark beside the ones that are interesting, intriguing, or capture the essence of the problem situation. You don't have to have a specific reason for all the hits you select. Often with this tool the choice is more intuitive, for example, it "grabs" you; you like it, but you can't really articulate why; it feels right. Be sure to deliberately select some novel hits even if you have to go back and look again.

When using this tool in a group, give each individual an equal number of hits, generally between 3 and 10 hits depending on how much data were generated—the more data, the greater number of hits. Allowing all group members an opportunity to select data enables the group to develop a shared understanding of the key factors in the situation.

Highlighting

Highlighting combines selection (hits), compression (clustering), and restatement (abstraction) into one tool. To use Highlighting, follow these steps:

1. **Review the principles for convergence.** Use the principles for convergent thinking to guide your use of this tool.

2. **Number all the options.** If you recorded your data on a sheet of paper you will need to number the data. If you used sticky notes to capture your data this is not necessary.

3. **Identify hits.** Select hits using the procedure already described.

4. **Cluster the data.** Examine only the hits to see if any of them are similar, have something in common, or could be productively grouped together. List the numbers of the hits that go together on paper or computer screen and circle them so you can see what belongs together. If the data are recorded on sticky notes, simply move like data into groups. The amount of hits in each cluster will vary—you can have "hot spots" that contain a number of options or a group of as few as two hits. Don't force all data into groups. Allow unique data points to stand alone.

5. **Label each cluster.** Identify a representative word or phrase that clearly and concisely captures the theme of each cluster. Ask yourself, "What is this cluster really about?" Restate what the cluster is about in a word or phrase that captures the meaning

and intent of all the hits inside. Restating may move you to a higher level of abstraction, which is a broader view of the data contained within that set. There is no need to restate single data points.

Using Convergent Tools Throughout the Process

The general nature of the Thinking Tools used for convergence in Assessing the Situation makes these tools useful in every step of the CPS process. These tools are all-purpose, and we will therefore refer to them when describing convergent thinking in subsequent chapters on the six remaining process steps. The selection function of Hits, in particular, makes this an all-purpose converging tool that can be used in every step of the process.

❖ GETTING AROUND IN THE CREATIVE PROBLEM SOLVING PROCESS: METACOGNITIVE TOOLS FOR DETERMINING NEXT STEPS

Recall that Assessing the Situation has two functions. The tools presented so far are designed to assist you in gathering data (i.e., the divergent tools) and selecting the most important data (i.e., the convergent tools). Now what? It is time to execute the second function of Assessing the Situation—determining where to go in the CPS process.

We present three metacognitive tools that help you to stand above the process to determine where to go next (see Table 5.4). The first tool, called the 4 I's, is designed to help determine whether or not it is worth applying CPS to the situation that has just been diagnosed. Not all problems require creative thinking; we recommend using the 4 I's to avoid putting creative energy into a problem that does not warrant this level of thinking. If you determine that it would be beneficial to apply CPS to the problem, you will then need to decide where to go next in the process. The next two metacognitive tools, Key Word Search and If-Then Process Analysis, are designed to help you identify the most appropriate process step after Assessing the Situation. These tools are used to make a bridge between Assessing the Situation and the most productive process step to apply to the problem. Because metacognitive thinking is required to guide progress through the CPS process, these tools can be used at the conclusion of each CPS process step to determine which step to use next. In many cases, this quick diagnosis will take you forward; however, sometimes the most productive action is to go back into a previous process step, skip forward several steps in the process, or simply exit CPS and use the new insights to take action.

4 I's

Before proceeding into any of the other CPS steps, you need to determine whether the situation requires creative thinking. If the problem does not require some new thinking—you already know what to do—then it makes little sense to use a process that will intentionally introduce new considerations that you don't really want. Thus, before going further into CPS, we recommend using a simple screening tool called the **4 I's** (Isaksen & Treffinger, 1985).

When examining the problem for which you identified the critical data, ask yourself whether this situation satisfies the following four criteria:

Influence: Will the individual or group who brought the problem forward be in a position to impact or change the situation? When a solution to the problem has been identified, will those who brought it forward have the authority or potential to implement the solution?

Imagination: Does the problem require creative thinking and does the individual or group desire new thoughts or approaches for the situation?

Interest: Is this an important problem, and does the individual or group recognize the need to spend time explicitly working on it?

Immediacy: Does the situation require attention now or in the near future?

The 4 I's is a metacognitive tool because it requires people to reflect on a basic process decision: "Does this problem warrant the use of CPS?" If the problem satisfies the four criteria, then CPS could be helpful, and the next process decision is to determine which of the six process steps would be most useful as a starting point.

Key Word Search

The words you use to describe a situation give an indication of the initial thinking required to make progress on the problem you face. In **Key Word Search,** you use verbs to determine where to go in CPS. Table 5.5 categorizes different verbs based on their relationships to the

Table 5.4   Assessing the Situation: Metacognitive Tool Overview

Tool Name	What the Tool Does	What You Do
4 I's Source: Isaksen and Treffinger (1985).	Helps an individual or group determine whether the problem identified is a good match for the CPS process.	Use the four criteria to evaluate whether the identified problem would benefit from the CPS process. Begin by determining whether the person or group that brought the problem forward can have a direct **Influence** on the situation. If so, then explore the degree to which **Imaginative** solutions will be sought. Finally, determine how much **Interest** there is in resolving the situation and the **Immediacy** of the situation.
Key Word Search Source: © 2005 Puccio, Murdock, and Mance. Reprinted with permission.	Presents a list of words that describe activities associated with different steps of the process. These key words can be used to help you identify where you need to be in the process.	After reviewing your converged list of data, create a task statement that captures the situation. Identify the verb used in your statement and compare it to the list of key words associated with the six remaining CPS steps. Use this list to create alternative task statements. Select a final task statement and proceed to the CPS step that is most associated with your task statement.
If-Then Process Analysis Source: Adapted from Miller, Vehar, and Firestien (2001).	This metacognitive tool locates people within the CPS process by presenting a list of If-Then scenarios. The "If" portion of the scenario describes the process need, while the "Then" aspect identifies the most appropriate process step to be taken. For example, if the need is to come up with ideas to overcome a challenge, then go to the Exploring Ideas step.	Consider what your process need is relative to the problem. Starting at the top of the table, read down the column of "If" statements until you find a statement that matches what you believe you need to do. Each "If" statement is paired with a "Then" statement that indicates which process step best fulfills your need. Find the process step that aligns with the If statement you identified and proceed to that step of the CPS process.

steps in the CPS process. For instance, when someone says he or she wishes to "consider," this indicates a need for Visionary Thinking and thus the Exploring the Vision step of CPS, whereas using the word "implement" suggests a need for Tactical Thinking, which is carried out in the Formulating a Plan step.

Table 5.5   Key Word Search

Exploring the Vision

Picture, dream, look at, forecast, contemplate, see, speculate, ponder, wonder about, etc.

Formulating Challenges

Clarify, untangle, explicate, define, decipher, clear up, uncover, discern why, etc.

Exploring Ideas

Come up with, invent, break through, originate, innovate, hatch, fashion, think up, find a way, make up, design a way, etc.

Formulating Solutions

Develop, elaborate, expand, evaluate, flesh out, strengthen, refine, analyze, maximize, build on, etc.

Exploring Acceptance

Sell, convince, market, promote, leverage, influence, persuade, pitch, position, introduce, advocate, popularize, recommend, etc.

Formulating a Plan

Execute, implement, do, script, orchestrate, devise, plot, outline, organize, roll out, sequence, act, carry out, etc.

SOURCE: © 2005 Puccio, Murdock, and Mance. Reprinted with permission.

Follow these steps to take advantage of the link between the use of language and the nature of our thinking:

1. **Form a Task Statement.** Review the converged list of data and form an initial task statement. A task statement is a one sentence description of the situation. It provides an at-a-glance summary of the work to be carried out. A task statement should be informed by the data gathered as part of Assessing the Situation and begin with "I/we want to . . ." Some sample task statements are:

- I want to *consider* new career options. [Exploring the Vision]
- I want to *uncover* reasons why my sales figures have declined. [Formulating Challenges]
- We want to *come up with* ways to streamline the amount of bureaucracy our clients must go through to access our services. [Exploring Ideas]
- We want to *strengthen* our after-school program. [Formulating Solutions]
- I want to *recommend* a new policy to central administration. [Exploring Acceptance]
- We want to *implement* a new software system by the end of the third quarter. [Formulating a Plan]

The language used in the task statement can provide clues about where to go next in the CPS process. In particular, the verb can point to the kind of thinking and, therefore, the process step that is best suited to address the task. After each of the sample task statements above, we indicated which CPS process step might be the most appropriate place to go after Assessing the Situation.

2. **Test Task Statement Using Different Verbs.** Identify the verb in your initial task statement. See which set of verbs it most closely matches in Table 5.5. Insert different verbs from this list, both within and across the process steps, to see which make the most sense or best capture your intent.

3. **Form Final Task Statement and Identify Matching Process Step.** After playing with alternative ways of phrasing the task statement, identify the statement that best captures your situation. That is the statement that best describes what it is you wish to do. When working in groups, use consensus decision making to select the final task statement. Using the key words listed in Table 5.5, identify which process step your task statement is most aligned with and go to that step.

If-Then Process Analysis

A straightforward approach for identifying where to go next in CPS is to identify which of the functions of the six remaining steps best suits your purposes. The metacognitive tool called **If-Then Process Analysis** helps you to stand above the CPS process and determine which step would be most helpful for you (adapted from Miller et al., 2001).

As with the Key Word Search, you form a task statement that starts with "I/we want to . . .". The task statement should be based on your key data and should summarize what you wish to accomplish. Once you have the task statement, use Table 5.6 to determine where you should be next in the CPS process. Think what you wish to accomplish and match this desire against the six "If" statements that describe the functions of each remaining CPS step. Read down the column of "If" statements and stop at the one that best describes what you think you need to do. When you find an "If" statement that describes your situation, read across to find out which of the CPS steps to go to next.

When working in groups, allow for consensus. Getting a group to make a decision about where to go next in the CPS process can help avoid going in circles. Many problem-solving meetings get off track because participants are actually working in different parts of the creative process. Explicitly coming to a group decision about which part of the process you are working in can save time, reduce frustration, and improve the outcome of your efforts.

Table 5.6   If-Then Process Analysis

If	*Then*
You need to establish the goal or the desired outcome of your efforts	Go to Exploring the Vision
You need to identify the obstacles or barriers that need to be addressed to achieve the desired outcome	Go to Formulating Challenges
You have identified a specific challenge (or challenges) that, if overcome, will move you in the direction of your desired outcome, but you do not know how to address this challenge	Go to Exploring Ideas
You have ideas that need to be transformed into workable solutions to overcome a challenge	Go to Formulating Solutions
You have solutions or a proposed change you wish to carry forward and want to ensure that the environment will support your thinking	Go to Exploring Acceptance
You have solutions or a proposed change and you are not sure what steps need to be taken, and in what sequence, to implement your thinking	Go to Formulating a Plan

SOURCE: Based on Miller et al. (2001).

❖ APPLYING WHAT YOU'VE LEARNED

For leaders, collecting information and using it to clarify, generate, or implement is a critical task. Sometimes there is only one piece of information on which a critical decision flies or fails. With practice, you can improve how you find, sort, use, and monitor large amounts of information. Try honing your Diagnostic Thinking skills by completing the following:

- Sharpen your general observation skills by closing your eyes and visualizing your office or a familiar room in your house. Then compare what you pictured to what is actually there. How well were you able to do this? Practice this on a regular basis to see whether your observation skills improve.
- Identify one personal or professional predicament or opportunity you have in your life. Diverge to gather all the data about it that you can think of. Use the divergent guidelines and really stretch for quantity and novelty; try to get at least 50 pieces of data. Include your feelings, hunches, and intuitions as well as facts. Examine the results. Were you surprised at any of the information? Was there anything new or different that you had not previously thought of?
- Look over your divergent list above. How can you begin to manage the amount of information you gathered? How will you know what is critical or not? What strategies do you usually use for this kind of decision making? Now apply the Hits tool to help you select the most important data from this list. How does this help in information management? Are there any actions you could take from just identifying and selecting key data?
- Get in the habit of thinking about your thinking. When you complete an activity or a task, take a few minutes to debrief it by asking, "What did I do to accomplish this?" "What was effective in my problem solving and what could I improve on?" Keep a notebook or list of these things for future development.

6

Exploring the Vision

Tools for Visionary Thinking

Chapter at a Glance

In this chapter you will learn about procedures that will help you to more skillfully engage in Visionary Thinking. Earlier we defined Visionary Thinking as an ability to articulate a vivid image of what you desire to create. Without this skill, a leader will find it difficult to identify meaningful goals.

This chapter begins by discussing why Visionary Thinking is an important leadership skill. This is followed by a description of the Exploring the Vision step. We will present three tools, Wishful Thinking, Storyboarding, and Success Zones, which are useful in facilitating Visionary Thinking.

❖ VISIONARY THINKING IN LEADERSHIP

The orator, philosopher, and politician Marcus Tullius Cicero said, "Let us not go over the old ground; let us rather prepare for what is to come." His quote describes the purpose of the CPS step Exploring the Vision because the goal of this step is to encourage forward thinking. A vision provides an image of where you want to go and helps you articulate your desired future. Having clarity in what you want to accomplish creates a singular lens through which creative efforts can be focused. Through this CPS step you will examine alternative views of future directions to pursue (i.e., the divergent phase of this step) and then identify which of these alternatives is the most productive pathway to reach that goal (i.e., the convergent phase of this step).

In some cases, a vision of the future is directed toward overcoming a predicament, as was the case with Mohandas Gandhi and his tireless efforts to establish home rule for India. As part of his quest to free India from British control, he initiated a campaign of noncooperation and self-reliance. He sought the revival of cottage industries as a means of establishing economic independence for India and adopted the spinning wheel as a symbol of the renewal of native Indian industry.

In other cases, you create a vision not as a response to a challenge, but because you see an opportunity you hadn't before. For example, consumers had not asked for a hand-held portable music playback device, but Sony's Akio Morita recognized that opportunity, and by identifying and developing this idea transformed the way people listen to music with the Sony Walkman. Along the way he also established Sony as one of the most recognized brand names worldwide. The Walkman was only one element within a larger vision, which was to establish a Japanese company whose brand image would be synonymous with quality. Morita established this vision in a time when Japanese products were viewed as anything but high quality. When Morita began his work, there was a strong view that Japanese products were inferior; consequently, many Japanese companies sold their products under another company's brand name. According to Kahan (2002),

> It was almost unheard of for a Japanese business to achieve brand status for its products. Yet, that is exactly what Morita set out to do. He was able to envision a day when his company, Sony, would be a brand that consumers would identify with the highest of quality. (p. 46)

Though there are certainly many factors that led to success at Sony, such as excellence in engineering and marketing, the ability to imagine new possibilities was a catalyst to later success.

Collins and Porras (1994) provided strong evidence for the importance of a vision in achieving organizational success. They carried out a detailed study to identify which factors enabled certain companies to become the "best of the best." They identified companies that had been prosperous for many decades, had gone through multiple product life cycles, had been in existence long enough to be led by a number of different executives, and had such strong brand recognition that their identity had been woven into the very fabric of society (e.g., Sony, American Express, Citicorp, General Electric, 3M, etc.). Each organization was then systematically compared to another organization in their respective industry. One of the chief differences that set the best companies apart from the rest was what they referred to as "Big Hairy Audacious Goals" (BHAG for short). As they explained, "A true BHAG is clear and compelling and serves as a unifying focal point of effort—often creating immense team spirit" (p. 94). These authors found that the visionary companies they studied had a history of establishing and then pursuing audacious challenges.

So central is vision to the creative process that Robert Fritz (1991), a composer and filmmaker, argued that the creative process begins with a concept of what it is you wish to create, and that it is the strong desire to bring your vision to fruition that actually engages you in creative thinking. Creation does not occur in a vacuum. Brilliant ideas and breakthroughs do not suddenly pop into our minds. As Fritz observed, "The popular misconception is that great ideas descend from on high and visit special mortals who are blessed or plagued with sudden realization, vision, and inspiration. This misconception adds to the erroneous notion that the creative process is mysterious and mystical" (p. 21). In Fritz's depiction of the creative process, you begin with a general notion of what you want and then form it into a more specific vision of the end result. As he noted, "First know where you want to go, then consider how to get there" (p. 25). The purpose of the Exploring the Vision step is to provide you, your team, or your organization with the tools and procedures to establish where you wish to go.

By internalizing Exploring the Vision in the CPS process, you enhance your ability to engage in Visionary Thinking and to draw out the future wishes and desires of others. Numerous leadership theoreticians and writers have cited the critical importance of Visionary

Thinking to leadership (e.g., Bennis & Nanus, 1985; Collins, 2001; Kouzes & Posner, 1995; Northouse, 2004; Palus & Horth, 2002; Tichy & DeVanna, 1990). Bennis and Nanus (1985), who studied 60 American CEOs, articulated how effective leaders engaged in Visionary Thinking. They noted that through a vision, leaders created an important bridge between the present and the future. Recently, in Collins's (2001) hierarchy of leadership capabilities, he defined Level 4, Effective Leader, as one who "catalyzes commitment to and vigorous pursuit of a clear and compelling vision, stimulating higher performance standards" (p. 20). To be effective, leaders must not only have the capacity to envision a future state that does not exist today, but must also be effective at drawing out the desires of others. Bennis and Nanus (1985) described the benefits of a vision:

> When an organization has a clear sense of its purpose, direction, and desired future state and when this image is widely shared, individuals are able to find their own roles both in the organization and in the larger society of which they are a part. This empowers individuals and confers status upon them because they can see themselves as part of a worthwhile enterprise. They gain a sense of importance, as they are transformed from robots blindly following instructions to human beings engaged in a creative and purposeful venture. Individuals in a team without a vision are likely to become disengaged and frustrated. (p. 91)

Kouzes and Posner (1995) presented an effective analogy for what it is like to be on a team that does not have a clear vision. Imagine you are in a presentation in which the presenter is using a digital projector to show a long PowerPoint presentation. Imagine that the projector is not focused and the presenter is oblivious to this fact. In this scenario it would be difficult to focus on the presentation, to be completely engaged. According to Kouzes and Posner, this is much like the experience people have when they work on a team that has no clear vision.

The purpose of this chapter is to present some practical procedures that will improve a leader's ability to engage in Visionary Thinking and to inspire this kind of thinking in others. Table 6.1 contains a list of reasons why Exploring the Vision is important to leaders.

❖ THE NATURE AND PURPOSE OF EXPLORING THE VISION

Sometimes, when looking at complex situations, you have only a vague notion of what needs to be addressed. For example, an individual may recognize the need to improve his or her health, a team may want to

Table 6.1   Key Reasons Why Leaders Need to Be Skilled at Exploring the Vision

- To be able to identify future opportunities
- To help others identify and work toward meaningful goals
- To ensure high levels of performance by engaging in forward thinking, anticipating what will be required in the future
- To create consensus among followers
- To provide others with a direction
- To create a sense of purpose
- To proactively initiate change by beginning with a clear image of the desired outcomes
- To discern which activities pose the greatest potential for forward progress for either the individual or group
- To inspire others to accomplish great feats

SOURCE: © 2005 Puccio, Murdock, and Mance. Reprinted with permission.

Box 6.1   Key Vocabulary

Some Key Concepts for Exploring the Vision

Exploring the Vision: The CPS process step used to create an image of a desired outcome.

Visionary Thinking: An ability to articulate a vivid image of what you desire to create.

---

radically improve performance, or an organization may decide that it needs to become more innovative. These are all worthy goals, but they are too vague for specific action. Imagine a superintendent who challenges the school district to raise achievement levels for all students, or a CEO simply sending out a memorandum indicating that from this day forward the company will be more innovative. How would you begin to respond to such broad goals? The pursuit of broad goals results in false starts, inefficiency, rework, frustration, and sometimes no action whatsoever. Have you ever asked a child, direct report, colleague, or friend to do something only to find out later that they were unable to respond effectively because you were too vague? The Exploring the Vision step is used when you recognize that something must be done and you need to focus in on what you want to attain. The tools presented here provide deliberate procedures for first exploring a variety of future states and then identifying the most productive vision to pursue.

Figure 6.1   Exploring the Vision in the Creative Problem Solving Thinking Skills Model

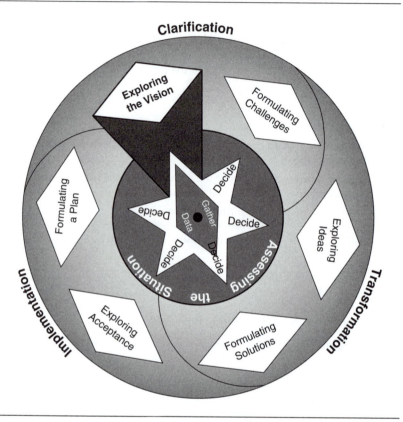

Exploring the Vision falls within the Clarification stage of the CPS process (see Figure 6.1). As such, this step has a close working relationship with the Formulating Challenges step. There is a natural transition from Exploring the Vision to Formulating Challenges; that is, from identifying the big picture of where you wish to go to identifying the obstacles that must be addressed successfully to get there. As a natural progression, Exploring the Vision will often lead to Formulating Challenges.

Exploring the Vision is the conceptually broader step within the Clarification stage of CPS. Here you are thinking about broader concepts, like goals and desires, versus pinpointing specific problems that operate as barriers to successful goal attainment, as you do in the Formulating Challenges step. As with the other three stages, you begin with a step in which you explore broader issues that are then used to formulate more concrete thoughts that help you move toward effective action.

The natural progression through the CPS steps, excluding the meta-step of Assessing the Situation, which is always the first step, begins with Exploring the Vision. As such, Exploring the Vision determines the focus for all other activities to follow. The identification of challenges, production of ideas, development of solutions, examination of the context, and creation of an action plan are designed to move you or your team toward some important goal. If, through Assessing the Situation, an individual or team is clear about the goal, then Exploring the Vision is not necessary. However, if an individual or team is uncertain about what direction to take, or there is a lack of consensus within a group, then Exploring the Vision must be your starting point.

In this chapter, we present two divergent tools and one convergent tool. These tools are designed to enhance your ability to identify important and meaningful goals.

❖ DIVERGENT THINKING TOOLS
   FOR EXPLORING THE VISION

You use divergent thinking in Exploring the Vision to make sure that you consider many possible future scenarios before committing to one. Although there are many divergent tools, we are presenting two that will help you explore various visions: **Wishful Thinking** and **Storyboarding**. Table 6.2 provides an overview of these tools followed by more detailed information on how to use them for Exploring the Vision.

Wishful Thinking

This tool is designed to help you think about many possible future outcomes, both positive and negative, regarding a particular topic or issue (see Isaksen & Treffinger, 1985). Throughout CPS, statement starters are used to help guide people's thinking. The statement starters used for Wishful Thinking are phrases such as "Wouldn't it be nice if . . . ," which can be abbreviated as WIBNI, and "Wouldn't be awful if . . . ," which can be abbreviated as WIBAI.

To use Wishful Thinking,

1. **Identify a general topic to explore** (i.e., a personal, team, or organizational situation). This topic will be the focus for

Table 6.2   Exploring the Vision: Divergent Tool Overview

Tool Name	What the Tool Does	What You Do
Wishful Thinking Source: Isaksen and Treffinger (1985).	Enables you to think broadly about the future, both in terms of desirable and undesirable future outcomes.	Use divergent thinking to generate a list of possible positive future outcomes. To do this, use the stem "Wouldn't it be nice if . . ." to explore future outcomes you wish to create. Do the same to generate potential negative future outcomes or situations you would wish to avoid. Use the statement starter "Wouldn't it be awful if . . ." to explore negative images of the future.
Storyboarding Source: Forsha (1995).	Defines a future goal and the steps required to attain the goal.	Create a panel with six squares. In the first square, draw an image of the present state. In the sixth square, draw an image of the desired future state. Fill in the remaining squares showing the key steps that must be taken to go from the current situation to the ideal future image.

SOURCE: © 2005 Puccio, Murdock, and Mance. Reprinted with permission.

Wishful Thinking and should be stated in a very broad and brief way. We suggest stating the topic as if it were a book title or a newspaper headline (e.g., The ACME Corporation Triples Sales; Smallsville School District Prepares Students for Positive Future).

2. **Using the statement starters WIBNI and WIBAI, generate many alternatives.** Follow the guidelines for divergent thinking and stretch for as many statements as possible, with a minimum goal of at least 30. Table 6.3 shows sample WIBNI and WIBAI statements related to a company's desire to pursue a new business opportunity.

3. **Identify key statements.** Use the Hits tool described in Chapter 5 to identify those positive situations (WIBNI statements) that seem most promising and those negative situations (WIBAI statements) that seem most crucial to avoid.

Table 6.3   Wishful Thinking: An Example

Wouldn't It Be Nice If . . .	*Wouldn't It Be Awful If . . .*
. . . we pursued markets outside of the United States	. . . we became stagnant
. . . we were able to partner with entrepreneurs in other countries	. . . there was a radical change in the market and our main business area dried up
. . . we franchised our business	. . . we stretched ourselves in too many directions
. . . we could sustain current operations while dedicating effort to some start-up ventures	. . . we lost one of our main customers

SOURCE: © 2005 Puccio, Murdock, and Mance. Reprinted with permission.

4. **Reverse any WIBAI statements.** If any WIBAI statements were selected, they should be reversed into wish statements to stay focused on the positive things you wish to create. For example, the WIBAI statement "We were unable to keep up with the technological development in our field" might become the WIBNI statement "We found a way to keep up with technological advancements."

When you have a long list of wishes you have finished this tool. Now what? It is time to complete the convergent thinking phase of this step and select one or a few wish statements to pursue. This can be done by looking at the results of the Hits tool to see which of the wish statements were identified as important to pursue. Alternatively, if you prefer to be more analytical in your decision making, you will want to use the Success Zones tool, which is described later in this chapter, or other selection tools that are familiar to you.

Storyboarding

Where Wishful Thinking relies on words, Storyboarding is primarily a visual tool. Forsha (1995) defined Storyboarding as "a series of panels showing clearly, using pictures, numbers, and words, important (significant) changes, in order of appearance, that taken together tell an interesting story" (p. 6). According to Forsha, storyboards have been used for many centuries as a means of communicating events. Forsha suggested that the ceiling of the Sistine Chapel is organized as a storyboard. Cartoon strips from the newspaper are excellent examples of storyboards. During the twentieth century, Storyboarding became a formal tool used to develop and organize plots for movies, television shows, and commercials (Forsha, 1995). Forsha indicated that storyboards can be used in a number of different ways. For the purposes of this book, we will use Storyboarding for its original purpose—to construct a story. Specifically, in Exploring the Vision we use Storyboarding to create a future story in panels that highlight the sequence of significant events from the beginning of the story (i.e., the present) to the desired outcome (i.e., the future).

To use Storyboarding,

1. **Identify the topic to be explored**. This might be a specific issue that a person is interested in working on, such as improving physical health; a team issue, perhaps attaining some accomplishment; or an organizational goal, such as entering a new market.

2. **Decide how many panels you want to have in your storyboard**. We recommend no fewer than six panels and no more than eight. On a large sheet of paper or on cards, draw the panels. These should be laid out in sequence like the panels in a cartoon.

3. **Define your current situation.** In the first panel, draw a picture that captures the essence of the situation as it is now.

4. **Project yourself into the future.** Consider what the ideal outcome would be for this situation. Be playful and imaginative. Remember to defer judgment as you consider this desired outcome. Once you have your desired future in mind, draw it in the last panel.

5. **Complete the story.** Now that you have the present situation and the desired future captured, consider what steps must be taken to move forward. The panels in between the present situation and the desired future should be completed so that they identify the sequence of major events or activities that represent progress toward the goal.

6. **Elaborate on the images in the panels.** The storyboard is not limited to just images. In some cases, it is helpful to complete the storyboard by briefly capturing in words the key issues, outcomes, obstacles, or insights associated with each panel. These can be recorded as brief statements in or around each panel.

If you are working on a team and individuals completed separate storyboards, you need to combine these independent storyboards into a single story. To do this, begin by giving individuals time to share their storyboards. Then identify and select elements from the individual storyboards to be combined into one final team storyboard. Elements can be selected through the Hits tool or through discussion. Again, you want to begin with the present state panel, move to the future panel, and then complete the panels in between.

As a reminder, the main thinking skill associated with the Exploring the Vision step is Visionary Thinking. According to Forsha (1995), "Storyboard concepts are useful in generating business plans, particularly in helping executives visualize a business process all the way from the initial idea through to the results" (p. 12). Thus, Storyboarding is an excellent tool for engaging in Visionary Thinking.

❖ CONVERGENT THINKING
   TOOLS FOR EXPLORING THE VISION

To successfully engage in Visionary Thinking, you must not only dream of future states, but must be able to determine what dreams are worth pursuing. Thus, divergent thinking regarding future opportunities must be balanced with convergent thinking. If you are faced with a number of alternative statements about the future, you must be able to sort out which options possess the greatest potential for delivering success. There are convergent tools that can help you make an effective choice. The Hits tool, which was described in Chapter 5, is useful in narrowing down a long list of options. Another tool that is particularly useful in examining competing statements of the future, Success Zones, is introduced in Table 6.4.

Table 6.4   Exploring the Vision: Convergent Tool Overview

Tool Name	What the Tool Does	What You Do
Success Zones Source: Treffinger (1992).	Enables you to examine competing future images to determine which are the most promising to pursue.	All options are evaluated against two criteria: degree of importance and probability of success. Once the future images are evaluated, each is placed in a graphic matrix that helps to identify those options worth pursuing.

SOURCE: © 2005 Puccio, Murdock, and Mance. Reprinted with permission.

Success Zones

This tool, adopted from Treffinger (1992), allows you to evaluate any number of goals, future scenarios or wish statements to determine which hold the greatest promise. The tool has two basic steps: evaluate the options against two criteria and then locate the options within a matrix. The two criteria that are used to evaluate each option are (1) degree of importance and (2) probability of success.

In general, the first criterion, degree of importance, refers to how critical the option is to you. If the option will ultimately contribute to success, then it probably is important. Here you might wish to consider whether the option aligns with your personal mission or the mission of your team or organization.

The second criterion is Probability of Success, which refers to how confident you are that you can attain the desired future state described in the option under consideration. You should consider how likely it is that a particular goal might be accomplished given current and antici-pated resources, as well as current or anticipated environmental forces. Some individuals and teams find it easy to imagine themselves accom-plishing almost any goal—the belief that anything is possible. To help differentiate one goal from another, consider how much energy and effort it will take to achieve the goal. In such situations, Probability of Success might be better thought of as ease of achievement.

The above are general descriptions of these two criteria (Degree of Importance and Probability of Success). Before evaluating future goals, make certain that these definitions work in your situation. If they do not, redefine these criteria so that they can be more directly applied to the options under consideration. It is particularly important in a group situation that everyone has a common understanding of the evalua-tion criteria. Therefore, before applying these criteria in a group, take some time to agree on the definitions for Degree of Importance and Probability of Success.

To use Success Zones,

1. **Evaluate the options against Degree of Importance.** For both criteria (Degree of Importance and Probability of Success), a scale ranging from 1 (low) to 9 (high) is used. A score of 1 is assigned to those future goals that are least important, while scores of 9 are given to those that are most important (i.e., Degree of Importance).

2. **Evaluate the options against Probability of Success.** A score of 9 is given to those that are most likely to be achieved or deemed easiest to accomplish (i.e., Probability of Success). In contrast,

those goals that are unlikely to meet with success or will take great energy should receive a score of 1.

3. **Create a grid with the two axes.** The matrix we recommend using is found in Figure 6.2. The X axis refers to Probability of Success and the Y axis refers to Degree of Importance. Each axis is broken into thirds (i.e., options that receive scores from 1 to 3, 4 to 6, and 7 to 9) and by crossing the two axes nine sections are created.

4. **Plot the results on the grid and consider the results.** Once all of the options have been evaluated they are placed in a matrix. To locate an option in the Success Zones matrix, begin by identifying where the option belongs along the continuum for Probability of Success (i.e., low, moderate, or high). Then place the option into one of the nine sections by identifying whether the option is low, moderate, or high in regard to Degree of Importance.

To provide some feedback, each box is labeled. The most promising opportunities are those options that are high in Probability of Success and Degree of Importance. These are future goals that should be seriously considered. "Creative Challenges" are those goals that will be difficult to achieve, but are deemed to be critically important by the individual, team, or organization. Options that land here are referred to as "Creative Challenges" because imagination and energy will be required to overcome barriers to success. These options are good candidates to pursue, but attention must be given to the identification of the challenges that will inhibit or prevent success. Equally important, but less challenging, are "Stretch Goals." The lower right corner is called "A Distraction." These options are believed to be easy to achieve but of little relative value. The lower left is called "Waste of Time" because not only are these options unlikely to be successful, but they are of low importance. If an option falls in the lower three sections, be cautious about pursuing it. Finally, the middle is labeled "Gray Area" because options that fall into this category are midway between Probability of Success and Degree of Importance. When comparing competing options, those that fall in the top row are the most promising to pursue, followed next by the middle row, and finally the bottom row.

❖ WHAT'S NEXT IN THE CREATIVE
   PROBLEM SOLVING PROCESS?

As we mentioned earlier in this chapter, the Exploring the Vision and Formulating Challenges steps are closely related. Therefore, the most

Figure 6.2.   Success Zones

	Low	Moderate	High	Key: Low 1–3 Mod 4–6 High 7–9
High	Creative Challenge	Stretch Goals	Promising Opportunity	
Moderate	Difficult Endeavor	Gray Area	Low-Hanging Fruit	
Low	Waste of Time	Why Bother?	A Distraction	
	Low	Moderate	High	**Probability of Success**

Degree of Importance (vertical axis)

SOURCE: Adapted from Treffinger (1992).

natural direction to take in the CPS process is to transition into Formulating Challenges to explicitly identify what obstacles must be addressed in order to reach the desired future you have just identified. Though this may be the natural progression through the CPS process, it is possible that you may have a different process need. In some cases, once a clear path forward has been identified or you know exactly what needs to be done to achieve the goal, you may no longer need CPS. You can use the If-Then tool in Chapter 5 to assist you in determining where to go next.

❖   APPLYING WHAT YOU'VE LEARNED

The intent of this CPS process step is to encourage leaders to engage in Visionary Thinking. By employing the tools shared in this chapter, a leader should be in a better position to describe a vivid image of a desired future and, furthermore, to articulate why that future is worth pursuing. Why might this be valuable? As Kouzes and Posner (1995) pointed out,

Envisioning the future begins with a vague desire to do something that would challenge yourself and others. As the desire grows in intensity, so does your determination. The strength of this internal energy forces you to clarify what it is that you really want to do. You begin to get a sense of what you want the organization to look like and be like when you and others have completed the journey. You may even write down your image or even draw a model of it. (p. 98)

Some Thoughts for Application

- Begin a wish list for your future. Ask yourself, "Where do I want to be 5 years, 10 years, or even 20 years from now?" Generate a list of 100 statements for all aspects of your life (Relationships, Career, Health, Money, etc.) using the stems, "Wouldn't it be nice if..." "Wouldn't it be awful if..." Converge on the promising ones and get to work!
- When working with a group, begin all new projects by creating a shared vision of the outcomes. Use tools such as Storyboarding or Wishful Thinking to create this vision.
- Identify some goals or wishes you are currently considering. Use the Success Zones tool to examine these options to assist you in identifying which are the best candidates to pursue.

7

Formulating Challenges

Tools for Strategic Thinking

Chapter at a Glance

How many times have you "solved" a problem only to have it come back again? There are many possible reasons why problems recur. Perhaps you addressed a symptom rather than the underlying problem. Sometimes the problem presented is not the problem at all; the real problem must instead be discovered, uncovered, or redefined.

In this chapter we will describe Formulating Challenges and discuss its importance to the CPS process. We will examine how a leader who considers a variety of perspectives and definitions of the problem can gain a deeper understanding of a predicament, uncover potential opportunities, and develop pathways from the present to the future.

We will then examine the dynamics of divergence and convergence in the context of this step and introduce the tools Statement Starters in Formulating Challenges and Web of Abstraction to support Strategic Thinking in this step of the CPS process.

❖ STRATEGIC THINKING IN LEADERSHIP

Martin Luther King, Jr. had a dream. When he so eloquently shared this dream with hundreds of thousands of people gathered at the steps of the Lincoln Memorial in Washington, D.C. in August 1963, he created such a compelling vision of the future that his speech is regarded by many as one of the most powerful of all time. For the full text of King's "I have a dream" speech, see the Web site www.stanford.edu/group/king. In Chapter 6, Exploring the Vision, we noted how important it is for a leader to portray a vision of the future that compels others to act. Martin Luther King, Jr. is an excellent example of this visionary leader. But it is not enough for a leader to have a vision; a leader must also have the ability to think strategically, that is, not only to dream, but also to recognize what must be done to manifest the vision.

Strategic Thinking is about articulating and addressing the challenges that stand in the way of achieving the desired vision and about creating a direction or pathway to the future. Consider again the case of Martin Luther King, Jr. How did he move people from the segregated society of the United States in the 1960s to a future in which there was equal opportunity for all? The challenges he identified and addressed included longstanding cultural norms and established laws that required him to be both creative and persistent. Some of the challenges that stood in the way of his vision were how to desegregate the schools, how to make public transportation and other accommodations open to all races, and how to eliminate discrimination in employment. One thing that made King remarkable as a leader was his ability to articulate the challenges standing in the way of his vision—some seemingly insurmountable—to create a path for others to follow. Many of the rights available today are a direct result of this Strategic Thinking.

In the previous chapter, we described Visionary Thinking, which in comparison to Strategic Thinking is broader and more future oriented. Strategic Thinking is concrete and focused on developing a direction or pathway to the future. **Strategic Thinking** involves *identifying the critical issues that must be addressed and finding the pathways to move toward a desired future.* A leader who thinks strategically builds bridges and highways to get from the present to the future. There are often a number of reasonable directions that might be taken toward the future; the role of the leader is to consider many possibilities before deciding on the most promising ones.

Box 7.1   Key Vocabulary

Some Key Concepts for Formulating Challenges

Challenge: An obstacle that stands in the way of achieving a vision (resolving a predicament or pursuing an opportunity).

Formulating Challenges: The CPS process step in which gaps are identified that must be closed to achieve the desired outcome.

Problem: A predicament or an opportunity, a gap between what you have and what you want.

Problem Finding: "Behaviors, attitudes, and thought processes that are directed toward the envisionment, posing, formulation, and creation of problems, as opposed to the process involved in solving them" (Jay & Perkins, 1997, p. 259).

Root Cause: The most basic reason, which, if eliminated, would prevent a recurrence; the source or origin of an event.

Strategic Thinking: Identifying the critical issues that must be addressed and finding the pathways to move toward a desired future.

We have highlighted the need for leaders to think strategically to move from the more abstract conceptual notion of a vision to the concrete pathways and clear direction toward the desired future. The CPS step of Formulating Challenges enables a leader to do this by exploring a number of potential pathways before deciding the best way(s) to proceed. See Table 7.1 for specific reasons why a leader needs to be skilled in Formulating Challenges.

❖   THE NATURE AND PURPOSE
     OF FORMULATING CHALLENGES

In natural process, Formulating Challenges is the companion to Exploring the Vision (see Figure 7.1). They, in turn, belong to the family of thinking skills whose purpose is to *clarify*. You do this naturally many times a day using such strategies as questioning, pausing, or rethinking. The deliberate use of CPS to help clarify situations leads to at least two specific benefits. First, you have the structure of the CPS

Table 7.1   Key Reasons Why Leaders Need to Be Skilled in Formulating
                     Challenges

- To break out of old ways of looking at the challenge
- To uncover opportunities that you didn't even realize existed
- To discover the root of the issue
- To identify sub-issues that may be hidden within complex challenges
- To avoid wasting resources, including time and money, in pursuing the wrong or poor-quality solutions
- To avoid rushing to a solution that might be adequate but not elegant
- To reframe the challenge to a productive level of abstraction or ownership for more efficient problem solving
- To define the issue more clearly and efficiently
- To test assumptions before moving forward

SOURCE: © 2005 Puccio, Murdock, and Mance. Reprinted with permission.

process to rely on, which takes a lot of the guesswork out of clarifying. Second, you have tools to support your deliberate efforts.

It can be very useful for a leader engaged in Strategic Thinking to use the CPS process to both support and guide thinking. The step of Formulating Challenges will clarify and often significantly modify perceptions of two major things that hinder effective problem solving: (1) the **scope** of the situation (Where does the problem begin and end?), and (2) the **direction** that your problem-solving efforts should take (What is the best way to approach the problem?).

In Formulating Challenges, you explore the obstacles that exist between the current situation and your vision of a desired future, focus on the ones that seem most significant, and frame them in a way that invites creative ideas. These decisions influence the scope of the challenge. In some cases, you will find that the road to a desired future is complex and contains many challenges and subchallenges that need to be addressed. In other cases, it may be that once you have framed the challenge accurately, the solution will become apparent. Albert Einstein once said, "The formulation of a problem is often more essential than its solution, which may be merely a matter of mathematical or experimental skill." This formulation of the challenge relates to the direction you want your efforts to take. That is why Formulating Challenges has a strong divergent push to it. Although you always diverge and converge in every step in the CPS process, the broad search for many different and original perspectives is especially useful early on to help you clarify messy, unclear, or tacit situations.

Figure 7.1   Formulating Challenges in the Creative Problem Solving
Thinking Skills Model

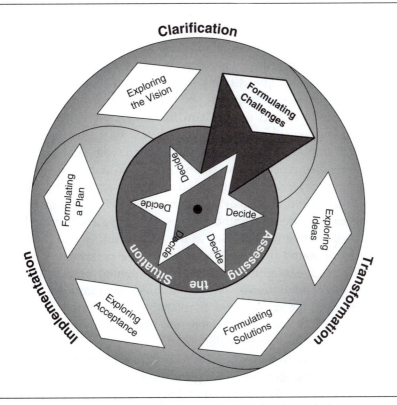

A problem may seem obvious to those who are anxious to generate ideas; however, time spent generating alternative perspectives that influence the scope and direction of the problem may be the most productive thing for a leader to do in the long run. The habit of looking at things the same way is a mighty enemy of creative thinking. To paraphrase an old maxim: *If you always think what you already thought, you'll always do what you already knew.*

Organizations involved in Total Quality Management efforts and Six Sigma use tools such as the Fishbone Diagram (Ishikawa, 1985) and Root Cause Analysis (Fagerhaug & Anderson, 1999). These tools help people to explore beyond the initial view of a problem, which may be a symptom, to a variety of possible underlying problems. Discovering a Root Cause, *the most basic reason, which, if eliminated, would prevent a recurrence; the source or origin of an event* (i Six Sigma, n.d.), provides a perspective on the problem that could directly lead to a successful solution.

The consideration of alternative perspectives is particularly helpful in Strategic Thinking. Your perceptions, values, views, or the simple fact that an approach was already on your mind to begin with will all influence your thinking. For example, what is the likelihood that if you consult first with a surgeon about a medical problem that you will decide that you need surgery to correct it? What if you had approached an internist or general practitioner first? Or a homeopath? The point is that the type of ideas or solutions you get in any problem-solving situation is directly related to how you frame or view it. For example, many self-employed business owners get their start after they are laid off or fired from their regular jobs. Rather than seeing unemployment as a failure, they redefine it as an opportunity to start a business. It is not uncommon for some of these individuals to even claim "Getting fired was the best thing that ever happened to me. I'm not sure I would have gone out on my own without the push." Doing a deliberate, broad scan for alternative ways to look at the current reality will shake you free of habit-bound thinking. These alternative perspectives provide powerful creative insights that open up the potential for new pathways that you might not otherwise have considered. For additional information on some of the important skills related to Formulating Challenges, see Box 7.2, which provides a brief review of the creativity literature on problem finding and problem definition.

Another way to look at this is to realize that often people enter this step thinking they are looking for things they know and end up uncovering things that they didn't know. This is the power of the creative process. The benefit of taking time to identify and define the most pressing challenges was articulated well by philosopher John Dewey when he said, "A problem is half-solved if properly stated."

Box 7.2   Research Note

Problem Finding and Problem Definition

The idea that problems, which include predicaments and opportunities, have to be found or discovered may come as a surprise to the average person who is trying to cope with a daily flood of unsolicited demands and decisions for which there is no readily apparent solution. In fact, in the creativity literature, this distinction goes back as far as the 1970s work of Csikszentmihalyi and Getzels (1971) and Getzels (1975), who identified a continuum of problem scenarios from presentation to discovery. These issues were also addressed in general by Wertheimer (1945) and Dewey (1933).

According to Jay and Perkins (1997), **problem finding** refers to "behaviors, attitudes, and thought processes that are directed toward the envisionment, posing, formulation, and creation of problems, as opposed to the process involved in solving them" (p. 259). In general terms, problem finding is viewed as the process or processes that precede problem solving. It is the umbrella term for activity that occurs before actual problem solving. It includes such things as problem discovery, problem construction, problem expression, problem posing, problem definition, and problem identification, some of which are similar, but are discussed in different terms in the literature.

Runco and Dow (1999) have suggested that problem finding is not a unidimensional concept, but rather it involves a set of highly interactive, complex skills. Most researchers agree with Runco's multidimensional conception of problem finding. For him, a comprehensive definition of problem finding encompasses (a) conceiving or envisaging problems or questions and forming possibilities in a situation (problem identification), (b) defining and formulating the actual problem statement (problem definition), (c) periodically assessing the quality of the problem formulation and its solution options, and (d) problem reformulation from time to time (Runco, 1994a).

The significance of identifying and defining the problem is highlighted by several researchers and scholars. Getzels and Csikszentmihalyi (1976) noted in their empirical research on the work of young artists, "Problem-finding appears to be a crucial component of creativity and what is more, it can be observed and assessed with satisfactory reliability and validity" (p. 115). Dewey (1933) talked about the act of discovering the problem as the first step in knowing.

If you are interested in more information on problem finding, look further at Dillon (1982), Jay and Perkins (1997), and Runco (1994b).

❖ DIVERGENT THINKING TOOLS FOR FORMULATING CHALLENGES

We mentioned earlier that Formulating Challenges has a strong divergent focus. Here is an overview of two divergent tools that work particularly well to create alternative perspectives on the scope and direction of a challenge. Also helpful is Brainstorming, which is described in Chapter 8.

Table 7.2   Formulating Challenges: Divergent Tool Overview

Tool Name	What the Tool Does	What You Do
Statement Starters in Formulating Challenges Source: Parnes (1967).	Enables you to articulate the challenge in a positive, forward-thinking framework that encourages idea generation and problem solution.	Place a statement starter at the beginning of each challenge: *In what ways might I (IWWMI) . . . ? How to (H2) . . . ? What might (WM) . . . ?*
Web of Abstraction Source: Basadur (1994); Hayakawa (1979); Isaksen, Dorval, and Treffinger (1994); Korzybski (1933); Parnes (1981).	Enables you to view a challenge from a wide variety of perspectives, including more abstract and more concrete views of the challenge as originally presented.	Begin with an initial challenge or statement of the goal. Ask "why" or "what's stopping me/us" to generate additional challenges that are more abstract or concrete perspectives. Ask "why else" or "what else is stopping me/us" to generate additional challenges.

SOURCE: © 2005 Puccio, Murdock, and Mance. Reprinted with permission.

Statement Starters in Formulating Challenges

Language is very powerful; how you frame a question has an impact on the type of response you will get. Consider the difference between these comments: *I need a new car* and *How might I get a new car?* Notice how one actually moves you toward a response and the other just sits in your head, not moving. Selecting the right words for the situation enhances your ability to communicate with others, and framing questions is a very powerful way to have people think deeper and more creatively. Those who facilitate groups, teach, or counsel know that a closed question—one that results in a yes/no answer—does not invite dialogue or deepen thought or communication. On the other hand, an open-ended question requires more thought to formulate a response and more elaboration in communicating the response. Have you ever noticed a number of awkward silences when someone is interviewing or questioning a child? Some of these are, of course, related to the maturity of the child, but many are related to the closed questions the person asked. "Did you have a good time?" "Was it fun?"

"Did you come with your mom and dad?" Although adults may feel the need to fill the awkward silence or elaborate, children just answer yes or no to the question they were asked.

In CPS, you use language as a tool by employing stems that "invite" or open up thinking. These stems set up open-ended questions. In Formulating Challenges, you can help yourself and others tap into creativity by framing issues as questions that invite ideas. Some of these questions include: *In what ways might I/we . . . How might I/we . . . How to . . . What might . . .* Put a questioning stem (*In what ways might*) together with someone to take action (*I*), add the action verb that tells what they will do (*eliminate*), finish the question with a receiver (*my bad habits*), and you have an invitation to solve rather than a statement of what is.

Parnes (1967) advised,

> The best way I know to move into problem-finding quickly and productively is by asking for "In what ways might I or we" (IWWMI) questions—perhaps pointing out that "How might I?" (or we) is just as reasonable, but does not emphasize quantity as well. Both connote the forward-thrusting, "ownership," action-oriented, infinite-possibility stance desired in the problem statements to be listed. (p. 127)

We recommend using Statement Starters with all tools in this step when phrasing challenges. The use of Statement Starters frames thinking in a way that is particularly helpful when working to identify challenges by "inviting" ideas that might solve the problem. These stems will be illustrated in the description of other tools in this section.

Web of Abstraction

The purpose of the Web of Abstraction tool, or Webbing for short, is to fully examine a diverse range of challenges associated with your vision or desired outcome. The Web of Abstraction encourages a 360-degree examination of related challenges at many levels of abstraction, depending on how concrete or abstract you are in wording them. At the center of the web is your vision or desired outcome, from which other ways of looking at the challenge are expanded by asking two basic questions: "Why" and "What's stopping me/us?" When you ask why, you generate broader, more abstract or higher-order challenges. The question "What's stopping me/us" tends to produce more concrete or operational challenges. As a result of responding to these two questions, you are able to map out many challenges. The example in Figure 7.2 relates to a personal goal, a faculty member at a college whose goal is to get promoted to the rank of professor.

To use Web of Abstraction,

1. **Identify a goal or desired outcome.** In the example, the goal is phrased as, "Wouldn't it be nice if I were promoted to full professor?" Write this goal or desired outcome in the center of a sheet of paper or flip chart.

2. **Ask "Why" and turn the answer into a question with a Statement Starter.** To begin to generate challenges, ask yourself the question "Why?" "Why am I interested in pursuing this vision or why is this important to me?" Your response should then be phrased as a question. In this example, the faculty member's initial reaction is driven by the desire to become better known. This statement is turned into a question beginning with an invitational stem: "How to enhance my reputation?"

3. **Ask, "Why else is this important to me?"** To further explore other challenges, you return to the vision. Again, the response is captured as a question. This time the faculty member responds by indicating that this promotion is important to her because she can earn more money. This response is converted into a new challenge, "How might I make more money?" Continue asking "Why else?" until the individual or team runs out of answers.

4. **Ask "Why?" and "Why else?" to those new challenges just identified.** This will extend the generation of challenges. So, for example, return to the challenge "How to enhance my reputation?" and ask the question "Why—why do I want to enhance my reputation?" In response, the faculty member thinks that an improved reputation will help make people more interested in her work (e.g., books, articles, training program designs, software, etc). This response leads to a new challenge: "How might I create products that have mass appeal?" This faculty member might then ask herself, "Why else is enhancing my reputation important to me?" which would lead to the identification of new challenges. It should be noted that in some cases, the response to "Why" or "Why else" is already captured in the web; in such situations, simply draw a line connecting the two challenges to show a relationship (in the example this is represented by the dotted lines). Continue asking "Why" and "Why else,"

branching out in a manner that allows many diverse challenges to be identified.

5. **Pose the question, "What's stopping me?" to explore more concrete challenges.** Return to the beginning vision or desired outcome. In the case of this faculty member, the question becomes "What's stopping me from being promoted to full professor?" Her initial response is that she does not believe she can get letters of support from key people; thus, a new challenge has been identified, "How to secure letters of support?" You would then follow up with the question, "What else is stopping me from being promoted?" This will encourage a branching out to identify parallel challenges. In response to what else might be stopping her, the faculty member indicates that she needs to publish more and now there is a new challenge, phrased as "How to publish more?"

6. **Continue asking "What's stopping me?" or "What else is stopping me?"** Continue exploring the lower part of the web by asking, "What's stopping me?" This will generate more concrete challenges. Drive down as far as you can go. Eventually the challenge statements will become so specific that it will just make sense to stop (e.g., How might I pick up the phone to contact people? or How might I put a stamp on the envelope to send out my application?). Use "What else is stopping me?" to branch out and generate more diverse challenges.

The example shows only a partially completed web. Generally you will generate many more challenges than the number shown in this example. Though the example may not be complete, it does illustrate the effects of using the Web of Abstraction tool. First, it demonstrates how quickly and effectively this tool helps to scope out the many challenges associated with a desired outcome. Second, it demonstrates how the "Why" and "What's stopping me/us" questions identify challenges at quite different levels of abstraction. Notice how the challenges at the top portion of the web highlight more global issues, such as leaving a legacy and achieving self-satisfaction. In contrast, as a result of responding to the question "What's stopping me/us," the challenges become more concrete, such as increased levels of networking, presenting at more conferences, and finding time to write.

There are two main benefits to the Web of Abstraction. First, by asking why and going up the web, individuals sometimes discover

Figure 7.2   Personal Example of Web of Abstraction

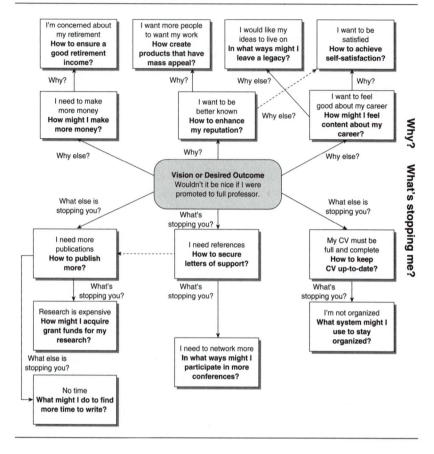

that the goal they thought was important was really overshadowed by some other goal. For instance, the faculty member in this example might discover that what is really important is not getting a promotion, but establishing financial security for retirement years. This type of insight can radically change where you focus your energy. For instance, the faculty member may decide to no longer focus on a promotion, but to explore ways to achieve financial security—getting a promotion is just one pathway to this goal. Second, the web may confirm an original goal and, as a result, map out the main challenge or challenges that must be addressed to achieve the goal. The process of completing the web takes those challenges that were looming in the dark, waiting to trip you up, and makes them visible. And now that they are visible, you can be more explicit about identifying what needs to be done to overcome these challenges.

❖ CONVERGENT THINKING TOOLS
FOR FORMULATING CHALLENGES

After you have generated a variety of questions related to your challenges, it is time to converge and select the one(s) that resonate with you. As in all CPS decision-making situations, use the principles of convergent thinking (Apply Affirmative Judgment, Keep Novelty Alive, Check Your Objectives, Stay Focused) to help you with your selection. Sometimes you will have an "aha" moment that is so strong you know exactly which challenge statement gets to the heart of the matter. In fact, once you have identified your challenge, you may be ready to move immediately out of this step in the CPS process. At other times you may need to sort through a variety of potential challenges before deciding where to go next. If the problem is complex, there may be sub-issues that you will need to tackle one at a time to clarify the situation even more. The convergent tools Hits or Highlighting (see Chapter 5) serve as well in convergence for Strategic Thinking as they do in other convergent phases of the process.

❖ WHAT'S NEXT IN THE CREATIVE
PROBLEM SOLVING PROCESS?

In completing the step of Formulating Challenges, you close down the function of Clarification and open the way for either Transforming or Implementing. Depending on whether or not you already have ideas that answer the challenges, you may or may not want to go directly to the first step of Transforming—Exploring Ideas. Or if you have ideas in response to the questions you generated in Formulating Challenges and don't want to push on the novelty of your initial thinking, you may want to transform those ideas into fully formed solutions in the Formulating Solutions step. Sometimes, after you step back and assess the situation, you may not need deliberate CPS to transform and will be ready to move on to the Implementing stage—using Exploring Acceptance and/or Formulating a Plan. In any case, the choice is yours and you will return to Assessing the Situation to make process decisions before moving on.

❖ APPLYING WHAT YOU'VE LEARNED

As a leader, you cannot merely create a compelling vision for others to follow. You must be able to help others see that this vision is attainable through concrete action. To determine the appropriate action, a leader must be able to examine, and help others to examine, the challenges that are standing between the present and the future.

Some Activities for Application

- Practice using statement starters on your own personal challenges. Think about something you have always wanted to do. Perhaps you want to start your own business, climb Mount Everest, or achieve some other distant goal. Once you have a vision of what you want, identify what is standing between you and your desired future. Use statement starters (In what ways might I . . . How to . . .) and generate at least 30 statements of these gaps or challenges. Identify the key statements of the challenge and analyze the implications for next steps.

- The next time you are working on a problem with a group or team, try reframing the challenges using statement starters. Turn progress-stopping statements, such as "Upper management will never go for it," into questions: "How might we convince upper management that this will work?" or "How might we find a champion within upper management to support this idea?" Again, generate a variety of challenges and then select those that seem most important.

- Identify a current goal. Try using the Web of Abstraction to help you stretch and generate many challenge statements related to this goal. Use it on your own or try using it in a group.

8

Exploring Ideas

Tools for Ideational Thinking

Chapter at a Glance

Who doesn't enjoy coming up with a great idea? If you watch the body language of someone who has just thought of a new idea, you will notice enthusiasm, excitement, and energy. It's hard to be blasé when you've just come up with a useful idea, something you had never thought of before.

In this chapter we will explore perhaps the most recognized element of the CPS process—Exploring Ideas. We will examine how a leader can generate ideas "on command" and also effectively bring out the ideas of others. We will discuss the nature of divergence and convergence in this step and introduce two tools, Brainstorming and Forced Connections, that will assist a leader in generating new, unusual, and useful ideas when they are needed.

❖ IDEATIONAL THINKING IN LEADERSHIP

Few would argue that leaders need to have ideas or that, in fact, leaders may be selected or elected because of their ideas. Once in positions of leadership, they are expected to have ideas to solve the difficult and complex problems their organizations and communities face. People admire leaders who have the ability to easily generate many ideas and refer to them as "idea men or women."

History is full of examples of prominent leaders who generated many unique ideas. For instance, one of the early colonial leaders in the United States, Benjamin Franklin, was a well-known statesman, inventor, and problem solver. As a politician, he had ideas about how a country might be created as a democracy rather than a monarchy. As Postmaster General, he determined mail routes and invented an odometer to keep track of the distances that were traveled to deliver mail. He invented the Franklin Stove to make it easier and safer for people to warm their homes and created the first fire company and fire insurance. And most people are familiar with the famous kite flying that led to his inventing the lightning rod. His ideas were a reflection of his curiosity, his talents, and a wide range of interests.

A more recent example of a leader with many ideas is Richard Branson, the CEO of Virgin Enterprises (Virgin Records, Virgin Airlines) and the owner of his own personal island. He clearly demonstrates the affective skill of playfulness mentioned in Chapter 3, and is known for his unique approaches. For example, he promoted a new venture by wearing a wedding gown for photographers. Randl Shure, managing director of BT Capital Partners Europe, said of Branson, "Not only does he come to us with great ideas, but he's willing to put in some of his own money to back them" (Flynn, Zellner, Light, & Weber, 1998, p. 2). He is such an "idea man" that it is a standing joke among Branson's top aides that they are paid to curb some of his outrageous schemes. "Richard comes up with ideas, and we say: Down Richard," jokes Virgin Atlantic CEO Steve Ridgway (Flynn et al., 1998, p. 3). Leaders such as Franklin and Branson, who generated many different ideas in a variety of arenas, illustrate the skill of Ideational Thinking.

Box 8.1   Key Vocabulary

Some Key Concepts for Exploring Ideas

Brainstorming: To practice a conference technique by which a group attempts to find a solution for a specific problem by amassing all the ideas spontaneously contributed by its members while actively following the four guidelines for divergent thinking.

Exploring Ideas: The CPS process step in which novel ideas are generated to address important challenges.

Facilitator: A person who is substantively neutral and has no decision-making authority in regard to the challenge who helps a group work together effectively to solve problems and make decisions.

Idea: Something, such as a thought or conception, that potentially or actually exists in the mind as a product of mental activity.

Ideational Thinking: Producing original mental images and thoughts that respond to important challenges.

Although a leader needs to able to think of ideas, it is unreasonable to expect that any leader, even one who is highly skilled in Ideational Thinking, will be able to generate ideas for every problem. The success of American Airlines during the difficult business climate that followed the September 11 attacks demonstrates how garnering employees' ideas can help organizations even in struggling industries such as the airlines (see Box 8.2). Just as an effective leader cannot do it all and must learn to delegate, a leader is not the source of all good ideas and must learn how to bring out the ideas of others.

The very nature of problems today—often complex, novel, and ambiguous—requires the best creative thinking in the organization. Ideas are everywhere, and often the people closest to the issue have the most productive ideas for solving the problem. Encouraging the ideas of others is the responsibility of leadership. By encouraging ideas, a leader is increasing the likelihood that followers will bring ideas forward in the future. It keeps the flow going rather than shutting it down. Often employees don't bother to even suggest ideas because they feel their ideas will not be welcome. Nelson (2003) noted that "only 41% of surveyed employees believe the typical company listens to their ideas" (p. 1).

Box 8.2   Real-World Example

Employees' Ideas Take American Airlines to New Heights

In 2004, American Airlines posted its first profitable quarter since the September 11 attacks. The remarkable success at American Airlines is due, in part, to a change in culture that takes seriously the ideas of its employees.

(Continued)

(Continued)

The staggering turnaround at American Airlines becomes even more impressive when one considers the management shakeup that occurred in April 2003. Shortly after two American Airlines unions had made financial concessions, CEO Don Carty made arrangements to give more than $40 million in retention bonuses to a small group of executives. Carty was forced to resign and the situation bred an atmosphere of mistrust between management and employees. A new CEO, Gerard Arpey, was soon appointed and this is when the turnaround began (Yoon, 2003).

With the new CEO came a new attitude toward employees. Arpey's operating philosophy is that employees are not management's problem; rather, employees are critical to the success of an organization. In Arpey's own words, "They have the best ideas; they know how to do the job more efficiently and more effectively. And we've got to lead by example and part of that leading by example is listening" (Goodwin, 2004). American Airlines management has not only listened to employees' ideas, but they have also acted on these ideas. These efforts led American Airlines to realize a reduction in annual costs of around $4 billion.

Here are some examples of the cost-saving ideas offered by employees. Rather than place mechanics in harnesses and suspend them in the air to repair jet engines, mechanics suggested that engines be oriented vertically and placed on lifts so that the engines could be maneuvered while mechanics work on them. The net result of having engines lowered to the floor while mechanics remain relatively stationary resulted in a reduction of 140 labor hours on every engine. This idea alone saves tens of millions of dollars a year. In light of the higher fuel costs in Los Angeles, one pilot suggested that planes going to Los Angeles from Dallas should carry enough fuel to return to Dallas for refueling. This idea led to a daily savings of $50,000. An employee familiar with drag racing suggested that flights leaving with empty seats should locate passengers in the rear of the plane, thus moving the center of gravity more towards the tail. The improved aerodynamics from this idea saves millions of dollars in fuel each year.

By actively soliciting employees' ideas, and acting on these ideas, American Airlines has had a direct impact on its bottom line. As CEO Arpey observed, "If we truly involve people—not pay lip service to them, truly involve them—we will make a better decision and we'll execute better on that decision" (Goodwin, 2004).

As noted in the American Airlines example, a leader sets the tone for how ideas are treated and whether generating ideas is really valued and rewarded. A leader who wants others to generate ideas must create a climate that supports and encourages individuals to bring their ideas forward. This includes encouraging playfulness, celebrating the generation of highly novel ideas, and providing space for individuals to follow their intuition and take risks. In Chapter 13 we will discuss this in more detail and explore the importance of climate for creativity.

In addition to being able to generate ideas on their own and being able to draw ideas out of others, leaders who are skilled in Ideational Thinking recognize the difference between an idea and a solution. Leaders need to understand that new ideas don't come out fully formed and ready to use. Ideas are often fragile and need to be nurtured and supported. In fact, a "half-baked" idea might just work if given time to develop. On the other hand, a seemingly wonderful idea may not look as good after some time has passed. It is important not to jump on the bandwagon too early and fall in love with an idea or abandon it too quickly because it looks odd or unusual. A leader skilled in Ideational Thinking encourages others to play with ideas, explore possibilities, consider alternatives, and to remember "It's just an idea."

The CPS step of Exploring Ideas assists you to generate many unusual ideas and to begin to sort them. Table 8.1 presents specific reasons why a leader needs to be skilled in Exploring Ideas.

Table 8.1   Key Reasons Why Leaders Need to Be Skilled in Exploring Ideas

- To get a breakthrough
- To have many, varied, and unusual ideas from which to find a solution
- To get a fresh perspective
- To go beyond the surface ideas that usually come up
- To be engaged in truly original thinking
- To create an environment where ideas are welcome
- To go to places you could never have anticipated
- To feel more energized; to be fully alive
- To create competitive advantage

SOURCE: © 2005 Puccio, Murdock, and Mance. Reprinted with permission.

❖ THE NATURE AND PURPOSE OF EXPLORING IDEAS

Exploring Ideas is the first step in the natural process of Transforming, that is, searching for solutions to your problem. Up to this point, either through CPS or your own natural process, you were clarifying the nature of the problem (see Figure 8.1). As you enter Exploring Ideas, you will

Figure 8.1   What's Next in the Creative Problem Solving Thinking
Skills Model?

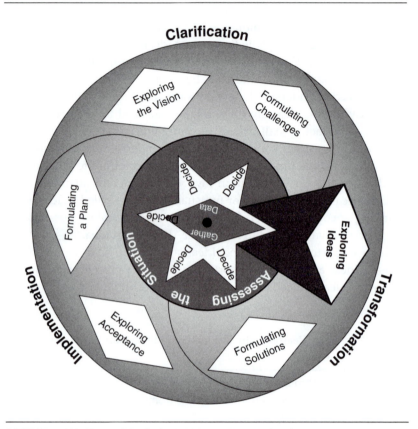

be seeking ideas for a focused statement of the challenge(s) that stand
in the way of solving the problem. When Osborn (1957, 1963) described
this step in the CPS process, he used the term "tentative ideas" because
the nature of this step is exploratory and open-ended. You may not
yet have solutions when you exit this step, but you will have some
ideas that you can transform through further scrutiny. In fact, the companion step in Transforming—Formulating Solutions—is the place in
the CPS process where ideas are evaluated and developed more fully
into solutions.

Exploring Ideas is also influenced by the process step of
Formulating Challenges. The more clearly the challenge is stated, the
more likely you are to get the kinds of ideas that can be used to solve
the problem. The interrelatedness between the two steps means that

you may find yourself going back to restate the challenge if the ideas you are generating really don't seem to be hitting the mark.

Exploring Ideas has a much more divergent than convergent feel to it. The focus here is more on generating ideas than converging and evaluating them, although in keeping with our CPS model, there are divergent and convergent phases in the step.

In addition to feeling more divergent, there is a great deal of energy produced at this point in Exploring Ideas. In a group setting you will often experience a sense of fun, laughter, and joy. When engaged in divergent thinking in Exploring Ideas, there is an explosion of novelty. Like popping popcorn, the ideas fly fast and furiously. Idea-generation sessions carried out in groups can be spirited, energetic, and just plain silly. Laughter fills the room and the rapid-fire generation of ideas may make it hard to record them all. Divergence in Exploring Ideas is about really letting loose, digging deep, and abandoning any preconceived notions about what you think might or should work to solve the problem in order to make room for novel solutions. Granted, not all sessions play out at full tilt; however, there is usually a sense of playfulness and humor. Adherence to the guidelines of divergent thinking (i.e., Defer Judgment, Go for Quantity, Make Connections, and Seek Novelty) ensures the right atmosphere is present for an all-out exploration of ideas.

The higher energy found in the divergent phase of Exploring Ideas must eventually give way to a focused search for the most promising ideas, which occurs during the convergent phase of this step. As with any convergent phase of the process, there will be a different feel to what is happening. You will need to be more deliberate, serious, and thoughtful as you begin the process of selecting and sorting ideas. Be sure to leave enough time for this. The fun and games part can be seductive. In a group setting, people generally enjoy themselves, and the danger in that is to stay too long in divergence. Think of all the meetings you have attended where you generated a huge list of ideas only to have time run out. Whatever happened to those ideas? The role of the leader is to manage the balance of divergence and convergence in Exploring Ideas so that ideas are both generated and considered.

❖ DIVERGENT THINKING TOOLS FOR EXPLORING IDEAS

The goal of divergent thinking in Exploring Ideas is to generate as many ideas as possible, and the guidelines for divergence will help you achieve this. We will present two tools, Brainstorming and Forced Connections, that are particularly helpful for Ideational Thinking.

Table 8.2 provides an overview of these tools. This is certainly not an exhaustive list; you may be familiar with other idea-generation tools that can be used in this step of the CPS process. Additional sources for tools that assist with Ideational Thinking include Goldenberg and Mazursky (2002), Michalko (1991), King and Schlicksupp (1998), and Van Gundy (1992).

One of the most common ways to begin divergence in Exploring Ideas is with Brainstorming. When working in groups, Brainstorming is a way to capture the ideas that are on the top of people's minds. Sometimes Brainstorming is the only tool that is necessary. If the divergent guidelines are being used effectively, you can generate many different and unique ideas just using Brainstorming. Often, however, people "run dry" and the ideas stop flowing. This is where it can be useful to introduce additional divergent tools.

Table 8.2   Exploring Ideas: Divergent Tools Overview

Tool Name	What the Tool Does	What You Do
Brainstorming Source: Osborn (1953, 1957, 1963).	Allows a group of individuals working together to productively generate a diverse set of options by encouraging them to follow the principles of divergent thinking.	Convene a group of five to eight individuals. Identify the challenge and state in the form of a question. Follow the guidelines for divergent thinking (Defer Judgment, Go for Quantity, Make Connections, Seek Novelty) to generate many possible solutions to the problem.
Forced Connections Source: Gordon (1961); Koestler (1964); Isaksen, Dorval, and Treffinger (1994).	Intentionally encourages flexible thinking by challenging the problem solver to generate solutions to the problem by using objects that are unrelated to the situation.	Collect a variety of objects that are unrelated to the problem. Any object will work, including common objects found in the room, outside in nature, toys, etc. Ask yourself or the group, "What ideas do you get from (object) for (the challenge)?" To stimulate additional ideas consider the size, shape, color, texture, the use of the object, memories that it evokes, etc.

SOURCE: © 2005 Puccio, Murdock, and Mance. Reprinted with permission.

Brainstorming

Brainstorming is the most well known of all the divergent tools. It has been so popular that it is often the only tool that people know and use to generate ideas—albeit not always accurately. Our training experiences have highlighted the fact that the word "Brainstorming" is widely diffused but not often well understood. We have found that most people recognize the word and have participated in a Brainstorming meeting; however, when we ask people what rules they followed during the Brainstorming session, they generally report only one rule consistently—"No judgment." To others, Brainstorming is synonymous not only with the entire CPS process, but also often with their view of creativity itself. To be clear about Brainstorming, we use the definition offered by Alex Osborn (1963), the man who developed this tool: "To practice a conference technique by which a group attempts to find a solution for a specific problem by amassing all the ideas spontaneously contributed by its members" (Osborn, 1963, p. 151). And to be more explicit, we would add "while actively following the four guidelines for divergent thinking."

We recommend the following steps when Brainstorming:

1. Convene a group of five to eight members. Identify five to eight people to participate in the Brainstorming session (fewer can effect the quantity of ideas and group energy level and more makes group dynamics and convergence hard to manage). Be thoughtful about who should be included in this idea-generation session. Do you want to include only those who have a vested interest in the resolution of the problem or do you wish to include some participants who might generate ideas but not participate later in the selection of the most promising ideas? Do you want people who are familiar with the situation? Do you want people who are fluent thinkers? Do you want people who bring a different perspective to the problem? Do you want to go for a diverse set of participants? In your invitation to these individuals, communicate the purpose of the meeting.

2. Identify and describe the challenge. At the beginning of the Brainstorming session, describe the specific challenge to be addressed. Be sure to frame the challenge statement in the form of a question, for example, "In what ways might we ... ?" "How might we ... ?" "What might ... ?" "How to ... ?" Write the challenge statement on flipchart paper for all to see. Provide key background information to help the meeting participants understand the challenging situation. This information might be presented in the form of bullet points, data organized within the Five Ws and an H categories (i.e., Who, What, Where, When, Why, and How), or via visual aids. Allow the participants some time to ask questions about the situation before moving into idea generation.

3. Generate ideas using divergent thinking. Review the guidelines for divergent thinking and then invite group members to generate ideas to resolve the challenge. Use flipchart paper to capture the ideas; record every response; don't paraphrase; have additional recorders if necessary. Continue generating ideas until the problem owner feels there are a sufficient number of ideas that might successfully deal with the challenge at hand. In classic Brainstorming, a recorder writes each idea on the flipchart. An alternative is to provide each person with a pad of Post-its™ and ask them to record their own ideas. When using this variation of Brainstorming, encourage the participants to say their ideas aloud, record one idea per Post-it™ sheet, and then post the sheet on a flipchart page for all to see.

The use of a facilitator can greatly enhance the productivity of a Brainstorming session. Borrowing from Schwarz (1994), we define the **Facilitator** *as a person who is substantively neutral and has no decision-making authority in regard to the challenge who helps a group work together effectively to solve problems and make decisions.* The facilitator is charged with managing the process of the meeting. This person does not make contributions to the content of the meeting; rather, his or her goal is to ensure that the meeting runs smoothly. Having a highly skilled facilitator will enable the group to stay on task, understand and maintain appropriate group roles, follow the guidelines for divergent thinking, manage group dynamics, and increase the likelihood of breakthrough ideas.

Brainstorming is a powerful and all-purpose tool to get novelty from divergence, and you can use it at any time and in any step or stage of the CPS process, such as to generate challenge statements in Exploring Challenges.

Box 8.3   Research Note

Some Comments on the Brainstorming Research Literature

Since Osborn (1953, 1957, 1963) introduced Brainstorming to the world in his book *Applied Imagination,* this group idea-generation tool has received great attention in the empirical literature. Indeed, there have been over 200 published articles on Brainstorming. A clear area of focus within this research is the comparison of idea production of groups engaged in face-to-face Brainstorming versus nominal groups in which ideas of individuals who work alone using divergent guidelines are later combined (e.g., Diehl & Stroebe, 1987, 1991). The apparent superiority of nominal groups led some researchers to conclude that the practicality of Brainstorming was seriously limited. For example, some authors have offered such statements as the "long-lived popularity of Brainstorming techniques is unequivocally and substantially mis-guided" (Mullen, Johnson, & Salas, 1991, p. 18). Many of these studies limited their scope of research to the number of non-redundant ideas generated, which is only one performance indicator of the effectiveness of Brainstorming.

We will return to this issue, but for now let's examine briefly the shortcomings of those studies that compared Brainstorming groups against nominal groups. The main drawback to these studies is that the use of Brainstorming within research investigations does not reflect the use of Brainstorming in organizations and other applied settings. Offner, Kramer, and Winter (1996) suggested that Brainstorming in research studies seems to be "totally divorced from reality and represents a clear 'disconnect' between research and practice" (p. 296). They identified the following specific limitations of these studies: use of newly formed groups; no or little training; groups operate without a facilitator; and no visual aids, such as flipcharts.

To make a more direct comparison between Brainstorming as it is used in practice and nominal groups, Kramer, Fleming, and Mannis (2001) used trained facilitators and various recording devices (e.g., flip chart or computer-aided recording) in conjunction with Brainstorming groups. Below are the results of this study, ranked in order based on the mean number of ideas produced.

- Brainstorming groups using computer-aided recording with facil-itator (M = 79.4)
- Nominal groups (M = 69.8)
- Brainstorming groups using flipchart with facilitator (M = 69.3)
- Brainstorming groups using flipchart without facilitator (M = 49.5)
- Brainstorming groups using computer-aided recording without facilitator (M = 49.1)

The results of this study were replicated in other studies, demon-strating that Brainstorming groups led by a trained facilitator generated as many ideas as nominal groups (see also Offner et al., 1996; Oxley,

(Continued)

(Continued)

Dzindolet, & Paulus, 1996). It should be noted that the difference between groups using the two recording methods was not statistically significant.

The study cited above used undergraduate students who worked on a college issue and examined only idea production as an outcome. Although it shows the value of a trained facilitator, the study sheds little light on the benefits of Brainstorming within organizational settings. In response to the assertion that nominal groups are more effective than Brainstorming groups, Sutton and Hargadon (1996) offered the following: "We propose that this conclusion is suspect because it is based largely on a single effectiveness outcome from studies that do not examine how and why organizations use Brainstorming" (p. 685). These researchers conducted an in-depth investigation within the design firm IDEO. They found that the use of Brainstorming groups supports organizational memory of design solutions, provides skill variety for designers, supports an attitude of wisdom, creates a status auction, makes an impression on clients, and provides income for the firm.

In conclusion, although some have criticized the practicality of Brainstorming, more recent research has demonstrated its value when properly applied, as well as highlighted the benefits beyond idea production.

Forced Connections

In Chapter 4 we described how the mind has a natural ability to create new ideas by making associations between unrelated concepts, an ability to borrow ideas from one context to solve a problem in other context. We called this the Make Connections principle of divergent thinking. Koestler (1964) referred to this as "bisociation." This is the association of two incompatible frames of reference. In the popular creative process method called "Synectics" (Gordon, 1961), the phrase "making the familiar strange and making the strange familiar" is used to describe the value of cross-fertilizing unrelated areas through the use of analogy to deliberately spark creative insights. The **Forced Connection** tool deliberately engages our minds in making connections. With the Forced Connection tool you intentionally "force" or stimulate your mind to generate new ideas by trying to see some connection between a random object and your challenge.

To use Forced Connections,

1. **Identify the challenge.** Begin with a clear statement of the challenge, framed as a question. Use invitational stems such as "How might . . . ?" "In what ways might . . . ?" For example, *How might I find a new job?*

2. **Select an object unrelated to the challenge.** Any object can be used, including those around you. A lamp, chair, couch, or plant are examples of what might be used to stimulate new ideas.

3. **Note the characteristics of the object.** What do you notice about the size, shape, color, general uses, texture, smell, and so on? For example, the plant is green, it has numerous leaves and branches, it needs to be watered and fertilized, it has multicolored leaves.

4. **Force a connection between the object and the challenge.** Ask yourself, "What ideas do I get for (insert your challenge) from (this object)?" For example, "What ideas do I get for finding a new job from the plant?" Ideas might include send flowers to a contact, cultivate new acquaintances, make my resume more colorful, branch out to other types of jobs. Remember to follow the principles of divergent thinking as you apply this tool.

5. **Repeat with additional objects.** What ideas do I get for finding a new job from the chair? The lamp? The couch? Keep selecting new objects to generate new connections and new ideas.

6. **Use other senses and modalities.** Beyond what you see, explore the other senses to make connections. For example, play music, touch objects, and so on. You might also use dance and motion to make connections kinesthetically.

❖ CONVERGENT THINKING TOOLS FOR EXPLORING IDEAS

Once you are ready to converge, you may have so many ideas that you don't know what to do with them all. Convergent thinking in Exploring Ideas is about sorting through these ideas and beginning to select those that are most promising, while still maintaining novelty. We presented two tools in Chapter 5, Hits and Highlighting, that will help you sort and select ideas. They will enable you to bring the "cream of the crop" of ideas into focus from all of the ones you have generated. The convergent guidelines will also support you in this process.

❖ WHAT'S NEXT IN THE CREATIVE
PROBLEM SOLVING PROCESS?

Something to remember at this point in the CPS process is that you do not have to make any commitments to the ideas you select as most promising. If you were to think of Exploring Ideas in terms of relationships and commitment, not only are you not getting married to the idea(s), you are not engaged or even going steady. At this point, you have met many new ideas and are now considering whether you might want to date any of them. Again, you might change your mind later, so don't worry about making a firm commitment at this point. If you wish to court these ideas, the next natural step would be to further examine these ideas in the Formulating Solutions step. On the other hand, "love at first sight" can happen and you may know exactly which idea(s) you want to implement and can move forward. The CPS process is flexible and allows you to move to any step in the process from here or to move out of the process completely. You can always go to Assessing the Situation to get your bearings and decide what to do next.

❖ APPLYING WHAT YOU'VE LEARNED

As a leader, building your Ideational Thinking skills will enable you to generate ideas when you need them, to bring out the ideas of others, and to recognize the difference between an idea and a solution. Ideas are the currency of creativity and they are free for the taking in every organization. This natural resource exists in every member of the organization, and tapping into it will energize individuals while also enabling the organization to change, make innovative leaps, and stay ahead of the competition. Ideas are everywhere. Just remember that they might look like diamonds in the rough and may need some cutting and polishing.

Some activities to try:

- Notice the number of ideas that you have considered in response to a personal challenge. Jot these ideas down. Now, use the divergent guidelines to expand your options. How many options do you now have? What were the benefits of using Ideational Thinking to tackle your challenge?
- Try the Forced Connections tool when you are working alone and stuck for ideas. Look around the room for objects that can be used to force a connection and generate new ideas. Remember to use the divergent guidelines.
- Facilitate a Brainstorming session with a group or team. Warm up the group by finding out how many are familiar with the guidelines for divergence. Reinforce the guidelines by reviewing them and having them visibly posted on the wall. Set a very high

target number to be generated, 40–50 ideas. As the group generates ideas, deliberately use the guidelines—have them make connections from ideas that have been generated, keep the pace moving, and remind the group to defer judgment and questions and discussion will happen later; encourage wild ideas.

- Identify a challenge for which you need some new thinking. Use the divergent guidelines or an idea-generation tool to produce as many ideas as you can to address this challenge. After generating a long list of ideas, switch to convergent thinking. As you begin to sort and select the ideas that will be most useful for your challenge, ask yourself which ideas

o Jump out at me immediately	o Stand head and shoulders above the rest
o Sparkle	o Make me smile
o Make me laugh	o Tickle my fancy
o Are unique	o Are intriguing
o Are "right on target"	o Fit the bill
o Are clear winners	o Add your own . . .

Force yourself to entertain some truly novel ways of approaching the challenge. Look again at the ideas you have not selected and consider which of them

1. would be fantastic if only you could figure out how to do them;
2. could really make a difference, but are difficult to implement;
3. you love, but wouldn't dare suggest to others;
4. seem silly, but still alluring.

Do you notice any difference between the two groups of ideas? The first are probably more easily implemented and are within your current reality. We would suggest that while there may be novelty in the first group, there may be even more novelty in the second group. We would advise you to be even more protective of the second group because otherwise it will not survive the first round of evaluation. Consider what it would take to implement some of the ideas in the second group. Which set of ideas presents the greatest opportunity for growth or for new experiences? Which set of ideas is most interesting and exciting to you? What benefits do you believe there are to forcing yourself to intentionally select ideas that are more novel?

9

Formulating Solutions

Tools for Evaluative Thinking

Chapter at a Glance

Have you ever had a great idea only to wake up the next morning and discover that it doesn't seem nearly as good as you thought it did the day before? What if you had acted on the idea in that initial raw, untested form? An error in judgment when moving an idea carelessly into action can cost thousands and even millions of dollars, not to mention serious "egg on the face."

This chapter contains information and examples about the CPS step of Formulating Solutions and addresses issues of Evaluative Thinking that are necessary for successful creative problem solving. We'll take a look at the basic function of Evaluative Thinking and identify three tools—Criteria; Evaluation Matrix; and Pluses, Potentials, and Concerns (PPC^O)—that work especially well when evaluation is needed.

❖ EVALUATIVE THINKING IN LEADERSHIP

Of all the demands that are placed on leaders in regard to expectations or responsibilities, few are greater than the demand for solutions. "What are we going to do? What is the answer? What's next?" and "What now?" are well-known refrains in leaders' experiences. The pressure to find a solution is a heavy responsibility for decision makers, whether working alone or in teams. It can be fun and challenging as well, but there is no need for it to be a guessing game. Using Evaluative Thinking takes some of the guesswork out of this important leadership task.

The French playwright Molière observed that "It is not what we do, but also what we do not do for which we are accountable." In **Evaluative Thinking** you *take the time to consider the reasonableness and quality of your ideas in order to develop workable solutions.* You may then decide to work further with them, hold some for later, or discard after you consider your accountability for actually making them work. Regardless, what you do or don't do is critical in preventing you from pursuing ideas that are not fully formed.

You may have heard the expression "You can't fit a round peg into a square hole," but, in fact, you *can* fit a round peg into a square hole if you add some padding to the base of the peg or modify the structure of the hole. The point is to envision the possibility of change, even though you may not see it at first, and then to evaluate in an affirmative, developmental way. Remember that in CPS it has been your job until now to bring some degree of novelty along with you no matter where you started in the process. In Formulating Solutions you need to continue to be aware of this and be willing to nurture the wilder options. Take your cue from former UCLA basketball coach John Wooden who said, "Don't let what you cannot do interfere with what you can do."

In today's business world, lack of foresight and failure to use thinking skills and tools that provide solid evaluation via divergence and convergence can be costly. Consider the meteoric rise and fall of the dot-coms. By the late 1990s, early 2000s, one in five dot-com ventures failed. In 2000 alone, an estimated 210 dot-coms went under (Sullivan, 2001). An examination of many of the critical factors cited as reasons for the widespread failure of these start-up ventures illustrates how lack of foresight and upfront awareness of this new business context undermined success. A quick glance at some reasons for dot-com failure (see Table 9.1) reads like a list of criteria that could have been generated to strengthen the now-defunct businesses before they ever left the conceptual stage. And although situations may seem clearer in hindsight, we still

Table 9.1   Reasons for Dot-Com Failures

1. **Customer Service Meltdown** Inadequate customer service provided via e-mail and telephone. 2. **Inadequate Order Fulfillment** Low inventory, missed shipping dates, and underestimated shipping costs. 3. **Use of Primitive Search and Transaction Tools** Slow and cumbersome systems frustrated users. 4. **Failure to Globalize** International surfers outspend U.S. surfers: Ventures that ignored the international market sometimes lost a competitive edge to those who did not. 5. **Building Community, Not Clientele** Failing to convert a network of users into paying customers.

SOURCE: Sullivan (2001).

make the case that some deliberate evaluation tied to solid divergence and convergence would have brought out many overlooked issues.

The widespread dot-com failures are a powerful reminder of the costly mistakes that can be made when poor evaluation and premature closure take over. Walters (2002) described it in this way:

> When the dot-com era blossomed, thousands of investors were only too happy to support an e-commerce start-up or anything with dot-com in the name. The words "online" and "e" gave companies the Midas touch, regardless of industry, resulting in a kind of greed-induced mass hysteria. Rather than following a visionspecific to and suited for the organization, dot-coms followed the few seemingly successful e-enterprises hoping to ride their wave. (p. 1)

This lack of solid Evaluative Thinking coupled with the rush to closure illustrated by the dot-com example can make life in the fast lane of new ideas precarious. The step of Formulating Solutions can be a leader's best friend on the road to successful implementation. It provides both the time and the structure to develop the inherent strengths of ideas and to anticipate and overcome weaknesses. Because leaders are accountable for implementing solutions and change, they need to be skilled in Evaluative Thinking. Table 9.2 highlights the reasons why we believe the Formulating Solutions step is important for leaders.

Table 9.2   Key Reasons Why Leaders Need to Be Skilled in Formulating
Solutions

- To strengthen the potential of wild, unusual, or different ideas so that they will be less strange to others
- To continue to keep an open mind on an idea's potential
- To deliberately think through the strengths and weaknesses of ideas
- To elaborate on a sketchy idea
- To turn ideas into viable solutions
- To determine the importance of what you need to do next; to begin to grow a plan
- To provide balance between novelty and usefulness
- To increase the chances that others will see the dazzle in a novel idea that you originally saw and felt
- To allow you to test your beliefs and intuition about ideas without external judgment
- To allow you to do your own evaluation before others see the final results

SOURCE: © 2005 Puccio, Murdock, and Mance. Reprinted with permission.

❖ THE NATURE AND PURPOSE OF FORMULATING SOLUTIONS

In the natural process, Formulating Solutions is the second step of Transforming (see Figure 9.1). Think of this step as being like the research and development wing of an organization—an incubator for newly arrived ideas that need some time and support to grow. Formulating Solutions provides a unique bridge from the speed, pace, and free-for-all nature of idea generation, which is designed to get you from novelty to usefulness without leaving the novelty behind. If in Exploring Ideas you set out to find and lasso the wild tigers of your imagination, in Formulating Solutions you set out to tame them without crushing their unique nature—after all, that's one of the reasons you used CPS to begin with—to get something unique and different.

There are two unique aspects that are fundamental to the nature of Formulating Solutions: (1) It is a transition point between ideas and implementation—and thus more closely related to the step that comes before it (Exploring Ideas) and the one that comes after it (Exploring Acceptance) than some other parts of the CPS process; and (2) divergence and convergence (and the tools that promote them) are more integrated in this step.

Figure 9.1   Formulating Solutions in the Creative Problem Solving
Thinking Skills Model

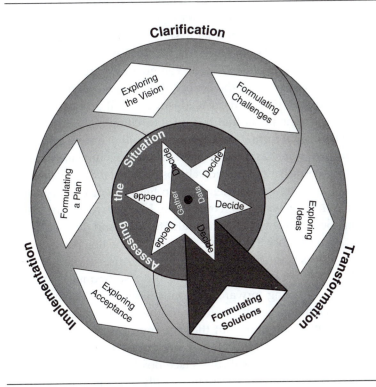

SOURCE: © 2006 Puccio, Murdock, and Mance. Reprinted with permission.

Box 9.1 Key Vocabulary

Some Key Concepts for Formulating Solutions

Evaluative Thinking: Assessing the reasonableness and quality of ideas in order to develop workable solutions.

Solution: An elaborated idea that has been examined and strengthened to develop the best possible fit with the proposed context in which it will be used.

Strengthening: A convergent thinking skill that keeps novelty alive by focusing first on the positive aspects of an idea and then seeking ways to overcome shortcomings associated with the idea.

Transforming: Changing something into a more refined or better articulated form. In the case of CPS, changing rough ideas into more elaborated and workable solutions.

The Bridge Between Ideas and Implementation

Because Formulating Solutions links with Exploring Ideas in the broader and more implicit natural process of **transforming** (see Box 9.1 for a definition), it is a crucial partner in securing answers to challenges that will actually work. As we noted in Chapter 8, novel ideas are fragile and rarely come out fully formed. The goal is to transform them. In Greek mythology, Athena, the beautiful daughter of Zeus, was not born in the normal way, but instead sprung full-grown from her father's forehead. The belief that beautiful or complete products simply come in their final form, rather than as a result of a sometimes ugly or messy process, is just as much a myth as Athena's unusual birth. As a process step, Formulating Solutions helps leaders take ideas that may need refining and strengthen them. It also helps them identify weaknesses and look for ways to overcome them. In other words, the step of Formulating Solutions helps you to evaluate fairly and deliberately.

We noted in Chapter 8 that in CPS there is a fine line between how people view ideas and solutions. Many people use the terms interchangeably, which is not only misleading, but also frequently dangerous in regard to rushing forward without thinking about what might be done to make things better, as we saw in the dot-com example. Ideas in CPS are *potential* solutions, but they are not fully formed solutions until they are strengthened, developed, elaborated, or evaluated. Thus, in CPS we reserve the term **solutions** (see Box 9.1 for a definition) for those choices and decisions that are more fully developed because it is the work that goes into developing solutions that creates the transition into the natural process of implementation—once you have committed to a solution it is natural to then think about what you need to do to implement it.

❖ DIVERGENCE AND CONVERGENCE IN FORMULATING SOLUTIONS: IT'S A BRAND NEW GAME

The second unique characteristic of Formulating Solutions is how divergence and convergence behave in this step. Have you ever been on a train trip and had to slow down or stop while the train switched from one track to another, or been driving on a road under construction when you saw a sign that read, "Caution, lane switch ahead?" When you begin the step of Formulating Solutions, you are entering such a critical juncture between the dynamic balance of divergence and convergence. In this step, you will notice a more convergent and focused feel to the thinking processes, tools, and activities. In CPS, convergence and selection occur in every step via dynamic balance, but in Formulating Solutions this balance is now heavily tipped toward Evaluative Thinking to increase the feasibility, and thus the quality, of wild or delicate new ideas you wish to take forward. It is in this step that your ideas will be turned into viable solutions or not. This requires a bit of slowing down, but it doesn't mean that you have abandoned divergence altogether. Navigating the lane switch between divergence and convergence in Formulating Solutions requires a more integrated approach to divergence and convergence than in the previous steps. In fact, several of the tools that are frequently used in this step contain both diverging and converging within the same general structure; therefore, we refer to these as integrative tools. The PPC^O and Evaluation Matrix that follow are examples of this integration (see Table 9.3 for a tool overview). Think of the function of diverging and converging in this step as similar to driving in city traffic where you will be going slower in general than on the open road and yet still have to speed up on occasion. The Dynamic Balance that we discussed in earlier chapters is still present; it just operates at a different pace as you move toward implementation.

Criteria

What did you have for dinner yesterday—a steak with mushrooms and onions and a giant salad? A grilled seafood platter? A vegetarian meal? A Weight Watchers frozen meal? A sandwich on the run? *Why* did you select the food and beverages that you did? Were you in a hurry? Are you allergic to seafood? Were you on a diet? Whether you were able to articulate them explicitly or not, you still had reasons for your dinner choices, and those reasons served as benchmarks or criteria to measure how near or far the selections came to meeting your expectations. Criteria help us to fill the gap between what you want and the actions you need to take to achieve it. They bring tacit needs and wishes to light so that they can be used to guide effective decision making.

In CPS, criteria are used to help you converge, specifically as a tool to screen or select from a large or small number of options. Interestingly, criteria are almost always present in our inner voice of judgment and can be productively applied in other steps when it is time to converge. We introduce them here because their powerful Evaluative Thinking function fits the heavier convergent demands of Formulating Solutions. In addition, criteria, although they can be used alone to evaluate, are a necessary component of another standard decision-making tool—the Evaluation Matrix.

Table 9.3   Formulating Solutions: Integrative Tool Overview

Tool Name	What the Tool Does	How to Use the Tool
Criteria Source: Noller, Parnes, and Biondi (1976).	Establishes benchmarks for evaluation; helps to screen ideas.	Generate a list of criteria in response to the questions "Will it . . . ?" or "Does it . . . ?" Select key criteria. Then select ideas that fit the key criteria. The closer an idea comes to meeting the criteria, the stronger it is.
Evaluation Matrix Source: Noller, Parnes, and Biondi (1976).	Illustrates relative strength of ideas in relation to criteria. Helps to make decisions about the most promising ideas to pursue.	When you have a large number of ideas (4 to 10), list them on the right side of a grid and put key criteria across the top. Compare and rate each idea by each criterion. Analyze the results for weak and strong points; consider these implications for further development or a final decision.
Pluses, Potentials, and Concerns (PPC°) Source: Miller, Vehar, and Firestien (2001).	Uses itemized checklists (pluses, potentials, concerns, and overcoming concerns) to evaluate one to three ideas. Strengthens ideas by identifying and addressing key shortcomings and highlighting key advantages.	Select one idea at a time and place each one at the top a sheet. List the letters P-P-C-O on the page. Underneath the first P, list as many pluses as you can come up with. Then move to the second P and list potentials (things that might happen). After these two rounds, list the concerns; word them as questions with an idea-inviting stem such as "How might . . . ?" Under the O, identify the major concerns and then diverge to overcome each of these concerns. Consider the implications for future action.

SOURCE: © 2005 Puccio, Murdock, and Mance. Reprinted with permission.

Have you ever thought that you knew what you wanted, only to discover after you got it that there were hidden aspects you had overlooked or not given appropriate attention to? Take buying a car for example. Just as with most thinking, there are some criteria, such as cost, that are on your mind because people always think that way. This is not to say that cost is not important to consider, but be cautious not to allow one criterion to mask other important criteria. For example, if you have always wanted a convertible because you just think they are cool, but you think you must buy a conservative family car, you may want to incorporate the more implicit criterion of "cool" into your mindset by trying to tease out what is behind the term that appeals to you. Is it the sense of freedom? Do you wish for a more daring image? Maybe you really can't put your finger on what it is—you just feel good about it.

Whatever your issues, it is diverging to generate varied, unusual, and even wild criteria that is likely to bring them out. You can diverge alone on criteria or you can convene a group and use a tool such as Brainstorming. When diverging, turn reasons into questions that will give you criteria. Use the stems "Will it . . . ?" or Does it . . . ?" Using the car example above, if a reason to consider in buying a car is cost, use the stem and turn that reason into a question such as "Will it be affordable?" Continue with the same stem/question approach until you get some quantity and novelty in your criteria: *Does it meet the family's needs? Will it make me feel good when I drive it to work? Will my mother-in law be able to get in the back seat? Will it get good gas mileage?* After diverging to your satisfaction, converge with an all-purpose tool and select with novelty in mind. Use these criteria to then select the ideas or options. Those that fit the most criteria are likely to be your best choices. Criteria can be used alone as a separate tool or you can take them forward into an Evaluation Matrix. Either way, making your reasons explicit and then using them as benchmarks to evaluate your choices or decisions helps you to sculpt your solutions to fit the context before you have to deal with outside opinions or demands.

Evaluation Matrix

The concept behind the **Evaluation Matrix** is to assess the relative strength of a large number (4 to 10 as a rule of thumb) of choices against explicit criteria and then to present the results in such a way that you can strengthen the weak points of any of the options, if you so choose. We mentioned earlier the advantage of deliberately generating and selecting criteria rather than using the first ones you think of, but regardless of how you obtained them, you will need criteria to guide your evaluation process.

To complete the Evaluation Matrix,

1. **Develop Criteria.** Generate and select criteria to evaluate your options (see previous tool).

2. **Check to see that the criteria are basically distinct from one another, positively worded, and written at about the same level of abstraction.** For example, "Will it be affordable?" and "Will it fit my budget?" are essentially the same thing. Choose the wording that will best encompass what you want to know. The budget issue is a little more concrete; would you be better served to deal with the general affordability issue, or do you prefer to keep your focus on the budget you have set? As a general rule, negatively worded criteria accomplish one thing—they make you think negatively about the issue before you even start to evaluate. There's nothing very creative about that, so don't waste your energy. Instead of "Will it make my spouse angry?" focus on "Will it make my spouse happy?" Make sure your criteria do not overlap or that one criterion is not subsumed by another. This can cause one criterion to have an undue influence on another.

3. **Build your matrix.** When you are satisfied that your criteria are worded in ways that will help you, write each one on the slanted lines of the matrix (you may prioritize or weight the criteria if some are more important than others). List the choices or ideas that you have selected down the left side of the matrix (see Figure 9.2 for a sample matrix).

4. **Select an evaluation system.** Identify how you wish to rate your choices—numbers (1–5); + – or 0 for neutral; ☺ ☻ ☺— whatever meets your need in relation to the complexity of the situation or your style. The more abstract the symbol, the broader the discrimination among the choices. Numbers are more concrete, as long as you don't fall into the trap of thinking you have to total them and use results as a substitute for analyzing what you have.

5. **Evaluate each choice.** Working DOWN the options, rate each option on the first criterion and put the evaluation results (number, symbol, etc.) in the box beside the choice. Working down the options helps avoid the halo effect where you might inadvertently rate a favored option higher. Move to the next criterion and do the same. If you find that a criterion you have selected doesn't work or doesn't represent what you intended

when you initially selected it, nothing bad happens; you have discovered the situation in time to make a correction before you take action. Simply change it on the matrix and rework your ideas around the modification. Continue evaluating options by criteria until all options have been evaluated.

6. **Review your matrix.** Look across all options and get a sense for which ones now appear to be the strongest. (Note: if you are using a number system, don't total the items and then assume the one with the highest score wins; the matrix assesses relative, not absolute strength.) Remember that you are working with items that you liked to begin with—items that have already made it through initial screening by their mere selection. Make an initial decision in regard to each choice. Identify whether you plan to accept the option as is, refine it to make it stronger, or reject it.

7. **Develop options and make a final decision.** Before you make a final decision, attempt to improve those options that were viewed as requiring some improvement (e.g., those in the "Refine" category). Let your intuition kick back in. Are there options with weak areas that you like? Re-examine the matrix and ask yourself, "How might this option be improved?" Those criteria for which an option does poorly might give you some areas to focus on for improvement. How might these choices be improved to better meet the criteria? Look at the big evaluation picture after additional strengthening and THEN make decisions to hold, modify, or go forward with different items.

Figure 9.2 shows an example of a completed Evaluation Matrix in which a team must decide which administrative software system to purchase for their organization. After generating and selecting pertinent criteria, the members of the team worked down each criterion to rate all of the selected software systems. They used a 0 to 5-point scale to evaluate the systems. As a result of the evaluation, two systems emerged as strong candidates. If you were to total the numbers, you might assume that this team would select the Omega system. However, note that they placed the Beta system in the refine category. Though the Omega system met most of the criteria, the group liked the user-friendliness of the Beta system. Therefore, they decided to speak with the developer of the Beta system to determine whether it would be possible to do some customization before installation (notice that this system received a lower score for the criterion "customizable"). If this were not possible, they would then go with the Omega system.

Figure 9.2   Evaluation Matrix Example: Selecting a Software System

Options	Fits our budget	User friendly	Compatibility	Customizable	Accessible support services	Accept	Refine	Reject
ACME	1	3	2	3	4			√
ABC	0	1	1	2	3			√
Alpha	3	3	3	3	4			√
Beta	4	5	5	3	5		√	
Omega	5	3	5	5	5	√		
New Century	1	2	3	3	3			√
Brand X	0	5	0	1	1			√

The first five data columns are headed **Criteria**; the last three (Accept, Refine, Reject) are headed **Decision**.

Rating Scale: 0 = poor   3 = good   5 = excellent

SOURCE: Format of matrix based on Isaksen and Treffinger (1985).

Pluses, Potentials, and Concerns (PPC°)

When you have a few ideas that you want to transform into solutions, the **PPC°** tool is helpful. This tool gets its name from the functions that each of its letters stands for—*Pluses, Potentials, Concerns, Overcoming Concerns*. Its purpose is to evaluate by strengthening (see definition in Box 9.1). This tool really packs a punch when it comes to making solutions workable. As we noted earlier, it has both divergent and convergent elements, making it a self-contained, abbreviated version of the CPS process itself, even though its primary function is still convergent. The PPC° is tailor-made for keeping novelty alive because there are two rounds of affirmative evaluation before you ever look at the concerns, and in addition, the "How to . . ." stem used to frame concerns easily leads to divergence to overcome the concerns.

The example we have used in Table 9.4 comes from a real-life issue in New York State. Prior to 1998, there was a five-year period for teachers to earn their master's degree; the Board of Regents then changed this requirement to a three-year limit. After a seven-month trial period, during which recent college graduates were burdened by loans to repay while they were adjusting to their very first classroom experiences and juggling family responsibilities concurrently, the Regents reconsidered and came out in support of the previous five-year term instead.

A quick look at our sample three-year option PPC° shows five sample pluses, one sample potential, three sample concerns, and an initial set of ideas generated to address the most critical concern (in a real situation, you would continue to diverge with more quantity until the concern was overcome or at least fully explored). Note that it is a good idea to have as many pluses as possible and a good list of potentials as well. In other words, use the divergent guidelines. These guidelines can be used to generate concerns in the next step of this tool. Notice that concerns are phrased in the form of a challenge statement (i.e., using statement starters such as How to . . . ? How might . . . ? What might . . . ?). Phrasing concerns in the form of a challenge invites ideas that may ultimately help you to strengthen the original idea being evaluated. Always begin with the Pluses and Potentials and then go to the Concerns.

In the final step of this tool, you generate ideas to overcome the most important concerns; always begin with the most crucial concern and use divergent thinking to pile as many ideas as possible on top of the concern. What often happens is that within the list of ideas are some that will help you to overcome that particular concern. The ideas selected to overcome the concern will ultimately make the solution stronger. This is why we write the "O" in the acronym for this tool as an exponent—it is the ideas generated to overcome the concerns that give new power to the solution being evaluated. Sometimes you are unable to overcome a concern. If this is the case, you can either go with the idea, recognizing its limitations, or decide to drop it and search for an alternative solution.

The PPC° is useful when you have one to three options to evaluate. You can evaluate only one option or compare competing ones by completing a PPC° on each and contrast the results to make a decision.

❖ WHAT'S NEXT IN THE CREATIVE
    PROBLEM SOLVING PROCESS?

The step of Formulating Solutions not only belongs with Exploring Ideas in the natural process of transforming, as we mentioned earlier it

Table 9.4   PPC°: An Example

Idea to Evaluate: Requiring New Teachers to Get a Master's Degree in Three Years

P luses (list what is good, positive about the idea)

- Increases level of content expertise
- Promotes even level of training
- Brings in more money to the State
- Gets it over quickly

P otentials (list what might happen if the idea were pursued, what are the possibilities)

- It might raise academic standards
- It might get young teachers to commit to the teaching profession

C oncerns (what are the shortcomings, weaknesses, or limitations of the idea)

- How to balance learning a new job along with the demands of graduate school?
- How to overcome the financial burden?
- How to juggle family responsibilities?

O vercome (generate ideas to overcome concerns, starting with the most important) Major concern: How to balance learning a new job along with the demands of graduate school?

- Give release time
- Cut back on school day one hour
- Provide teacher aides to teachers who are in graduate school
- All teachers in graduate school to take personal days to help manage their schoolwork
- Provide daycare for teachers
- Have graduate courses delivered in the schools

SOURCE: © 2005 Puccio, Murdock, and Mance. Reprinted with permission.

has an interesting transformational function in implementation as well. A colleague of ours, Ed Pettitt, an engineer and inventor at Delphi International, describes this from his experience in product development. Formulating Solutions in product development, he maintains, is a matter of getting solutions ready to fit the context, whereas in Exploring Acceptance you are trying to get the context ready to accept the solutions. Whatever direction you determine, you will need to assess the situation, gather the appropriate data, and make a process decision.

If your solutions hold up to deliberate evaluation, you will be ready to look at how to get them accepted by others in Exploring Acceptance, or if this is clear, you may want to go straight to action. It is possible, however, that you will find that your initial ideas don't hold up to the scrutiny of deliberate evaluation, so you may need to go back to Exploring Ideas and pick up some new ones. Or perhaps, after you have carefully examined the solution, the whole direction is not satisfactory, and you decide that you need more clarification. In that case, a return to Exploring the Vision or Formulating Challenges might be helpful. Use the If-Then tool in Chapter 5 to guide you toward the next process step.

❖ APPLYING WHAT YOU'VE LEARNED

Thomas Edison once said, "Opportunity is missed by most people because it is dressed in overalls and looks like work." The deliberate work required in Formulating Solutions is such an opportunity. A leader needs to recognize and value what this step can do to strengthen decisions and actions, despite the pressure to produce quick and easy solutions. The step of Formulating Solutions provides an experimental laboratory where leaders can test their initial thinking and ideas by deliberately evaluating before they leap to implementation. The fate of a leader's success in implementing change often rests here, for as motivational speaker Anthony Robbins observed, "It is in your moments of decision that your destiny is shaped."

Here are some activities designed to help you develop your Evaluative Thinking skills:

- What idea have you been thinking about implementing? Better yet, what idea has you intrigued, but you've eliminated it from consideration because you can't imagine how you would make it happen? Before giving up totally, do a deliberate strengthening of the idea by completing a PPC°. In addition to stretching for many pluses and potentials, be sure to state the concerns in the form of a challenge (questions with invitational stems) and generate many ideas to overcome the key concerns. What insights do you have now about this idea?

- Practice generating criteria for evaluation when you are given an assignment. What would an excellent outcome look like? Will it . . . ? Does it . . . ? Use this process as a method of establishing the benchmarks for evaluation of your work.
- Next time you make a major purchase or an important decision, use the Evaluation Matrix. Generate criteria that will help you select among the options, select the most important criteria, and build yourself a matrix. Rate each option against the criteria and see whether it helps you make a good decision.

10

Exploring Acceptance

Tools for Contextual Thinking

Chapter at a Glance

Have you ever been enamored with an idea that you introduced with great fanfare, only to be let down by others' lack of enthusiasm? In this chapter, we will examine how to increase the likelihood that your ideas and proposed creative changes will eventually be adopted. To be successful, leaders must be able to look beyond what they want to create and assess how the environment will respond to the proposed change. Thus far in the CPS process we have focused on evolving an effective idea, solution, or proposed change. Now let's shift from this internal focus to an external one. In Exploring Acceptance, you engage in Contextual Thinking: understanding the interrelated conditions and circumstances that will support or hinder success.

In this chapter, you will learn about how Contextual Thinking enhances leadership effectiveness. Specifically, we will introduce two new tools, Assisters and Resisters and Stakeholder Analysis, to help you scan the environment where the creative change will be introduced to determine what forces will help or hinder your implementation.

❖ CONTEXTUAL THINKING IN LEADERSHIP

The purpose of this chapter is to provide leaders with the mindset and tools to effectively engage in Contextual Thinking. To be effective at implementing solutions and introducing creative change, leaders need to anticipate the reaction, both pro and con, to ideas they wish to implement. This is particularly true when they are introducing a new concept, service, or product because novel ideas are often resisted or viewed with some degree of suspicion. Consider the power of the status quo in keeping novelty from being embraced. Furthermore, it is sometimes necessary for leaders to engage their team in Contextual Thinking, especially when a team has fallen in love with its own idea. By engaging a team in the Exploring Acceptance step, leaders can introduce some objective thinking to a situation and potentially enhance the degree to which a change will be successfully adopted.

Consider the successful introduction of some recent products and services. The Apple iPod was introduced at a time when the music-listening and technology-savvy consumer was copying and sharing music CDs, while at the same time, the music industry confronted issues of profit and artist rights. The compact, technologically advanced Apple iPod, which can be used to download purchased music and much more, responded to all of these issues and has been wildly popular.

Another example of introducing responsive products and services is the successful entrepreneur, who is adept at understanding the market and creating new business opportunities. In fact, in response to the needs of busy working people, services such as personal shoppers, dry cleaning delivery, gourmet take-out, and even dog daycare have emerged. On the other hand, misreading the environment can be problematic, even for large corporations.

Do you recall the disastrous introduction of New Coke? In the early 1980s, the number one soft drink, Coke, was beginning to lose market share to Pepsi. Blind taste tests featured in the Pepsi Challenge campaign showed that Coke drinkers preferred Pepsi. In response, Coca-Cola began to experiment with new formulas for Coke, and in 1984, Coca-Cola produced a new formula for Coke that beat Pepsi in blind taste tests by a margin of 6–8 points. While Coca-Cola experimented with new formulas, it tested consumers' reactions to a possible change to the flavor of this popular soft drink. Specifically, market research carried out by Coca-Cola between 1983 and 1985 showed that the consumers strongly opposed the idea of changing Coke's flavor.

However, Coca-Cola was so taken by the positive results of its own blind taste tests that New Coke was quickly brought to market. According to Bastedo and Davis (1993),

> All discouraging market research was tossed into the rectangular file. On April 23, 1985, New Coke was released to a great deal of fanfare. By the middle of June, people were "Saying NO to New Coke." The reaction to New Coke was swift and humiliating. (p. 3)

The failure of New Coke is a classic example of implementing an idea with little consideration for how the idea will be received. An interesting twist on the Coca-Cola story is that the company responded rather creatively to the negative response by reintroducing the original formula as "Classic" Coke.

We can once again turn to the dot-com failures to highlight a more contemporary example of how a lack of Contextual Thinking, or *understanding the interrelated conditions and circumstances that will support or hinder success,* can lead to a failed venture. In Chapter 9 we discussed how many dot-coms failed as a result of moving too quickly from idea to implementation. Specifically, we noted that many dotcom ideas were not well developed through careful evaluation, the kind of thinking that is applied through the Formulating Solutions step of the CPS process. However, not all dot-coms failed because they were good ideas that were not well developed; there were plenty of dot-com ventures that failed simply because they were not good business ideas from the outset. For example, one dot-com company was built around the belief that pet owners would find it more convenient to buy supplies for their animals over the Internet (Kaplan, 2002). Unfortunately, many pet owners made their purchases only when necessary and were not in a position to wait for their supplies to arrive by postal delivery. Similarly, a dot-com makeup company soon discovered that many shoppers were unwilling to buy cosmetics, such as lipstick, via the Internet because they preferred to try out such products in person (Kaplan, 2002). Further examples of dot-com ideas that failed principally as a result of poor Contextual Thinking are found in Table 10.1.

Leaders operate in a social context. To be a leader means, by definition, that you work with others. To successfully introduce novel solutions or to bring about creative change, leaders must learn to skillfully work within their social contexts. As Mumford et al. (2000) observed,

Table 10.1   Some Dot-Com Examples That Might Have Benefited From Good Contextual Thinking

Dotcom	Nature of Business	Reason Cited for Failure
Iam.com	Online portfolios of actors and models intended for use by casting directors. Approximate cost for startup was $48 million.	Casting directors prefer to work with talent agencies; it saves them time as the talent agencies serve as an initial screening mechanism.
Third Voice	A free browser plug-in that allowed users to place "sticky notes" on Web sites. These notes would then be seen by others who visited the Web site. Startup costs approximately $15 million.	Controversy broke out soon after the launch of Third Voice. Sticky notes often degenerated into virtual graffiti and Webmasters were concerned that they would lose control of their sites.
Mercata.com	A "group buying" site that attempted to band consumers together so that they could purchase merchandise at wholesale prices. Startup costs almost $90 million.	One of the factors believed to contribute to the demise of Mercata.com was the fact that manufacturers were reluctant to sell directly to consumers as they did not want to damage relationships with retailers.

SOURCE: Kaplan (2002).

From a leader's perspective, organizational constituencies and stakeholders pose significant potential restrictions. Thus, leaders' solutions must be built upon consensus, which implies a broader point. Leaders must develop and implement solutions in a distinctly social context. . . . The need to develop and implement solutions with and through others places a premium on social skills. (p. 15)

You may recall from Mumford and his colleagues' (2000) model, presented in Chapter 2, that three sets of skills play a primary role in yielding effective leadership performance. One set of skills relates to CPS, while another refers to social skills, and a third to knowledge. Through the Exploring Acceptance step, we hope to enhance both the cognitive and affective skills that will enable leaders to introduce solutions that work and change that sticks. Table 10.2 provides some specific reasons why we feel these skills are so crucial to effective leadership.

Table 10.2   Key Reasons Why Leaders Need to Be Skilled in Exploring Acceptance

- To ensure that the rollout of a new idea or change goes as smoothly as possible
- To build a coalition of support
- To avoid being blindsided by critics or hidden trip wires
- To inform the plan of action with wisdom and social intelligence
- To respond effectively in a fast-paced global economy
- To introduce change into multicultural and multinational contexts
- To ensure psychological, emotional, and social support for proposed solutions and creative change
- To attract resources necessary for success
- To ensure alignment with organizational goals and mission
- To facilitate an objective look at how to position an idea or change so that it will be supported by others

SOURCE: © 2005 Puccio, Murdock, and Mance. Reprinted with permission.

Box 10.1   Key Vocabulary

Some Key Concepts for Exploring Acceptance

Contextual Thinking: Understanding the interrelated conditions and circumstances that will support or hinder success.

Exploring Acceptance: The CPS process step used to increase the likelihood of success when implementing new solutions.

Stakeholders: Individuals, groups, or organizations that have a vested interest in the proposed solution or change.

❖ THE NATURE AND PURPOSE
OF EXPLORING ACCEPTANCE

The purpose of the Exploring Acceptance step is to pause for reflection before rushing forward to implement a solution or creative change (see Figure 10.1). Think of it as the decompression chamber between the euphoric feelings often associated with the breakthrough thinking that occurs in the idea generation and solution development and the implementation of the results. Through the Exploring Acceptance step, you intentionally inject Contextual Thinking into your creative process to

Figure 10.1   Exploring Acceptance in the Creative Problem Solving
Thinking Skills Model

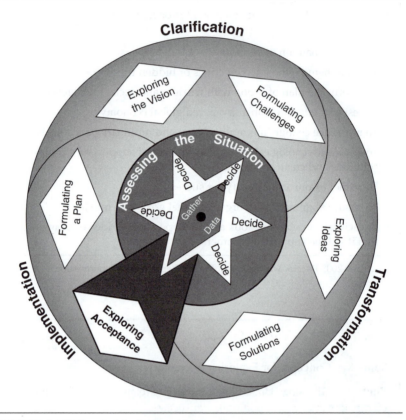

SOURCE: © 2006 Puccio, Murdock, and Mance. Reprinted with permission.

develop an understanding of the environmental conditions that might
help or hinder the successful implementation. Contextual Thinking
involves scanning the environment in which you wish to introduce a
solution or change. Through this environmental scan, you become
aware of factors such as people, resources, conditions, and so on that
will either support or block the new idea. By anticipating these factors,
you can develop actions to enlist sources of support and overcome
sources of resistance. Does Contextual Thinking guarantee that your
ideas will not fail? No, but it increases the likelihood of success.

There is an important link between the steps of Exploring
Acceptance and the Formulating a Plan (both of which fall within the
Implementation stage of natural process). The Contextual Thinking in

Exploring Acceptance informs actions in the implementation plan. When Exploring Acceptance precedes Formulating a Plan, there is a greater likelihood that a more robust set of action steps will be created, thus increasing the potential for success. Without Contextual Thinking, the plan may be too narrowly focused on the mechanical steps that must be followed to implement a solution or change and may not sufficiently consider how forces in the environment will respond.

To skillfully engage in Contextual Thinking and to carry out the Exploring Acceptance step, individuals rely on effective divergent thinking to thoroughly scan the environment in which an idea or change will be introduced. Overlooking one key ally or foe can severely limit success. Thus, particular emphasis is applied to the divergent phase within the dynamic balance between divergent and convergent thinking. After completing an exploration of the environment in which the solution or change is to be introduced, convergent thinking is then applied to identify those factors that are most important to consider as the solution or change is carried forward. For this reason, we will introduce you to two new divergent thinking tools aimed specifically at promoting sound Contextual Thinking. Tools previously discussed can be applied to carry out the convergent phase of Exploring Acceptance.

❖ DIVERGENT THINKING TOOLS FOR EXPLORING ACCEPTANCE

Divergent thinking in Exploring Acceptance ensures that you have sufficiently examined the environment for things that will either support or undermine the success of your idea. Without divergent thinking, you are more likely to overlook critical planning factors. The goal of divergent thinking in this step is to cast a wide net to identify as many factors as possible that should be considered when you build an implementation plan. Many factors that are captured in this net will not come as a surprise, particularly for those already well in tune with their environment; however, divergence often leads to surprises that alert you to critically important planning contingencies that otherwise might have been overlooked. Table 10.3 provides a brief overview of two tools that are useful in helping you to engage in divergent Contextual Thinking. You may already be aware of other tools that achieve the same end; we encourage you to use whatever you have at your disposal to carry out an environmental scan.

Table 10.3   Exploring Acceptance: Divergent Tool Overview

Tool Name	What the Tool Does	What You Do
Assisters and Resisters SOURCE: Isaksen and Treffinger (1985); Noller, Parnes, and Biondi (1976).	Sorts planning contingencies into two categories: those sources that will help (assisters) and those that will hinder (resisters) success.	The basic questions of who, what, where, when, why, and how are used to identify what factors will assist or resist implementation of the new solution or change. Divergent thinking is applied to generate options within each of these categories.
Stakeholder Analysis SOURCE: Mason and Mitroff (1981).	Identifies key people who have a vested interest in the solution or change and categorizes these individuals into those who will support and those who will reject the change.	Create a list of those individuals who have a vested interest in the solution or change. For each person, identify his or her position along a scale ranging from strongly support to strongly oppose. Determine where each person needs to be, in regard to support, in order to successfully implement the solution or change. Generate action steps for those individuals that need to be moved from one position to another (e.g., strongly oppose to moderately support).

SOURCE: © 2005 Puccio, Murdock, and Mance. Reprinted with permission.

Assisters and Resisters

The **Assisters and Resisters** tool is quite straightforward. Divergent thinking is used to generate options within two broad categories: factors that will assist in implementing a proposed change and factors that will serve to resist the change. To fully explore these factors, we recommend that you use the categories in the Five Ws and an H tool (i.e., who, what, where, when, why, and how) to organize the search for assisters and resisters. Table 10.4 provides some questions that are useful in discovering sources of assistance and resistance within each of the categories. When generating sources of assistance and resistance, read through the categories in Table 10.4 and create a column of potential sources of assistance and a column of potential sources of resistance.

Table 10.4   Searching for Sources of Assistance and Resistance

	Sources of Assistance	*Sources of Resistance*
Who	Individuals or groups that will help progress	Individuals or groups that will hinder progress
What	Things (e.g., resources, attitudes, beliefs, systems, policies, procedures) that will help the proposed change	Things (e.g., resources, attitudes, beliefs, systems, policies, procedures) that will hinder the proposed change
When	Issues with regard to timing that will facilitate progress (e.g., Are there particularly good times to roll out the change?)	Issues with regard to timing that will inhibit progress (e.g., Are there particularly bad times to roll out the change?)
Where	Physical locations or places that would support success	Physical locations or places that would hinder success
Why	Reasons that might be provided in support of the proposed change	Reasons that might be offered to block the initiative
How	Actions others might take in support of the idea	Actions others might take to undermine the idea

SOURCE: Isaksen, Dorval, and Treffinger (1994).

In some situations, the same factor can be both a source of assistance and a source of resistance. For example, if you are unaware of a key decision maker's (e.g., the boss's) attitude toward the idea, then this person may be listed as a possible assister and possible resister. After generating as many possible sources of assistance and resistance as you can, you will need to identify those that will have the greatest potential impact, both positive and negative, on the proposed change or solution. A convergent tool like Hits is useful for this. These key sources of assistance and resistance would then be used to help identify the necessary action steps to carry out the change or to implement the solution. Action steps that take advantage of the sources of assistance and overcome sources of resistance should become part of the implementation plan (see Chapter 11, Formulating a Plan).

Stakeholder Analysis

Mason and Mitroff first introduced **Stakeholder Analysis** in 1981. Since its introduction, Stakeholder Analysis has been widely adopted in strategic planning efforts. Figure 10.2 shows an example that was created by an organizational consultant, Tim Switalski (personal communication, September 16, 2004), and is based on the work of Mason and Mitroff (1981).

Over the last several years in Buffalo there have been discussions about whether the Peace Bridge, which connects downtown Buffalo to Fort Erie, Canada, should be replaced by a "signature" bridge or maintained as it is with the addition of a duplicate bridge. Many agreed there was a need to upgrade the situation, but there was some debate about the best way to proceed. Figure 10.2 is based on the assumption that the Bridge Authority has decided that the best option is a signature bridge and that they now wish to move this idea forward for acceptance. We present this merely as an example to illustrate how stakeholder analysis works and not as a data-based example. The example shows the key stakeholders and an estimation of current levels of support, along with projections of the level of support needed to initiate the project successfully. Note that even when the stakeholder is exactly where you wish, such as the Tourism Board in this example, it may still be useful to think about how this stakeholder can help to have a positive influence on others.

To use Stakeholder Analysis,

1. **Generate a list of all stakeholders. Stakeholders** are those *individuals, groups, or organizations that have a vested interest in the proposed solution or change.* They are in a position of decision-making authority or are influential with respect to the success of the idea. If a long list of stakeholders is generated through divergent thinking (more than 20), it might be useful to trim the number down to those that seem most crucial before carrying out an analysis. Evaluation of too many stakeholders can be overwhelming, particularly when action steps are placed into a plan for implementing the solution or change.

2. **Identify their current level of support**. Once all stakeholders have been generated, identify their current level of support for the solution or change.

3. **Estimate where level of support needs to be.** Once you identify where you believe a stakeholder's current level of support is, then estimate where the stakeholder needs to be to ensure the successful adoption of the solution or change. Ask yourself, "Where do I think this stakeholder needs to be in order for me

Figure 10.2   Stakeholder Analysis Example: Building a Signature Bridge

Stakeholder	Strongly Oppose	Moderately Oppose	Neutral	Moderately Support	Strongly Support	Required Actions
City Government (U.S.)			X		O	Put plan forward that would show how a bridge can be the beginning to downtown revitalization.
Residents in close proximity to bridge (U.S. & Canada)	X			O		Identify a reasonable offer for property. Provide relocation services. Focus on new opportunities associated with relocation.
City residents in general			X	O		Begin a campaign highlighting various benefits of a signature bridge.
Congressman Smith		X			O	Demonstrate how a new signature bridge would resolve many local issues and challenges, as well as contribute to national concerns (e.g., border security).
Regional Government (Canada)			X	O		Highlight the benefits of a signature bridge versus a twin span.
New York State Government			X	O		Invite key politicians to a town meeting to discuss bridge issue.
Truck drivers and businesses that use bridge			X		O	Demonstrate how a signature bridge would save time and money.
Tourism Board (U.S. & Canada)					X	Use economic impact studies provided by tourism boards to influence other stakeholders.

X = Where are they now?   O = Where do they need to be?

to have this solution or change successfully implemented?" Ask the same question of each identified stakeholder.

4. **Generate action steps to close the gap.** Finally, action steps are identified to close the gap between where each stakeholder is and where the stakeholder needs to be.

❖ CONVERGENT THINKING TOOLS FOR EXPLORING ACCEPTANCE

The two divergent tools presented in this chapter have a common core structure. Each operates like a ledger, tracking the assets and liabilities that are likely to influence the eventual success of a proposed solution or change. At the beginning of this chapter, we indicated that the purpose of the Exploring Acceptance step is to help individuals and teams take some time to reflect before leaping to implementation. This time of reflection allows you to scan the environment in which you are introducing a new solution or change so that later you are not surprised by what appears. Divergence in Exploring Acceptance encourages a broad search for many factors that need to be considered for the solution or proposed change to be effective. Convergent Thinking allows you to focus on those factors that will be most crucial to consider as you go forward. It would probably be difficult to build an action plan around 40 anticipated sources of resistance, 53 stakeholders, or 28 helping forces. We recommend using tools like Hits to narrow down a larger set of options to a smaller, more manageable number. For instance, Hits could be used to identify key sources of assistance and resistance or key stakeholders.

❖ WHAT'S NEXT IN THE CREATIVE PROBLEM SOLVING PROCESS?

What comes next after Exploring Acceptance? Before we answer that question, let's first focus on the outcome of this step. After completing Exploring Acceptance, you should have a sense of what to consider as you roll out your solution or change. What are the helpful aspects and the potential hurdles? With these insights in mind, you may decide that you need to formulate a more systematic and explicit plan, for example, if the situation involves greater complexity or when you are working with a team, the implementation needs to be coordinated more fully. In such cases, we recommend using information gained through Exploring Acceptance to inform the action steps in implementation. When Contextual Thinking precedes the development of an implementation plan, it injects greater wisdom and foresight into the process—ultimately enhancing the probability of success. As we noted earlier, the outcomes of the Exploring Acceptance step lead quite naturally into the Formulating a Plan step. If you feel you are not prepared to go into the Formulating a Plan step, then use the If-Then tool found in Chapter 5 to make your next process decision.

❖ APPLYING WHAT YOU'VE LEARNED

At the heart of leadership is the ability to facilitate and lead change. To successfully introduce creative change, leaders must be keenly aware of the environment. They must possess an astute ability to anticipate those forces that will support or impede the proposed change. This anticipatory thinking may prevent failure, and in some cases, disaster. To paraphrase Confucius, people who take no thought about what is distant will find sorrow near at hand.

Some activities to try:

- Practice scanning your context to see how astute you are at noticing details, reactions, and environmental clues. Observe a meeting or social interaction and jot down behavioral indicators of how people might be feeling or what they are thinking about the topic or situation. Pay particular attention to nonverbal signals (tone of voice, gestures of engagement, withdrawal, etc.) that might show assistance or resistance to the topic or idea. How effective were you at "reading" the situation?
- Think of a time when you (a) successfully interpreted and (b) unsuccessfully interpreted the context or environment into which you introduced an idea or situation that others were not prepared for. Analyze what worked and what didn't in each situation. List what you might have done differently.
- Identify a solution you have developed and are ready to implement. Review the sources of assistance and resistance to making this solution a reality. Generate ideas to overcome the key sources of resistance, and consider how you might leverage your assisters to overcome any resistance. Note what new insights you have gained from using this tool.

- As the leader of a team, consider a decision or action you want to implement that requires that all members of the team are on board and committed. Using the Stakeholder Analysis, review where you believe each individual team member currently stands on this issue and where he or she needs to be for it to be successfully implemented. What do you need to do to move individuals to a different position?
- Find a newspaper article in which a new idea is being proposed. Read through the article and identify sources of assistance and resistance in regard to the idea addressed in the article. Consider what you might do to overcome the sources of resistance.

11

Formulating a Plan

Tools for Tactical Thinking

Chapter at a Glance

"Just do it." This Nike slogan certainly reflects one approach to implementing solutions. We would suggest, however, that doing some planning before implementing will increase the likelihood of a successful outcome.

Have you ever overlooked a very important detail, requiring you to back-track and incur extra expense or loss of time and energy? Perhaps there was a deadline approaching, and in a rush to implement an exciting solution, you did not take the time to think through the steps required for implementation.

In this chapter, we will discuss planning and the Tactical Thinking that is used in this step of the CPS process. We will examine a creative approach to planning and introduce four tools, Generating Action Steps, How-How Diagram, Sequencing, and Performance Dashboard, that will help you successfully implement your solution or creative change and monitor the results.

❖ TACTICAL THINKING IN LEADERSHIP

In CPS, we define **Tactical Thinking** as *devising a plan in specific and measurable steps for attaining a desired end and monitoring its effectiveness.* Although not always visible or heralded, it is Tactical Thinking that creates great results for leaders. The outcome of solid Tactical Thinking is that ideas get implemented, events go off without a hitch, and complex projects are effectively completed on time and on budget. In other words, planning allows leaders time to reflect on tasks that must be accomplished, to establish timetables and deadlines, to align necessary resources, and to manage all of the other details that must be taken into account to successfully implement a solution or change.

The planning leaders do is not often visible as it happens off-line or behind the scenes. The fact that you only see the final product means you may not fully appreciate the amount of work required to make it possible. However, you can get a glimpse into the importance of planning when you think about major events and imagine all of the details that must be managed.

Consider the 2004 Summer Olympics in Athens and the controversy around the effectiveness of the planning. There were fears as early as 2000 that the city would never be ready for the August 2004 opening because planning milestones were not being met. There was a lack of visible progress, and there were concerns about the Greek management team that was in charge of organizing the event. In fact, in April 2000 International Olympic Committee President Juan Antonio Samaranch stated that "unless there was a drastic improvement in planning for the event, the 2004 Olympics could be taken away from the spiritual home of the Games" (BBC News, 2000). Gianna Angelopoulos-Daskalaki, who had led the bid to bring the games to Athens, was brought in to take over operations. Obviously a leader skilled in Tactical Thinking, she organized details, restructured tasks, and monitored the activities of the whole team until there was a flow of action toward the goal, and the 2004 Olympics went on as scheduled. In reference to incomplete venues and transportation infrastructure, Angelopoulos-Daskalaki noted, "It will take a great effort to get these things done. But we haven't come this far to let challenges like these stop us now" (BBC Sport, 2004, p. 1).

Another arena where effective Tactical Thinking is necessary is in military operations. Perhaps one of the most impressive illustrations of this was the World War II invasion of Normandy, France on June 6, 1944. Imagine the amount of planning required for this massive military operation. The Public Broadcasting System presented a special program commemorating the 60th anniversary of D-Day that highlighted some of the logistics that were involved. A transcript of the program described the action:

> An invading army had not crossed the unpredictable, dangerous English Channel since 1688—and once the massive force set out, there was no turning back. The 5,000-vehicle armada stretched as far as the eye could see, transporting over 150,000 men and nearly 30,000 vehicles across the channel to the French beaches. Six parachute regiments—over 13,000 men—were flown from nine British airfields in over 800 planes. More than 300 planes dropped 13,000 bombs over costal Normandy immediately in advance of the invasion. War planners had projected that 5,000 tons of gasoline would be needed daily for the first 20 days after the initial assault. In one planning scenario 3,489 tons of soap would be required for the first four months in France. (PBS, n.d.)

Although these examples—planning the Olympics and a massive military operation—are certainly dramatic and complex, they also have elements in common with the planning that all leaders do. In each case, the thinking skill that is utilized is Tactical Thinking. This is no longer the "what if" approach found in Exploring the Vision or Exploring Ideas, but the "what now" thinking required to make something happen.

Just as it is important to plan, a leader must also know when to stop planning and begin implementing. It is certainly possible to create elaborate plans that attempt to consider every contingency. However, in this day and age, when speed of implementation is critical to competitive edge, it is important to identify the critical elements and discard the irrelevant ones. Just as it is possible to fall into "analysis paralysis" when evaluating an idea, you can "plan to plan" and never move forward. When this happens you may be exhibiting an aversion to taking the risk to implement or letting your style preference override the need to move forward. As World War II General George S. Patton once said, "A good plan today is better than a perfect plan tomorrow." In Table 11.1, we outline some of the reasons leaders should be skilled in Formulating a Plan.

Box 11.1   Key Vocabulary

Some Key Concepts for Formulating a Plan

Action Steps: Concrete, observable activities undertaken by individuals and groups that lead to a desired outcome.

Formulating a Plan: The CPS process step focused on developing a plan before moving to implementation.

Tactical Thinking: Devising a plan in specific and measurable steps for attaining a desired end and monitoring its effectiveness.

Table 11.1   Key Reasons Why Leaders Need to Be Skilled in Formulating a Plan

- Ideas are just ideas unless you do something with them.
- Communicating a plan to others says that you are serious about making it happen.
- Deliberate planning helps you avoid forgetting something critical.
- You will avoid some of the costs of backtracking—wasted resources, paying more for convenience items if needed at the last minute, overtime pay, etc.
- It helps you to frame tasks in sequence and see how they play out, avoids putting steps out of order.
- You can see how actions/events interact with each other.
- It helps you to deal with detailed, multi-layered situations.
- It creates a "can-do" attitude, "This is not so hard."
- It provides a "stop and think it through" step for those prone to rushing to implementation.

SOURCE: © 2005 Puccio, Murdock, and Mance. Reprinted with permission.

❖   THE NATURE AND PURPOSE OF FORMULATING A PLAN

Formulating a Plan is a straightforward step in the CPS process. This is the concrete "What do I actually need to do to make this happen?" step. If you are moving into this step, you have a solution to a predicament or a proposed change for an opportunity that you have evaluated, refined, and tested with others and are ready to move forward to implementation (see Figure 11.1). You may have used other steps in the CPS process to get here, or you may have just spent some time in Assessing the Situation and realized that you are ready to plan.

Figure 11.1   Formulating a Plan in the Creative Problem Solving Thinking
Skills Model

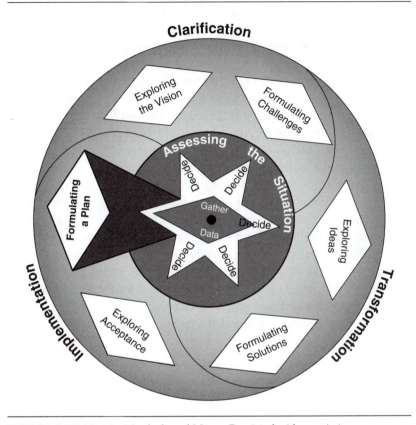

The purpose of this step is to help you search for all of the possible
action steps that will enable you to successfully implement your solution or change, identify key elements and sequence them in a logical or
effective order, and leverage people against tasks to make things happen. Have you ever rushed to implement a solution or roll out a change
and had difficulty because in your rush you overlooked important
aspects of the plan? Perhaps you overlooked some details and had to
backtrack. Maybe your efforts were not well coordinated and implementation was delayed, or key people were not consulted and, as a
result, the initiative was put on hold. When preparing to introduce a
novel solution or change, particularly in a high-stakes situation, it is
helpful to be explicit about the steps required to ensure success.

The Formulating a Plan step enables you to be explicit because by its nature it is very detail oriented and concrete. It will seem familiar to anyone who regularly generates a to-do list, or who has been involved in a major project implementation. In its dynamic balance, this step has a more convergent than divergent feel, although divergence is still present. For example, making a to-do list usually involves listing tasks off the top of your head. In Formulating a Plan, you use the divergent guidelines to search for many tasks that you might want to accomplish and then, using convergent guidelines, make your final selections.

There is a feeling of accomplishment at this step in the CPS process as you approach the point where "the rubber meets the road" and you prepare to make a commitment to implementation. You have moved from "That's a good idea" to "Hey, I can make this happen." In fact, breaking down implementation into concrete action steps makes it seem more manageable and can create a sense of clarity, focus, and an energy that comes with feeling that something is possible. Once you have created an explicit plan and you have a realistic appraisal of what is involved in making a solution happen, there is still one more opportunity to decide whether the outcome is worth the effort required for implementation.

The divergent and convergent tools presented here will guide you through this planning as you put the tactics in place for action.

❖ DIVERGENT THINKING TOOLS FOR FORMULATING A PLAN

The divergent tools presented below are designed to focus your thinking on what you need to do to carry a solution or change forward. We present two tools, but we encourage you to incorporate others that you know as well. Project management books, courses, and software are good places to find planning tools. Table 11.2 provides a brief overview of two basic divergent tools that are useful in Tactical Thinking.

Generating Action Steps

How often do you begin a day by first listing all the things you need to do that day? The tool **Generating Action Steps** (Isaksen et al., 1994; Isaksen & Treffinger, 1985) parallels the creation of a "to-do" list. Just as some people create to-do lists when faced with many activities and assignments, the same can be done when it is time to consider all the steps that might be required to carry out a creative solution or change. **Action steps** *are concrete, observable activities undertaken by individuals and groups that lead to a desired outcome.*

Table 11.2   Formulating a Plan: Divergent Tool Overview

Tool Name	What the Tool Does	What You Do
Generating Action Steps SOURCE: Isaksen and Treffinger (1985); Isaksen, Dorval, and Treffinger (1994).	A broad search for the steps required to implement a solution or change.	Use divergent thinking to generate the steps required to implement a solution or change. Follow the divergent thinking guidelines to amass all the action steps associated with the successful rollout of a solution or change.
How-How Diagram SOURCE: Higgins (1994); Majaro (1991).	Helps individuals and groups dig deep to identify specific action steps necessary to carry out a solution or change.	Identify a solution or change you wish to implement. Ask the question "How can this be achieved?" Record the responses to this question. These become the first layer of action steps. For each of the initial action steps, again ask "How can this be achieved?" Record the responses. Continue asking "How" until you reach the logical limits.

SOURCE: © 2005 Puccio, Murdock, and Mance. Reprinted with permission

To use Generating Action Steps,

1. **Describe the solution or change.** Write a description of a proposed solution or creative change. As with other tools, the use of a statement starter helps to focus thinking. Try beginning the description of the solution or change with "I/we are committed to pursue . . .". Feel free to replace the verb in this statement with other action verbs suited to your situation (e.g., create, propose, develop, produce, offer).

2. **Diverge on Action Steps.** Ask yourself, "What do I/we need to do to implement . . . ?" Use the divergent guidelines to generate a comprehensive list of action steps. Use other tools like Brainstorming to help explore more potential steps. When it appears you have exhausted all possible action steps, stretch further by asking, "What else do I/we need to do to implement . . . ?" Continue generating until you believe all possible action steps critical to success have been identified in this list.

If you are entering the CPS process at Formulating a Plan, it is a good idea to use one of the Exploring Acceptance tools before you generate action steps, to make sure you have sufficiently considered the context. Assisters and Resisters or Stakeholder Analysis, for example, helps identify factors that will facilitate or hinder success. Be sure that action steps are generated for each of the key forces that will help or hinder acceptance of the solution or change. For instance, some action steps may be required to draw in and enlist the support of some of the identified sources of assistance, while other action steps should be focused on overcoming potential sources of resistance. Make your thinking here formal and specific. Have the results of whatever Exploring Acceptance tool you used visible while generating action steps, and be sure that the list of action steps takes these planning factors into consideration.

How-How Diagram

While the Generating Action Steps tool is a broad and intuitive search for action steps, the **How-How Diagram** introduces more specificity and structure (Higgins, 1994; Majaro, 1991). This procedure encourages you to first identify general action steps and then drill down to very concrete actions and activities.

To use the How-How Diagram,

1. **Identify the solution or proposed change.** Begin by writing the solution or change on the left side of a piece of paper or flipchart. Use the statement starter "I am or we are committed to pursue . . .".

2. **Ask "How?" and record responses.** Consider the proposed solution or change and ask yourself, "How?" "How am I or are we going to accomplish this?" Record your initial responses as action steps to the right of the solution or change.

3. **Ask "How?" again and record responses.** After the initial action steps have been listed ask the "How" question again, but this time pose the question "How can this be achieved?" for each initial action step. List the various responses to the right of the action steps, respectively.

4. **Continue to ask and record.** Continue asking "How?" until you reach the logical conclusion for each thread of thought.

When you use this tool, follow the guidelines for divergent thinking. As a result, you may generate more action steps than you will

Figure 11.2   Sample How-How Diagram

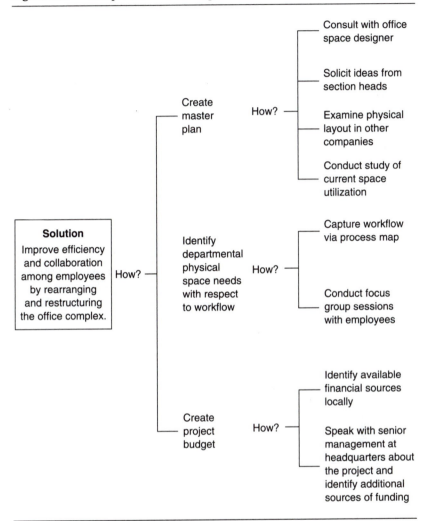

actually use, but it is important to first diverge before selecting the action steps you intend to pursue. By diverging first, you improve the probability of finding key actions that are important to overall success.

Figure 11.2 provides an example of a How-How Diagram. This diagram describes a fictitious business. In this situation, employees in a local office within a large organization have experienced tremendous growth and, as a result, they have not been attentive to their use of physical space. In many cases, departments have outgrown their physical space. As a consequence, some members of the same department are located in different areas, offices that have critical relationships are not located near each other, and there are physical storage issues. In this example, we show how the solution of rearranging and restructuring the office building breaks down into specific action steps through the use of the How-How Diagram. This example stops after two rounds of asking "How?" In real situations, you would typically carry on asking how until you reach some logical conclusion or get to the point where you are generating very narrow and concrete behaviors that are obvious (e.g., pick up the phone to make a call, turn on the computer to send an e-mail message).

❖ CONVERGENT THINKING TOOLS
   FOR FORMULATING A PLAN

Both of the divergent tools in this chapter are designed to help you conduct a comprehensive search for the actions that should be taken to successfully implement a solution or change. Once these long lists of action steps are created, you need to identify which actions are most important. The tool Hits is a useful procedure for identifying the most important action steps. Once a short list of actions has been identified, you can work further with them. Two possibilities are to sequence them along a timeline and to create a method for monitoring progress. To accomplish this, we present two convergent tools. The first, **Sequencing**, helps you arrange action steps along a time continuum. The second, **Performance Dashboard**, provides a playful and visual method for tracking the progress of the solution or change. Table 11.3 provides an overview of these two tools. Again, you may already be familiar with other tools that help organize an individual or group's activities in carrying out a solution or a change; feel free to use them as well.

Sequencing

Earlier we drew a parallel between creating a "to-do" list and the divergent tool Generating Action Steps. When a "to-do" list contains many items, people typically find some way to prioritize the items so that they can focus their efforts in a productive manner. Some might, for instance, decide to tackle their "to-dos" in order of importance. Action steps can also be organized according to time. **Sequencing** is a tool that can help you to be more explicit about which action steps are undertaken

Table 11.3   Formulating a Plan: Convergent Tool Overview

Tool Name	What the Tool Does	What You Do
Sequencing SOURCE: Isaksen, Dorval, and Treffinger (1994).	Organizes action steps along a time-line.	Define the deadline by which you wish to implement a solution or change. Define four blocks of time within this time horizon (immediate, short term, intermediate, and long term). Sort the action steps into these four blocks of time.
Performance Dashboard SOURCE: Senge et al. (1999).	Provides ongoing feedback on progress made toward a goal.	Identify the key outcomes that would demonstrate progress toward the goal. For each outcome, define a graphic performance indicator that provides visual feedback. Monitor progress by checking the performance indicators.

SOURCE: © 2005 Puccio, Murdock, and Mance. Reprinted with permission.

when (Isaksen et al., 1994). When done individually, it enables you to pursue a goal in an efficient manner and to monitor progress. When done by a group, it allows members to coordinate their efforts and to keep each other accountable for making progress toward the goal.

To use Sequencing,

1. **Confirm the solution or change.** If you have not already confirmed the solution or change you wish to implement, complete the statement "I/we are committed to pursue ...". If you are working in a group, make certain that all members agree on the proposed solution or change.

2. **Determine the time horizon.** In light of the solution or change, define the desired time horizon for full implementation. Consider the optimal date by which you would expect to have the solution or change fully implemented. The time horizon will vary greatly based on the nature and complexity of the task. In some situations it may be as short as a week, and in others it may be years.

3. **Break down the timetable.** Identify four distinct blocks of time: immediate, short term, intermediate, and long term. We suggest that the immediate time frame be defined as one to two days. These are actions that must be pursued right away to get the solution or change in motion. The goal here is to prevent the solution or change from dying on the drawing board by at least carrying out some initial action steps. The remaining three blocks of time (i.e., short term, intermediate, and long term) are defined with respect to the implementation deadline set in Step 2. For instance, if the deadline for full implementation is one year out, the short-term time frame might be two days to one month from today, intermediate may be one month to six months, and long-term might be six to twelve months. Again, the time frames will vary in accordance with the time horizon, but establishing them concretely will give you clearer milestones to assess progress.

4. **Organize the action steps.** Once the time frames have been defined, organize the action steps into the four blocks of time. Take each action step in turn and place it into the immediate, short-term, intermediate, or long-term time frames.

5. **Check for overlooked action steps.** Review the action steps once they have been sequenced into the four blocks of time to determine whether any important action steps have been overlooked. Ensure that the action steps present a logical flow and that there are no gaps between the steps.

Once action steps are sequenced, you have a road map that outlines how to proceed toward the desired outcome. To bring greater structure and accountability, the list of action steps can be placed in a broad implementation plan. An implementation plan is a way of elaborating on the action steps by pinpointing when the action will be completed, to whom the successful completion of the step will be reported, and, if working in a group, who is responsible for carrying out the action step. To illustrate what an implementation plan might look like, we use our own experience as a university department that wanted to offer a distance graduate program (see Figure 11.3).

Performance Dashboard

The thinking skill used in Formulating a Plan is Tactical Thinking. You may recall that we defined Tactical Thinking as an ability to devise

Figure 11.3   Example Implementation Plan

Goal: We are committed to offering a graduate program to distance students.

Action	By Whom?	By When?	Report Completion to Whom?
Immediate (two days): a. Seek approval of dean	a. Department chair	a. Within two days	a. Department staff
Short Term (two months): a. Design program format	a. Faculty committee	a. Within one month	a. Department staff
b. Secure financial support to hire program coordinator	b. Department chair	b. Within one month	b. Department staff
c. Hire program coordinator	c. Department chair	c. Within two months	c. Department staff & dean
Intermediate (two to nine months): a. Register program with university administration	a. Department chair	a. Within three months	a. Department staff & dean
b. Create promotional material	b. Program coordinator	b. Within three months	b. Department chair
c. Conduct recruitment campaign	c. Program coordinator	c. Four to nine months	c. Department chair
Long Term (nine months to one year): a. Complete logistical preparation	a. Program coordinator	a. Within nine to ten months	a. Department staff & chair

SOURCE: © 2005 Puccio, Murdock, and Mance. Reprinted with permission.

a plan that includes specific and measurable steps for attaining a desired end and methods for monitoring its effectiveness. The tools presented thus far focus on the first part of this definition. Effective

Tactical Thinking requires more than a list of action steps; you must also be able to monitor progress. The feedback provided through continuous monitoring allows you to recognize when course corrections must be taken or further problem-solving efforts must be applied to ensure success. The purpose of the tool **Performance Dashboard** (Senge, Kleiner, Roberts, Ross, Roth, & Smith, 1999) is to provide visual stimuli that keep track of progress toward the desired end. Many of us have seen the fundraising boards posted on the lawns of various organizations. Typically they are shaped like a thermometer. The height of the red line signifies funds raised to date. This visual cue gives any onlooker immediate feedback as to how the fundraising efforts are progressing. When the red line reaches the top, the goal has been achieved.

Performance Dashboard works in the same way as these fundraising thermometers. Car dashboards contain many instruments that monitor various aspects of a vehicle's performance and provide feedback via warning signals. In Performance Dashboard, you use the car dashboard as a metaphor to create your own feedback instruments. You create visual instruments, like the dashboard of a car, that monitor important outcomes associated with your goal. For example, in regard to the implementation plan presented in Figure 11.3, the group might determine that the key indicators of success are the number of inquires received regarding the graduate program and the number of applications received. A graphic instrument that could be used to keep track of inquiries might look something like a speedometer, and it might be called the "Inquiry-o-Meter." We might determine that 0 to 5 inquiries per week was slow progress, 6 to 10 was moderate, and 11 or more meant we were racing along. With this in mind, we would now create a graphic instrument that has a needle that indicates how many inquiries were received for that week. With regard to the number of applications received, the group might determine the target goal and then create a graphic illustration that looks similar to the temperature gauge in a car. For instance, the needle in this graphic indicator might move from cold to hot as the number of applications increase until it hits the target number. This could be called the "Application Gauge."

To summarize, begin creating a Performance Dashboard by defining the important outcomes that represent progress toward the goal. Select and define graphic instruments that provide visual feedback with respect to the performance indicators. You may want to be playful in how you name the instruments. Check the performance indicators on a regular basis. Use the information depicted by the performance indicators to determine whether progress is on schedule or whether corrective action needs to be taken to overcome impediments.

❖ WHAT'S NEXT IN THE CREATIVE PROBLEM SOLVING PROCESS?

The direct application of the principles and procedures of CPS may come to an end as you pursue the actions outlined in the implementation plan. However, things often do not go as planned. The monitoring of the action steps, perhaps through the Performance Dashboard or by simply tracking the completion of the action steps, might highlight an unexpected problem. In such cases, it may be useful to briefly return to the CPS process to address this problem. Begin by using Assessing the Situation to determine the kind of problem-solving effort required to get things back on track (e.g., Is there a need to come up with ideas for an unexpected challenge? Is there a critical stakeholder who needs to be brought on board? Was a critical action step overlooked?). Once the appropriate problem-solving response is identified, employ a procedure to address the need, and when completed, incorporate the outcome of this thinking into your action plan and keep moving.

❖ APPLYING WHAT YOU'VE LEARNED

Tactical Thinking skills will serve a leader well in making final preparations to implement a solution. The ability to be explicit about the logistics and details will make the actual implementation run smoothly. Using a creative process to think through all of these action steps will also increase the likelihood that unintended consequences, both good and bad, are uncovered prior to implementation. Also, expect as a part of this creative process that you will discover things you could not have anticipated otherwise.

As a leader, it will be important for you to have and to engender respect and understanding in others for this part of the creative process. When there is a rush to implement, you may need to be the one to put on the brakes, rather than fuel the fires by calling for rapid action. Take the time required to use this step thoroughly because when it comes to planning, it's "Pay me now or pay me later."

Some activities to try:

- Identify a complex, multi-task project that you are ready to implement. Using the divergent guidelines, stretch and generate many possible action steps. Using the Hits tool, select those that seem most critical. Use the Sequencing tool to create a timeline of these actions. Notice what insights you have gained from taking a creative approach to planning this implementation.

- Use the Performance Dashboard tool in your next group task. Develop a graphic to represent the visual indicators of progress on this task. Use this as a way to define outcomes for the task and to later monitor progress once the task has been implemented.
- Call together a group to help you create an implementation plan for something that has been hanging over your head, something you have wanted to get around to but can't seem to get off the ground. Use the How-How diagram to generate specific action steps. Use Sequencing to create a timetable for taking action.
- Analyze a current "to-do" list. How deliberate and comprehensive is it? What might you do to strengthen your implementation? Can you sequence the items in this list?

PART III

Additional Factors That Influence Leaders

12

Psychological Diversity

Leading People With
Different Creativity Styles

Chapter at a Glance

The purpose of this chapter is to explore psychological diversity in how people approach creativity and change. Everyone has the capacity to be creative and to introduce change, but how they go about doing this varies. Norman Rockwell and Pablo Picasso were both highly creative artists, but their work reflects different creativity styles. Where Rockwell sought to represent the beauty and humor of everyday life, Picasso challenged our perceptions by developing a new way of representing life. In this chapter, we examine how the ways people engage in creativity differ. We will examine two major approaches for understanding psychological diversity that relate directly to creativity, and we will then draw connections to leadership.

❖ PSYCHOLOGICAL DIVERSITY
AND LEADERSHIP EFFECTIVENESS

Over the last several decades, people in organizations have discussed the importance of diversity. The general argument has been that for organizations to be successful in today's complex economic environment, they must employ a diverse workforce (Loden & Rosener, 1991). Work by Michael West, a professor at the Aston Business School, has drawn a close connection between a diverse workforce and innovation. West (1997) argued that "the more diverse the workforce, the more likely it is that an organization will be innovative, just simply because of the variety of alternative perspectives that are brought to bear" (p. 95). Through a number of research studies, West (2002), West and Wallace (1991), and De Dreu and West (2001) assessed the impact of diversity on innovation in teams. West and his colleagues found, for example, that culturally similar teams were more successful over the short term, while culturally diverse teams tended to be more innovative over the long term. They also discovered that teams with higher levels of skill and professional diversity were more innovative than teams whose members had a restricted set of skills and a narrow range of disciplinary backgrounds. West and his colleagues' research clearly demonstrated that diversity can be directly linked to innovation in teams, thus supporting the assertion that a diverse workforce is beneficial in organizations. As West (1997) concluded, "The conflict of perspectives generated by heterogeneity is the stuff of innovation; it is through managing conflict and diversity associated with heterogeneity that creativity and innovation are generated" (p. 95).

When diversity in organizations is discussed, the focus is typically on what Loden and Rosener (1991) define as **primary dimensions of diversity**. Their six primary dimensions of diversity are: age, ethnicity, gender, physical abilities/qualities, race, and sexual/affectional orientation. They defined primary diversity as "those immutable human differences that are inborn and/or that exert important impact on our early socialization and an ongoing impact throughout our lives" (p. 18). According to Loden and Rosener, these six primary dimensions of diversity exert a constant and profound influence on self-perceptions and on how people view the world. They also identified secondary dimensions of diversity, which can be changed, modified, or discarded (e.g., marital status, work experience, religious beliefs, educational background). Loden and Rosener suggested that primary forms of diversity have the greatest impact on experiences in the workplace. The creativity literature (Basadur, Graen, & Wakayabashi, 1990; Kirton, 1994;

Puccio, 1999; West, 1997) leads us to suggest adding a seventh dimension—psychological diversity—to their set of primary dimensions.

Psychological diversity refers to *differences in how people organize and process information as an expression of their cognitive styles and personality traits.* As with the set of six primary dimensions of diversity, psychological diversity is established early in life, has an ongoing influence on people's self-image, and influences their perceptions of others (Kirton, 1994). Also, like the other forms of primary diversity, individuals' personality traits and cognitive styles are not readily changed. However, in contrast to most of the primary dimensions of diversity such as age, ethnicity, and gender, psychological differences are not always apparent at first glance. For example, in a team there might be two individuals who possess the same six primary forms of diversity, yet who are completely opposite with regard to their personalities and cognitive styles.

Although it may not be immediately visible, psychological diversity can have a profound impact in the workplace. This is perhaps most evident in teams or work units in which individuals have close interactions with one another. Psychological diversity becomes evident over time through individuals' behavior in such things as the way they approach problems, the kinds of ideas they generate, how they handle tasks, and the nature of their interactions with others.

Why might it be important for leaders to understand psychological diversity, particularly as it relates to creativity? First, leaders who understand themselves are in a much better position to leverage their strengths and to find ways to compensate for their deficiencies. Second, to lead means to influence others. It is hard to influence others when you don't understand them. An appreciation for psychological diversity enables leaders to communicate more effectively, coordinate change efforts more successfully, and draw out the creative talents of others. It is critically important for leaders to understand that not everyone thinks and behaves in the same way. Third, leaders must be effective at managing process. Any time a team comes together to solve a problem, either by design or default, the team members are engaged in a process, and often this is a creative process. To improve their ability to manage process, it is valuable for leaders to understand how different members of the team engage in the creative process. Like the conductor of an orchestra who has to combine varying musical talents to make a symphony, or a coach who has to make differences among athletes work together for the betterment of the team, a leader must be sensitive to the psychological diversity on a team and be adept at coordinating these differences to bring about increased harmony and performance.

Although there are many ways in which people differ with respect to personality traits and cognitive styles, we will focus on two approaches to psychological diversity that relate directly to how people express their creativity. Kirton's Adaptor-Innovator theory (1976, 1994) is an early description of different creativity styles. Kirton was the first to argue that people's style of creativity is unrelated to their level of creativity. According to Kirton, people express their creativity either in an **adaptive style**, *a preference for improving existing ideas,* or an **innovative style**, *a preference for challenging current paradigms.* While Kirton's theory broadly examines creativity styles, a second approach to psychological diversity is focused on how people prefer to engage in the creative process. This approach, which is assessed through an instrument called *FourSight* (Puccio, 2002), holds that people vary in the amount of energy they have for different stages of the creative process. For example, while one person working on a team might be drawn naturally to generating ideas, another person may have a clear preference for gathering information to clarify the problem.

❖ KIRTON ADAPTOR-INNOVATOR THEORY: TWO DISTINCT AND VALUABLE APPROACHES TO CREATIVITY AND CHANGE

A theory that has done much to expand our understanding of creativity was put forward by British researcher Michael Kirton (1976, 1994). Kirton's work draws a distinction between two fundamental views of creativity in individuals. Historically, creativity researchers were focused on understanding what characteristics and qualities distinguish highly creative people from less creative ones. This more traditional approach has been called the level approach because it places people on a continuum from low to high creativity. In contrast to the focus on how much creativity people possess, Kirton suggested another way to think about creativity—the style approach. Style of creativity is concerned with the way in which people express their creativity, not the degree or amount of creativity they possess. According to Kirton, an individual's style of creativity can be identified along a continuum that ranges from an adaptive orientation—creating through continuous improvement of existing ideas and systems—to an innovative orientation—creating by introducing radically new ideas that challenge the current way of doing things. Although quite different in the way they express their creativity, adaptors and innovators possess the same potential for reaching high levels of creative productivity.

The distinction between level and style is quite important because it shatters the misconception that there is only one way to be creative. Consider how two artists, Pablo Picasso and Norman Rockwell, achieved high levels of creative productivity in different ways. Rockwell typifies the adaptive style of creativity while Picasso exemplifies the innovative one. Rockwell painted American life in a traditional manner with great attention to detail. Author and art curator Christopher Finch (as cited in Vaux, 2002) said,

> Norman Rockwell created a world that, because of its traditional elements, seems familiar to all of us, yet is recognizably his and his alone. He is an American original who left his mark not by effecting radical change but rather by giving old subjects his own, inimitable inflection. His career has been an ode to the ordinary, a triumph of common sense and understatement. (p. 1)

Picasso's cubist works, on the other hand, created controversy. He distorted reality, modified scale, and broke images apart. Picasso mastered traditional art images but then broke away from them and created work that helped to define a new paradigm called modern art.

Just as both of these fine artists expressed their style preferences, people anywhere in between can achieve great levels of creative productivity. The opposite is true as well. Because creativity style and level of creative success are independent, it is possible to find low-level creative adaptors and low-level creative innovators.

The origins of Kirton's theory grew out of his study of corporate change initiatives in the 1960s (Kirton, 1961). The purpose of the study was to develop an understanding of how significant change takes place in organizations from conception to implementation. Kirton found that some managers tended to put change initiatives forward that worked within the constraints of the existing system. As a result, these ideas tended to be readily accepted. In contrast, others took a more radical approach to change and offered ideas that threatened prevailing thought and practice. As a result, these ideas were often resisted and their initiators treated with suspicion. As already noted, Kirton referred to the former as an adaptive approach and the latter as an innovative one.

Kirton has argued that all people can be located along his style continuum, ranging from a clear preference for the adaptive orientation to a clear preference for the innovative orientation. Indeed, Kirton (1976) developed a self-report paper-and-pencil measure that places respondents along his adaptor-innovator continuum. This measure, called the

Kirton Adaptor-Innovator Inventory (KAI), has been adopted into research and practice around the world (e.g., Foxall & Bhate, 1993; Goldsmith, 1986, 1994; Isaksen & Puccio, 1988; Kubes & Spillerová, 1992; Prato Previde & Carli, 1987). Table 12.1 contains a list of characteristics that are associated with the adaptive and innovative styles of creativity (Goldsmith, 1994; Kirton, 1976, 1994, 1999). The stronger a person's preference toward either the adaptive or innovative style, the more likely he or she will be to display these characteristics. As you read through the two lists, you might wish to think about your own preferences. Do you feel more inclined toward the adaptive or innovative style of creativity, or perhaps you are a balance of the two?

Table 12.1   Characteristics of Adaptors and Innovators

Characteristics of Adaptors	Characteristics of Innovators
• Precise	• Undisciplined
• Reliable	• Impractical
• Thorough	• Think tangentially
• Methodical	• Methodical
• Prudent	• Risk takers
• Conforming	• Catalysts to settled groups
• Dependable	• Unsound
• Rarely challenge rules	• Challenge rules and past practices
• Provide stability and continuity	• Provide a break with the past
• Prefer short-term efficiency; concerned with the details associated with implementation	• Seek long-range effectiveness; willing to trade off short-term efficiency
• Sensitive to people, good team players	• Independent minded; often threaten group cohesion
• Prefer to develop a few original ideas at a time and evaluate these ideas for potential effectiveness	• Prefer to proliferate original ideas and are less attentive to the practicality of such ideas
• Create by finding ways to improve existing ideas and systems	• Create by producing more radical change that challenges current ideas and systems

SOURCE: Goldsmith (1994); Kirton (1976, 1994).

Adaptors and Innovators in Organizations: Bias and Coping

Although there are clear personality distinctions between adaptors and innovators, Kirton has argued that there is no difference in their respective creative potential. However, our experiences in delivering creativity workshops and courses, as well as our research on lay people's perceptions of creativity, indicate that U.S. culture has a bias towards the innovative style of creativity. We believe that when most people in the U.S. think of creativity or a creative person, they are more likely to think of Kirton's innovator.

Puccio and Chimento's (2001) research with a U.S. sample of lay people showed that their implicit views of creativity favored the innovator. The same bias was also found in Argentina (González, 2003) and Singapore (Ramos, 2005). If the prevailing culture assumes that innovators epitomize what it means to be creative, then the creative talents of half the population may be devalued. What does this mean? People who have adaptive tendencies may be mislabeled as being less creative, thus eroding their self-esteem with respect to creativity. This labeling may also result in undervaluing the creative contributions of adaptors. The reality is that societies and organizations need both adaptive and innovative creativity. As Kirton (1994) suggested,

> The innovative approach is obviously needed in any organization that is to survive. Yet any organization that is large and has been successful over a long period of time must inevitably be adaptively oriented to guard against unacceptable risk—inherent in making drastic changes over a broad front over a short space of time. (p. 9)

Organizations need a balance between ideas that focus on finding better ways to do what they currently do (i.e., continuous change) and ideas that challenge prevailing thought (i.e., discontinuous change). This bias toward the innovator style raises a concern about how people are treated within organizations. The push for innovation in the workplace may create organizational environments that favor innovators and at the same time become uncomfortable for adaptors. This may place undue pressure on adaptors to begin to act like innovators, and it may also upset the natural balance that occurs when both adaptive and innovative orientations are supported. To be effective in decision making and change initiatives, leaders need to honor and support both the adaptive and innovative styles of creativity.

Although a focus on innovation may create a work environment that does not support adaptive creativity, the reality in organizational climates is that they are more highly concerned with adaptive creativity, if they are interested in creativity at all. Many organizations pay only lip service to innovation, mentioning it in the mission statement or talking about it during employee "pep rallies," but in reality what is expected on a day-to-day basis is adaptive creativity. In such organizations, employees are required to focus on efficiency, consistency, conformity, and ideas that support the status quo. Furthermore, the daily operations may necessitate low-level adaptive creativity where there is no need for employees to think creatively at all. They simply need to carry out tasks as prescribed. Using a modified version of the KAI, the work of Puccio and his colleagues (Puccio, Joniak, & Talbot, 1995; Puccio, Talbot, & Joniak, 2000; Puccio, Treffinger, & Talbot, 1995) supports this. They found that on average, employees in three different organizations said their work environments required them to be more adaptive than they ideally wanted to be at work. In a follow-up interview, one employee in Puccio's (1990a) study noted,

> I had only been with the company for six months when I completed the survey. I came from a very small company where I had to do the engineering, sales, and a lot of project work all in one job. The only system that mattered was my system. Then I came to a large company with a well-established system. Yes, maybe I was rebelling a bit against it. I hated it. In my present job I am learning things about this business that I didn't get at the other company. I am also getting more money. But the actual concessions I had to make to conform to the system have been quite vast in comparison to my preferences and experiences.

According to Kirton (1994), when work environments force people to adopt a creativity style that is not natural for them, they engage in coping behavior. Kirton (1994) defined **coping behavior** as "a departure from preferred style by the minimum amount for the least time needed" (p. 6). Given the great variety of situations and tasks you face professionally and personally, it is natural on occasion to engage in coping behavior for short periods of time; however, problems may arise when you are compelled by your circumstance to operate for longer periods of time in a style that is not preferred. Kirton suggested that coping behavior costs energy and that over prolonged periods of time this may lead to stress. So what are other consequences of coping behavior? Puccio (1990b) found that a large gap between the creativity style employees believed was required by their jobs and the style they preferred resulted in lower levels of job satisfaction and higher levels of stress. Additionally, Puccio et al. (2000) found that when a misfit existed between the person and the environment, the extent to which employees reported producing creative work went down. This was particularly true for innovators. The creative efforts of innovators who believed they were required to be adaptive at work suffered much more than those of adaptors who believed they were required to be innovative.

Leaders have much to do with establishing the nature of the psychological climate at work; therefore, it is incumbent on them to be sensitive to constructing work environments that facilitate the creative talents of both adaptors and innovators. Chapter 13 will explore the kind of work environments that encourage creative thinking.

Adaptor-Innovator Styles in Teams

Adaptor-innovator style preferences have clear implications in teams and groups. Kirton (1999) has reported that particular groups tend to have mean adaptor-innovator preferences that reflect the responsibilities of their job or function within the organization. For instance, data collected on engineers, bank managers, civil servants, and accountants show that all have more adaptive group preferences, while R&D managers, marketing teams, and planning teams have more innovative mean scores. Kirton (1994) suggested that "teams, to carry out their tasks successfully, need to have skewed A-I means, often on a permanent basis" (p. 69).

Hammerschmidt (1996) provided empirical evidence to support Kirton's contention that teams with particular adaptor-innovator mean scores may be better suited for certain kinds of tasks. Hammerschmidt studied the success rates of managers engaged in a team problem-solving activity (i.e., the Hollow Square: A Communication Experiment). Over a period of four years, Hammerschmidt worked with 119 different 8-member teams. The teams were evenly divided into two subgroups, each having a specific role to play in the problem-solving activity (i.e., some members participated in a subgroup of "planners" who were responsible for devising instructions for an activity to be carried out by the second subgroup, called the "implementers"). To successfully solve the problem, the subgroups had to find a way to work cooperatively. Hammerschmidt used the managers' KAI scores to construct the subgroups. In some cases, he assigned managers to role-consistent subgroups and in other situations to role-inconsistent subgroups. That is, Hammerschmidt believed the responsibilities associated with the planning subgroup were better suited for the more adaptive managers and that the implementer subgroup was best suited for those with an innovative orientation. (It should be noted that in order to successfully solve the problem, the implementer subgroup must challenge some of the assumptions associated with the task.) Hammerschmidt also manipulated the difference in mean scores between the two subgroups. In some cases, he arranged the subgroups so that the difference between the overall adaptor-innovator preferences of the two subgroups (i.e., planners and implementers) was small and in other cases it was large. Why? According to Kirton (1994), communication will become more strained between individuals and groups as the difference between their preferences increases.

The two-by-two matrix found in Figure 12.1 shows the four kinds of teams created by Hammerschmidt and the respective success rate of these teams. As a point of comparison, Hammerschmidt also examined the success rate of teams that were randomly put together. What is most striking is the fact that teams with two strikes against them, subgroups who were far apart on the A-I continuum and who were in style-inconsistent roles (i.e., adaptors as implementers and innovators as planners), were successful in solving the problem less than half the time. The greatest level of success came for those teams whose members were assigned to role-consistent subgroups (82.35% and 87.50% successful, respectively). Hammerschmidt (1996) noted that "subteam collaboration difficulties virtually disappeared and were never part of recorded observations with the introduction of homogenous (same score) subteams" (p. 66). It is interesting to note that the teams with relatively small differences between subgroup means, yet who worked in style-inconsistent roles, were also quite successful. Hammerschmidt attributed their success to the small cognitive gap between the subgroups. He commented that "as subgroup members are more like each other they tend to perceive, solve, and communicate the problem in a similar fashion resulting in better intra-team communication and a higher success rate" (p. 66).

So what implications do the results of Hammerschmidt's study, and knowledge about adaptor-innovator scores relative to teams, have for leaders? For one, leaders need to understand that the success or failure of a team may, in part, be due to the adaptor-innovator composition of those individuals within that team. Understanding the makeup of a team's cognitive style will help a leader recognize those tasks that will more readily fit the predispositions of the members of that team.

Figure 12.1   Adaptors and Innovators: Problem Solving in Teams

	Roles Style Consistent	Style Inconsistent	
Small	82.35%	77.27%	Teams put together randomly = 52%
Large	87.50%	42.85%	

Cognitive Gap Between Teams

SOURCE: Hammerschmidt (1996).

This is not to say that a leader cannot make an assignment that is outside of the cognitive style preferences of a team or individual. Rather, leaders need to understand that for some tasks, teams will engage in the task with little hesitation, as it is well suited to the members' adaptor-innovator preferences. In such cases, there is likely to be a flow to the work process, resulting in little need for intervention on the part of the leader. However, in other cases, where the responsibilities of the task do not match the natural inclinations of the team, there is likely to be a mental wrestling match between the team and the task. They may literally struggle to get their minds around the task. In such cases, the leader may need to facilitate the team or bring other strategies and resources to bear in support of the team.

Finally, leaders should be aware that cognitive style differences can impact effective communication in teams. Teams that have a wide range of creativity style preferences among their members may experience communication challenges. When this occurs, leaders need to recognize that the cognitive style differences, not misguided motives, may be the cause of the communication problems. Additionally, leaders need to be aware of their own adaptor-innovator preference and to understand how their approach to creativity, change, and decision making influences their interactions with members of the team. An innovative leader on a relatively adaptive team will face quite different dynamics than an innovative leader on a team of relatively innovative members. Know that your cognitive style has a profound effect on your actions and will also influence how others perceive you.

❖ FOURSIGHT: UNDERSTANDING HOW PEOPLE ENGAGE IN THE CREATIVE PROCESS

In addition to Kirton's broad distinction about the existence and impact of style and level of creativity overall, people also have diverse ways of interacting with the creative process. Have you ever been in a problem-solving group where some people had more energy for particular parts of the process? One minute they were eagerly engaged in generating ideas, but when it came time for implementing these ideas, they lost interest and enthusiasm. CPS gives us an explicit description of a fluid creative process in which we all engage to a greater or lesser degree. It is natural to expect that some people will find aspects of it easier to perform, while struggling with other parts of the process.

In this section, we will focus on a developing theory that describes people's preferences for interacting with the creative process, and then we will look at an instrument used to assess these preferences. This theory of creative process preferences is based on the following foundational points: (a) the creative process is a natural process that all people engage in, and CPS is one way of describing this creative process; (b) the steps of the creative process require mental activities, and the nature of these activities varies from step to step; and (c) people possess different preferences for thinking and processing information. Therefore, because the creative process involves different mental activities, and people possess different preferences for mental activities, it might be expected that people will express differences in how they prefer to engage in the creative process. This approach is operationalized through a self-report instrument called *FourSight* (Puccio, 2002), which identifies people's preferences for four fundamental mental activities within the creative process (i.e., clarifying the problem, generating ideas, developing solutions, and implementing solutions).

If you accept the assertion that leaders need to be able to manage the creative process, then it is important that leaders understand how they engage in this process. Once leaders recognize these tendencies in themselves and others, they are in a much better position to bring their effectiveness to the next level. Where these process tendencies are often apparent is in meetings. One person may be stuck in analyzing information, another wants to generate ideas, a third is focused on developing a solution, and still another is ready to "just do it."

FourSight gives you a window to view these interactions as preferences rather than distractions, and thus maximize the benefits of diversity.

The Four Preferences: Using FourSight to Improve Personal Performance

FourSight, the initial research version of which was known as the *Buffalo Creative Process Inventory*, enables individuals to identify the degree of energy they have for four different process preferences. These preferences are called **Clarifier, Ideator, Developer,** and **Implementer.** Both research (Puccio, 1999, 2002; Rife, 2001) and experiences gained through the use of *FourSight* with numerous groups have led to insights into the qualities and characteristics associated with each of the four preferences. Table 12.2 provides a summary of the key qualities associated with each of the preferences measured by *FourSight*. As you examine this table, think about yourself in light of these descriptors. Which ones sound like you? Which ones sound completely foreign to how you think and behave? Some people have a strong inclination for just one of the four preferences. Others have combinations of peak preferences (e.g., a person might enjoy and have great energy for both the Clarifier and Implementer preferences). As you read these columns, place a check next to those items that describe you. Be honest with yourself. This quick self-assessment may help you gain insight into your approach to the creative process.

FourSight is a value-neutral assessment of creative process preferences. Having a strong preference in one area over another is not inherently good or bad; each preference has its characteristic assets and potential liabilities. The value is in understanding your preferences. This information can show you areas of strength and unearth blind spots in your interactions with people and process. It can help you understand why you have been successful in some situations and why you are frustrated by others. The goal is to use this information to arrive at a deeper understanding of how you personally approach the creative process and then to use this information to enhance your effectiveness.

Individuals with a strong preference for Clarifier are drawn to, and have a great deal of energy for, uncovering facts that determine the most productive way of defining the task or problem. Clarifiers are good at examining the details and analyzing situations. They are cautious about leaping to conclusions or solutions. Because any preference taken to an extreme can become a liability, high Clarifiers run the risk of suffering from "analysis paralysis" by overanalyzing situations to such a degree that they are slow to resolve a challenge or to capitalize on an opportunity.

Table 12.2   An Overview of the *FourSight* Preferences

Clarifier	Ideator	Developer	Implementer
Clarifiers are	*Ideators are*	*Developers are*	*Implementers are*
Focused	Playful	Planful	Persistent
Orderly	Social	Pragmatic	Determined
Serious	Flexible	Concrete	Action oriented
Methodical	Independent	Cautious	Decisive
Deliberate	Imaginative	Structured	Assertive
Organized	Adventurous	Disciplined	Risk takers
Clarifiers need	*Ideators need*	*Developers need*	*Implementers need*
Order	Room to be	Time to	The sense that
The facts	playful	consider the	others are
and history	Constant	options	moving just as
Access to	stimulation	Time to	quickly
information	Variety and	evaluate and	Timely responses
To ask	change	develop ideas	to their ideas
questions	The big picture		
Clarifiers annoy others by	*Ideators annoy others by*	*Developers annoy others by*	*Implementers annoy others by*
Asking too many questions	Drawing attention to themselves	Being too nit-picky	Being too pushy
Pointing out obstacles	Being impatient when others don't get their ideas	Finding flaws in others' ideas	Readily expressing their frustration when others do not move as quickly
Identifying areas that have not been well thought out	Offering ideas that are too off-the-wall	Getting locked into one approach	Overselling their ideas
Overloading people with information	Being too abstract	Being too critical	Showing their impatience in regard to group process
Being too realistic	Not sticking to one idea		

SOURCE: Puccio (2002). Reprinted with permission.

     High Ideators excel at generating ideas. They are fluent and flexi-
ble thinkers who find it easy to generate out-of-the-box ideas. If you
need ideas, go see an Ideator; they have plenty. They are intuitive,

global, and conceptual in their thought process. Because they tend to think in more abstract terms, they sometimes struggle when working with details. They may overlook the details, leave them to someone else, or find that working out the details drains their energy.

Developers enjoy refining ideas. They are energized by the kind of thinking required to analyze and critique ideas. Developers may not generate a lot of ideas, but they are good at selecting ideas that can become highly workable and practical. Individuals who are Developers tinker with ideas. They enjoy crafting and polishing ideas. The potential downside to this preference is that Developers may sometimes become preoccupied with perfection and not be willing to push an idea forward because they feel it can still be improved.

High Implementers have little patience for deliberate creative process methodologies such as CPS. They like to see things happen. They are action oriented and therefore may be quick to express impatience with deliberate process. Implementers move quickly from concept to reality. Their ideas have little chance of growing any moss. They take great pride in seeing their ideas come to fruition. Although Implementers are adept at getting things done, the potential risk they run is rushing too quickly to action and thus implementing ideas that are not fully developed.

There are also people who do not express a peak preference for any of the four areas (i.e., all of their preference scores are rather similar). These individuals are called **Integrators** because they are adaptable. Integrators can go with the flow of the process, moving easily from step to step. They can also look at situations from many different perspectives. Integrators tend to be good team players who can communicate readily with others who have different process preferences and have a concern for maintaining harmony in teams. The potential challenge for Integrators is to make sure that they diagnose situations for themselves and do not simply follow the lead of others who express strong opinions.

Think about how you naturally approach the creative process and consider ways in which this approach has served you well, but also consider how your preferences have inhibited success. As one student wrote in regard to her *FourSight* preferences, "I must not shy away from that which I do not enjoy, but rather recognize it, embrace it, and improve it." This is using foresight.

FourSight is one approach to identify process preferences relative to CPS. Basadur and his colleagues (1990) have designed another measure of process preferences called the *Creative Problem Solving Profile*. For information on their approach see Box 12.1.

Box 12.1   Research Note

Basadur's Creative Problem-Solving Profile

In 1990 Basadur, Graen, and Wakayabashi published a detailed description of a paper-and-pencil inventory designed to help people identify their preferences within Basadur's version of CPS, called Simplex®. They named this measure the *Creative Problem-Solving Profile* (CPSP). According to Basadur et al. (1990), people can be located along two perpendicular information-processing dimensions: how people gain knowledge and how people use knowledge. Knowledge can be gained in either direct or abstract ways. People then use this knowledge for ideation (i.e., divergent thinking) or for evaluation (i.e., convergent thinking). As Basadur and his colleagues noted,

> Each individual could thus be characterized as having a unique set of relative preferences on these two information-processing dimensions. . . . Considering these two dimensions makes it possible to create four quadrants of different combinations of gaining and using knowledge. (p. 113)

These four quadrants are used to identify four different process preferences. High preference for gaining knowledge through direct experience and using knowledge for ideation is called the Generator style. The combination of the acquisition of knowledge through abstract thought and a preference to use information for ideation is called the Conceptualizer style. The third process preference is called Optimizer, which combines a preference for knowledge brought about by abstract thinking and a preference to use knowledge for convergence. Finally, the Implementor style brings together a preference for knowledge acquisition through concrete experiences and the use of this knowledge for convergent thinking.

The CPSP uses 12 sets of 4 words to identify individuals' preferences. Each word in the set relates to one of the four poles on the two underlying dimensions. A respondent examines the set of words and ranks them in terms of how descriptive they are of his or her "problem-solving style." The CPSP has been used in a number of research studies (Basadur & Head, 2001; Basadur, Wakabayashi, & Graen, 1990; Houtz, Selby, Esquivel, Okoye, Peters, & Treffinger, 2003). A study of particular note with respect to the notion of psychological diversity is Basadur and Head's (2001) examination of the problem-solving performance in teams composed of members with homogenous CPS styles (i.e., all of one CPSP style), moderate homogeneity (i.e., members represented two of the four CPSP styles), and heterogeneous blends (i.e., members represent all four CPSP styles). These researchers found that MBA students working on a business problem in teams with the greatest mix of CPS process styles significantly outperformed the homogenous groups on three of five measures of innovative performance. For a look at the CPSP, go to Basadur et al. (1990), and for further information on Basadur's Creative Problem Solving model, Simplex®, go to Basadur (1994).

Using CPS Principles and Procedures to Complement Your Creative Process

Now that you have a deeper understanding of how you engage in natural creative process, this may give you a better idea of what areas could be strengthened. What do you do if something does not come naturally to you? The CPS process described in previous chapters provides deliberate principles and tools that can support you in improving your creativity skills. Therefore, if you have a low tendency for a particular *FourSight* preference, you can learn various CPS principles and tools to assist you with the steps of the process for which you have less energy. If, for example, you are a low Ideator, it may be valuable for you to learn and apply the divergent thinking guidelines and such tools as Brainstorming and Forced Connections. Although you may not possess a natural tendency to be an Ideator, it is possible, when necessary, to learn to think and act like an Ideator. Table 12.3 provides some examples of CPS principles and tools that individuals with low preferences might find useful to learn and apply. Knowing your preferences allows you to dip into CPS and extract those principles and tools that complement your natural tendencies.

The combination of understanding the steps to the creative process, such as those associated with CPS, and understanding how you personally engage in the creative process will enhance your self-management skills. For instance, if you know your high Implementer preference often causes you to move quickly to action, and as a consequence perhaps to solve the wrong problem, you might then consider how the steps associated with the Clarifying stage of CPS might help you to be more effective. In other words, if you know you get overly focused on certain steps of the process, you can, with intent, decide to more evenly distribute your energy and effort. Also, by knowing your biases, you may be able to avoid the tendency to push the task you are

Table 12.3   Using CPS to Support Low *FourSight* Preferences

Low Clarifiers Might Benefit From	Low Ideators Might Benefit From	Low Developers Might Benefit From	Low Implementers Might Benefit From
Principles: • Stay Focused • Check Your Objectives	Principles: • Defer Judgment • Go for Quantity • Seek Novelty	Principles: • Apply Affirmative Judgment • Allow for Incubation	Principles: • Stay Focused • Keep Novelty Alive
Tools: • Success Zones • Five Ws and an H • Web of Abstraction	Tools: • Brainstorming • Forced Connections	Tools: • Evaluation Matrix • PPC^O • Generating Criteria	Tools: • Generating Action Steps • Implementation Plan

SOURCE: Puccio, Murdock, and Mance (2005). Reprinted with permission.

working on into your own comfort zone (e.g., when high Clarifiers diagnose tasks they may have a tendency to see a need for more clarification, or high Ideators see the need always to move into idea generation). This might be achieved by using concepts taught in the Assessing the Situation chapter to more skillfully diagnose situations. Research has shown that people with different *FourSight* preferences respond differently to CPS training (see Puccio, Wheeler, & Cassandro, 2004). For example, while people with certain preferences associated great value with particular tools, others found different tools and aspects of the process to be useful. The advantage of the CPS process is that it offers a wide range of principles and procedures that complement people's natural creative inclinations, thus strengthening their ability to manage the full creative process.

Using FourSight to Improve Team Performance

As with the adaptor-innovator theory, *FourSight* also has implications for teamwork. All teams, whether they are aware of it or not, engage in the creative process. To varying degrees, all teams analyze situations, identify opportunities, address predicaments, produce ideas, hone solutions, and implement their best thoughts. Now cross the fact that all teams engage in the creative process with the fact that each member of a team has his or her own biases with respect to this process. This synergy of differences can lead to creative potential or can cause conflict, which can undermine this potential. To be more specific, imagine you are an Ideator who works on a team dominated by Implementers. Or imagine you are a leader who has a clear preference for the Implementer orientation, and your team is made up of individuals whose dominant preferences fall into the Clarifier and Developer areas. Can you see the potential for conflict in these situations? In the former, the lone Ideator might feel quite frustrated by the team's tendency to aggressively push ideas into production. In the latter scenario, the leader with a strong Implementer preference might experience a constant tug-of-war with a team of individuals with preferences for the Clarifier and Developer orientation. While the leader pushes for action, the team might still be evaluating the situation and working to perfect the best solutions.

At the beginning of this chapter, we talked about psychological diversity. Sometimes psychological differences lead people to form negative judgments of others. In other words, people sometimes ascribe negative characteristics to those who do not think and behave like they do. Pejoratively speaking, others may see Clarifiers as overly cautious, stuck in a rut, or dogmatic. Ideators might be called fuzzy-minded, cavalier, dreamers, or show-offs. Developers may be seen as overly critical, nit-picky, wet blankets who always dwell on the negatives. Implementers can be perceived as going off half-cocked. They take the ready-fire-aim approach to problem solving and may be perceived as pushy or abrasive.

These negative perceptions can cause friction in teams. This friction can come in at least two forms. The first form comes from personality clashes. As described above, people often make judgments and draw negative conclusions about others because their personalities are different from their own. As a result of such pejorative views, team members may begin to tune others out; communication breaks down. The team may splinter with the most like-minded members forming subgroups, or people may simply avoid one another.

Leaders, in particular, must be wary of their own tendency to judge team members who possess different process preferences. In fact, it would be wise for leaders to embrace those who provide a different perspective because they stand the greatest chance of challenging rigid perceptions and groupthink. Furthermore, in order to draw the best from individual members and the team as a whole, leaders must build climates where psychological differences, such as creative process preferences, are honored.

A second form of friction is a process clash in which people with different process preferences may pull in different directions when working on a task. For example, while Ingrid the Implementer is pounding the table saying "Enough discussion; let's make a decision!," Danny the Developer is still running final calculations through his mind. In the same meeting you might also have Isabel the Ideator who is generating yet more ideas and who, in turn, is frustrating Cole the Clarifier who is still asking questions to figure out whether the correct problem is being solved. When a team like this comes together to work through the creative process, particularly when they are not following an explicit process like CPS, it is easy for individual process preferences to drive how the process unfolds. A good example of this kind of process clash occurred during a team-building workshop with a small training and development organization. As part of the workshop, the team received feedback on their *FourSight* preferences. When the team profile was posted for all to see and discuss, the manager of the unit had an immediate revelation. He turned to one of his colleagues and said, "I now know why you drive me crazy. While I'm still trying to assess whether we have a market for a newly proposed service, you are already launching a marketing campaign." The manager was the only Clarifier on the team, and the person to whom he addressed his comments had the strongest Implementer score. When these diametrically opposed process approaches were discovered and productively discussed, it was possible to dissipate some of the tension in the team.

Often, on the way to a goal teams can get derailed by their process. We suggest this might be a result of personality or process clashes among team members who possess different *FourSight* preferences. A leader who is aware of CPS can employ this process to circumvent both personality and process clashes; CPS can become a great leveler. One of the key advantages that CPS provides with respect to teamwork is that it creates an explicit framework within which to operate. By using CPS, the team members focus their problem-solving energy in one direction and together progress through the process. By sharing the same process framework, the team is likely to arrive at a better solution and experience less frustration along the way.

A Comment on Psychological Inventories

In this chapter, we have focused on two approaches for understanding and measuring psychological diversity with respect to creativity. These two theoretical approaches, Kirton's adaptor-innovator continuum and *FourSight*, rely on psychological inventories to identify people's preferences. There are standards applied to psychological measures that help differentiate research-based measures from simple personality surveys like the kind found in magazines. These psychological tools are subjected to research to test their soundness. Box 12.2 provides some technical information regarding the KAI and *FourSight.*

Box 12.2 Research Note

Technical Aspects of the Kirton
Adaption-Innovation Inventory and FourSight

Since its introduction in 1976, the KAI has been used in hundreds of research studies. A number of these studies focused on the reliability of the KAI. For example, in the KAI manual, Kirton (1999) reported reliability coefficients for the KAI's total scale and the three subscales that all exceeded the standard convention of .70. The KAI has also shown good stability over time, with test-retest coefficients ranging from .82 to .86 for time periods that ranged from 5 to 43 months. It has also been demonstrated that creativity training has no effect on people's KAI scores (Murdock, Isaksen, & Lauer, 1993).

Numerous studies have examined the validity of the KAI. Many of these studies have focused on Kirton's contention that creativity style is unrelated to ability. For instance, the KAI has been correlated with a variety of intelligence measures, and in all cases the coefficients were near zero—no relationship (Kirton, 1999). Adaptor-innovator preferences have also been compared to measures of leadership effectiveness and management competencies. No relationship was found for leadership effectiveness (Kirton, 1999), and only 1 of the 11 management competency scales showed a significant relationship to the KAI (Schroder, 1994). These findings underscore the fact that neither adaptors nor innovators hold the advantage over the other with regard to leadership effectiveness.

A number of investigations have directly examined the degree to which Kirton's creativity style continuum is related to creativity measures (Kirton, 1999). Recall that Kirton suggested that creativity style is independent from level of creative ability. These studies have yielded mixed results (i.e., significant relationships with some creativity measures while not significant with others). Kirton's (1999) analysis and interpretation of these findings suggest that some creativity inventories are pure measures of style, others are more measures of ability, while still others mix level and style. Thus the KAI's relationship to these measures varies based on the nature of the creativity measure to which it is being compared. For further information on research related to the Adaptor-Innovator theory and measure, see Kirton (1999) or Kirton (1994).

(Continued)

(Continued)

FourSight is a younger creativity style instrument. Its development began in the early 1990s. Over this period of time more than eight different versions of this paper-and-pencil self-report measure were tested (Puccio, 2002). The items found in *FourSight* were designed to articulate the different mental operations associated with the various steps of the CPS process. The phrasing of the questions and the response scale were designed to elicit a respondent's strength of preference for these various creative process operations. Factor analysis and statistical evaluation of internal reliability of items in *FourSight* were used to modify, improve, or drop statements. The technical manual for *FourSight* reports Cronbach alpha coefficients, indicators of internal reliability, as follows: Clarifier = .78, Ideator = .81, Developer = .79, and Implementer = .81 (Puccio, 2002). In a recent study of the relationship between *FourSight* preferences and the type of knowledge used by workers, Chan (2004) reported the following alpha coefficients: Clarifier = .79, Ideator = .75, Developer = .83, and Implementer = .86.

Recent research has begun to focus on testing the validity of *FourSight* (Puccio, 2002). One method of establishing validity is to compare a newly developed measure to well-established ones. For instance, *FourSight* has been correlated to Kirton's measure of creativity style and the popular measure of psychological type called the *Myers-Briggs Type Indicator* (MBTI; Myers, McCaulley, Quenk, & Hammer, 2003). A number of theoretically expected correlations emerged from these comparisons. In the handful of studies that compared *FourSight* with Kirton's measure, one clear and consistent outcome emerged. The Ideator scale was significantly correlated (correlation coefficients ranged from .43 to .76) with Kirton's subscale called "Sufficiency of Originality." This indicates that as the Ideator score goes up so does an individual's tendency to produce many original ideas. A number of these studies also showed that the Clarifier and Developer preferences were significantly correlated with Kirton's Efficiency subscale. This would indicate that Clarifiers and Developers tend to be more concerned about the details and being precise—which would seem to readily match these particular process preferences.

One study ($n = 53$) was carried out to assess the relationship between *FourSight* and the MBTI. Here the Ideator preference was positively correlated with intuition on the MBTI ($r = .68$), while high scores for Clarifier ($r = -.52$) and Developer ($r = -.54$) corresponded with clearer preferences for the judging scale (i.e., a tendency to desire closure and order). These and other studies (i.e., Puccio et al., 2004; Rife, 2001) begin to provide initial evidence for the validity of *FourSight*. For further information on the technical aspects of *FourSight*, see the manual (Puccio, 2002).

❖ APPLYING WHAT YOU'VE LEARNED

Psychological diversity is all around, in families, at work, among friends, and so forth. Although it may not be immediately visible, its effects influence the interactions between a leader and his or her team or among members of a team. The following activities will help you to become more aware of your own approach to the creative process and the preferences of others and can create a better understanding of the implications associated with this form of psychological diversity.

- Think back to a challenging task or problem you faced recently. Identify your creativity style; consider yourself with respect to the adaptor-innovator continuum, the four *FourSight* preferences, or other information you might have that says something about your approach to creativity. Describe how your creativity style influenced, either positively or negatively, what you did in regard to this task or problem—both the process you engaged in and the outcome of your efforts. In light of your creativity style, what might you do differently the next time you are faced with a complex challenge?
- Identify a person with whom you have an important work relationship. Using information from this chapter, compare and contrast your approach to creativity against his or her approach. Describe the implications of the similarities and/or differences between the two of you. How are the respective preferences beneficial to the relationship? How might the interaction between you and your colleague's preferences inhibit high performance? How might an awareness of you and your colleague's creativity preferences assist you in improving the relationship?
- Think back to a recent team project in which you were involved. Consider the behavior of the members on this team and see whether you can identify people with different adaptor-innovator preference or *FourSight* preferences. What specific behaviors led you to conclude that certain people on this team possessed particular creativity preferences? If different preferences existed on this team, what were the implications of such differences?

13

Building a Climate for Creativity

How Leadership Sets the Tone

Chapter at a Glance

Have you ever had a job in which the work day seemed to just fly by? Time went by quickly because you were engaged, productive, happy, and creative. How about the opposite experience—have you ever had a job where the work day seemed to drag on and on? In this case you may have felt inhibited, unproductive, frustrated, and uncreative. Such feelings about work are often a response to the work environment itself.

The combined influence of climate and leadership in the work environment is a one-two punch that can either support or hinder your creativity. Therefore, in this chapter we will present basic information about psychological climate, identify some research-supported aspects of creative climate, and discuss the leadership implications of it.

❖ INTRODUCTION: SOME BASICS ABOUT CLIMATE

If you take a highly creative person and put her into a work environment or classroom setting that rigidly blocks change or inhibits new ideas, what do you suppose happens to her creativity? Although she may have a capacity to imagine new possibilities, the immediate situation may undermine such efforts; consequently, creativity is unlikely to flourish. Early creativity research focused on individual attributes that predisposed people to achieve high levels of creativity. More recent research has considered the effects of a person's environment on his or her ability to be creative (Amabile & Gryskiewicz, 1989; Ekvall, 1991; Isaksen & Lauer, 2002; Lapierre & Giroux, 2003; Rickards & Bessant, 1980; Siegel & Kaemmerer, 1978; Turnipseed, 1994).

Research on organizational climate, a specific line of investigation within the broader area of environment, has shown clear implications for creative thinking and innovation in the workplace (Lauer, 1994). Swedish researcher and organizational psychologist Göran Ekvall has devoted the last 30 years to identifying and understanding the dynamics of climate (Ekvall, 1983, 1991, 1996, 1999; Ekvall & Arvonen, 1984; Ekvall, Arvonen, & Waldenstrom-Lindblad, 1983). Ekvall (1991) defined **organizational climate** as the *"recurrent patterns of behavior, attitudes, and feelings that characterize life in an organization"* (p. 403).

When the term "climate" is used in this manner, it is a metaphor to describe how the psychological atmosphere in an organization affects members' experiences (Ekvall, 1987). Much like physical climate—such as the weather in a region—has an impact on people's attitudes, so does psychological climate. By **psychological climate** we mean *a person's perceptions of the behaviors, attitudes, and feelings that typify everyday life in a particular setting.* How do you feel when you wake up on a warm, bright, sunny morning versus an overcast, cold, damp one? Your perception of climate in organizations can be like either one of these metaphors—some workplaces are perceived as psychologically sunny and bright; others may be perceived as cold and uninviting. As Ekvall (1999) observed, "Social and behavioral scientists studying organizations have adopted the climate metaphor as a theoretical construct for understanding, explaining, and describing organizational processes and their effects" (p. 404).

What are the effects of organizational climate? Research has shown one key area that is influenced by organizational climate is creativity (Amabile & Gryskiewicz, 1989; Ekvall, 1991; Rickards & Bessant, 1980; Siegel & Kaemmerer, 1978). Ekvall (1991) offered the following statement to describe the dynamic role climate plays in organizations:

I regard organizational climate as an intervening variable which affects the results of the operations of the organization. The climate has this moderating power because it influences organizational processes such as communications, problem-solving, decision-making and the psychological processes of learning and motivation. (p. 74)

Among the organizational results or outcomes specifically affected by climate are innovation, quality, productivity, job satisfaction, and profit (Ekvall, 1991). His research further demonstrated that employees' perceptions of the organizational climate were significantly related to the innovativeness of an organization or department.

Organizational climate can be distinguished from another often-discussed environmental variable called corporate culture. **Culture** consists of *patterns of basic assumptions, values, beliefs, symbols, and meaning that define the standards, norms, and expectations of how people should think, feel, and behave* (Ekvall, 1991). Culture is based on deep-rooted assumptions and operates on such a preconscious level that it is often taken for granted. It is stable over time. Climate, on the other hand, is more illustrative of day-to-day events (Schneider, 1990). It is more changeable than culture, and should be regarded as a manifestation of it. Schein (1985) has described this level of climate within culture as "artifacts" of it, such as visible behavior patterns. Ekvall (1999) also observed, "Climate is a derivative of culture. Climate is nearer the observable reality than culture" (p. 404). Because climate is more easily influenced than culture, it is more likely to be a local phenomenon that can vary from unit to unit or workgroup to workgroup within the same organization. For review, Box 13.1 contains a summary of some of the fundamental terms associated with the workplace environment described above.

Box 13.1   Key Vocabulary

Some Key Definitions in Climate and Leadership

Environment: A general biological term used to describe the surroundings of an organism.

Culture: Patterns of basic assumptions, values, beliefs, symbols, and meaning that define the standards, norms, and expectations of how people should think, feel, and behave.

(Continued)

(Continued)

> **Leadership Style:** The ways leaders influence those with whom they work in formal or informal interactions.
>
> **Organizational Climate:** The recurrent patterns of behavior, attitudes, and feelings that characterize life in an organization; the combined perceptions employees have of the psychological climate.
>
> **Psychological Climate:** A person's perceptions of the behaviors, attitudes, and feelings that typify everyday life in a particular setting.

❖ THE LEADERSHIP-CLIMATE CONNECTION

One of the critical determinants of organizational climate within a department, unit, or team is leadership. Research supports a direct link between leadership and creative climate. Ekvall (1999), for instance, reported that leadership behavior accounted for a range of 30% to 60% of the variance in his creative climate research. Ekvall (1999) noted,

> The cause of the climate variation between subunits of the organization to occur, in spite of obvious similarities in, say, tasks, work routines, formal regulations, technology, premises, competencies of the staff, and general mission goals, is to be found in the local leadership, both formal, executed by the manager, and informal, exerted by one or more subordinates with leadership drives and competencies. (p. 404)

Ekvall specifically indicated that leadership style directly affects the climate for creativity. **Leadership style** in this chapter refers to *the ways leaders influence those with whom they work in formal or informal interactions.* Goleman (2000) reported on similar connections between leadership and climate from the Hay/McBer data (Kelner, Rivers, & O'Connell, 1996). They found that 53% to 72% of employees' perception of climate could be traced back to the leader. He specifically examined how different leadership styles impacted the work climate and identified six leadership styles that affect organizational climate and, in turn, performance. His data came from over 3,000 executives in a database developed by the consulting firm of Hay/McBer. He examined the relationship between leadership style, organizational climate, and financial performance. The six climate factors he used were flexibility, responsibility, standards, rewards, clarity, and commitment. The leadership styles he identified were:

1. **Coercive**—the leader demands compliance. ("Do what I tell you.")

2. **Authoritative**—the leader mobilizes people toward a vision. ("Come with me.")

3. **Affiliative**—the leader creates harmony and builds emotional bonds. ("People come first.")

4. **Democratic**—the leader forges consensus through participation. ("What do you think?")

5. **Pacesetting**—the leader sets high standards for performance. ("Do as I do, now.")

6. **Coaching**—the leader develops people for the future. ("Try this.") (pp. 82–83)

Each of these styles relates to an attitude and commensurate strategies that both influence and are influenced by climate. Interestingly, two of these leadership styles can have a negative impact on climate and thus performance. Can you spot them? Here's a hint: One creates resistance and resentment and the other overwhelms people and creates burnout. What are your experiences with these leadership styles? What kind of environment would each style perpetuate? What combinations of style might be needed under different circumstances?

According to Ekvall (1999), the leadership style conducive to a creative climate is most akin to transformational leadership (see Chapter 1 for a description). The behaviors transformational leaders engage in that help to foster an organizational climate that facilitates creative thinking include

- Being open to change
- Involving followers in problem-solving efforts
- Responding positively to new ideas
- Being supportive of new ideas
- Encouraging debate and entertaining different perspectives
- Allowing freedom and autonomy, not being controlling
- Encouraging risk-taking and accepting failure

How leaders behave certainly has a large impact on the nature of the climate in a particular setting; however, it is not the only factor. Ekvall (1999) suggested that goals and strategies, structure, personnel policy, resources, and workload help to determine the nature of the climate. In the next section, we will move away from the factors that influence climate to explore specific qualities in a climate that either inspire or undermine creativity. Before moving to the next section, however, read the research note found in Box 13.2. We believe that how a team manages its process also has an impact on environment. The Box contains a description of a study supporting how groups trained in CPS enjoyed a much more positive work atmosphere than groups who were not trained in CPS.

Box 13.2   Research Note

Leadership Styles and Organizational Climate

One of our colleagues, Roger Firestien, provided clear evidence for the productive outcomes created when people and processes interact effectively in a positive environment (Firestien & McCowan, 1988). Firestien wanted to understand how communication behaviors in small groups facilitated or inhibited the development of ideas. In his study he gave 45 groups, each with approximately 5 members, a real business problem. Twenty groups received training in CPS; the remaining 25 received no training. All groups were videotaped while they generated potential solutions to the business challenge. Raters analyzed the videotapes and compared the trained and untrained groups. The results of the study are listed below (all comparisons between trained and untrained groups are statistically significant).

	Untrained	Trained
Total Responses	26	39
Verbal Criticism	2.2	0.9
Verbal Support	1.4	3.7
Laughter	2.1	6.0
Smiles	2.6	6.7
Ideas Generated	13	27

Comparing the trained and untrained groups, the total number of responses indicated that there was more interaction among those groups trained in CPS and that the nature of this interaction was more positive. Analysis of the videotapes revealed that members of the untrained groups were twice as likely to verbally criticize ideas. In contrast, participants in the trained groups provided more verbal support for one another, laughed more, and smiled more often. These data also showed that the trained groups generated twice as many potential solutions to the problem than the untrained groups. Later, following the publication of the original study, the business owners of the problem rated the quality of the ideas. This analysis showed that groups trained in CPS generated significantly more high-quality ideas (see Puccio et al., 2006).

Goleman et al. (2002) noted that "when people feel good, they work at their best" (p. 14), and a variety of research studies support a similar climate connection (e.g. Bartel & Saavedra, 2000; Barsade & Gibson, 1998; Isen, 1999; Totterdell, 2000; Totterdell, Kellett, Teuchmann, & Briner, 1998). The Firestien study highlighted not only how the CPS process enhanced group output, particularly when working on a task that required divergent thinking, but also how CPS training helped group members create a more positive work environment. Do you dread going to meetings? One reason why people dislike meetings relates to the negative psychological atmosphere that often accompanies meetings. Poor process skills can produce negative meeting environments. Improve group members' process skills and the atmosphere in a meeting is likely to be more positive.

❖ CREATIVE CLIMATE IN ORGANIZATIONS: WHAT TO LOOK FOR

What makes a climate conducive to creativity? What conditions are necessary or sufficient to it? Research and practical workplace implications of such people as Ekvall and Harvard business professor Teresa Amabile help to articulate key factors.

Amabile's Stimulants and Obstacles

Teresa Amabile, who has researched creativity and innovation in the workplace for almost 20 years, has been especially interested in the conditions that help or hinder creativity in work environments (see Table 13.1). Her early work with colleagues at the Center for Creative Leadership in Greensboro, North Carolina, identified basic obstacles (what hinders) and stimulants (what helps) to creativity in the workplace (Burnside, Amabile, & Gryskiewicz, 1988).

"Creativity in the Wild"

In an extensive recent study, Amabile and her associates collected almost 12,000 daily journal entries from 238 people working on creative projects in seven companies in consumer products, high-tech, and chemicals industries (Amabile, Constance, & Steven, 2002). She commented, "The diary study was designed to look at the creativity in the wild. We wanted to crawl inside people's heads and understand the features of their work environment as well as the experiences and thought processes that lead to creative breakthroughs" (in Breen, 2004, p. 75).

Table 13.1   Stimulants and Obstacles to Creativity

Stimulants	freedom, effective project management, adequate resources, collaborative atmosphere, recognition, sufficient time and challenge
Obstacles	too much bureaucracy, inappropriate rewards, lack of cooperation, organizational disinterest, not enough resources, time pressure and a need to maintain the status quo

SOURCE: Burnside, Amabile, and Gryskiewicz (1988).

As a result of the study, she identified six myths about creative environments in the workplace (in Breen, 2004, pp. 76–78):

1. Creativity Comes From Creative Types

Not so, says Amabile's research. Regular people with at least average intelligence are capable of doing creative work. Factors such as experience, knowledge, technical skills, talent, the ability to think in new ways, and the ability to push through uncreative times can be activated in people who are happy with their work. Intrinsic motivation—working at what they do for the sheer love of it, rather than for some external reward such as money—is a key factor in people's creativity.

2. Money Is a Creativity Motivator

When asked about rewards on a regular basis, participants in the diary study often said that the question "wasn't relevant." For them, thinking about money wasn't a day-to-day issue. This is also supported by Torrance's (1987) earlier study on inventors, in which the inventors he studied identified the intrinsic love of inventing as their top motivation; the external reason of money was a distant fourth. Amabile has maintained that people want the opportunity to engage in their work and to make room for genuine progress.

3. Time Pressure Helps Creativity

Although participants gave lip service to the positive influence of deadlines on their creativity, actual data showed that they were least creative when fighting against time pressure. Not only were they less creative in general, there was a kind of "time pressure hangover" that continued to influence them adversely not only on deadline day, but for the next two days as well.

4. Fear Forces Breakthroughs

The data in the journal entries were coded for the degree of fear, anxiety, sadness, anger, joy, and love that people were experiencing on a given day. They found that creativity was positively associated with joy and love and negatively associated with anger, fear, and anxiety. Entries indicated that people were happiest when they came up with creative ideas, and that they were even more likely to have a breakthrough if they were happy the day before. Thus Amabile makes the case that "one day's happiness often predicts the next day's creativity" (in Breen, 2004, p. 78).

5. Competition Is More Important Than Collaboration

Amabile's research showed just the opposite—when people compete for recognition, they stop sharing information, and information or data, as we noted it in Chapter 5, is critical for creative success. No one person can be expected to have all the information that is required to be successful in complex tasks.

6. If an Organization Is Streamlined, It Is Creative

Amabile noted that "creativity suffers greatly during downsizing" (in Breen, 2004, p. 78). She and her colleagues studied 6,000 people in a division of a global electronics company for the entire time of a 25% downsizing, which took 18 months (Amabile & Conti, 1999). In this case, every one of the stimuli to creativity in the work environment went down significantly. Both the anticipation of the downsizing and the follow-up time after it greatly affected creativity.

Amabile's creativity-in-the-wild myth breakers and earlier stimulants and obstacles add to our understanding of what creative climate looks like and can provide a checklist of conditions that leaders can use to plan or make decisions to help their teams be more creative. For example, a better understanding of the impact of time pressure on our ability to produce new or different ideas or outcomes could change how project timelines are set up. This could be as simple as building short amounts of incubation time into a project plan. Or it could be developed into a more formal norm as at the design firm of W. L. Gore and Associates, where patience and long-term thinking are valued, and associates are expected to spend time tinkering with ideas. Amabile's findings are also useful for the transformational leader. For example, encouraging joy and meaning in work not only changes how people do things, but also has an impact on how employees develop as people. Regardless of the angle, explicit creative climate data help shape a leader's thinking about important factors that might otherwise be invisible or neglected.

Ekvall's Climate Dimensions

Another view of the conditions that constitute creative climate comes from Göran Ekvall, who, working in the early 1970s with Swedish companies that appeared to be either innovative or stagnated, traced the evolution of novel ideas and their development in companies. His results are the basis for the identification of 10 climate dimensions (nine positive and one negative) that impact creativity in organizations. Table 13.2 contains a definition of each of these dimensions and some exemplar positive and negative behaviors associated with each that you can use to identify creative climate in your own organization (Ekvall, 1996).

By making some conditions for creative climate more explicit, Ekvall gives leaders a language to identify and describe the status of climate in their environments. Let's see how this can be done by looking at a current example of creative climate in a company and comparing the behaviors described there to Ekvall's creative climate dimensions.

Working at W. L. Gore: Breaking Old Rules or Adhering to Creative Climate Dimensions?

Imagine working in "a place where nerds can be mavericks; a place that's impatient with a standard way of working, but more than patient with nurturing ideas and giving them time to flourish; a place that's humble in its origins, yet ravenous for breakthrough ideas and, ultimately, growth" (Deutschman, 2004, p. 56). At W. L. Gore, a well-known design firm, you would find such an opportunity. Deutschman described Gore's climate as "strikingly contradictory." He noted that "Gore's uniqueness comes from being as innovative in its operating principles as it is in its diverse product lines. This is a company that has kicked over all the rules that most other organizations live by" (p. 56). And sure enough, Gore's so-called new rules of business begin with the maxim "Start breaking old rules." These rules, however, are not new to followers of creative climate; in fact, they look very familiar. Let's further examine how Ekvall's climate descriptors can be identified within Gore's maxims.

Gore Rule # 1: There Is Power in Small Teams

Gore tries to keep its teams small so that everyone can get to know one another and work together with a minimum number of rules. They even have a policy of capping the size of their manufacturing plants at 200.

> **Climate Dimension Parallels:** The emphasis on small size and minimum rules as they relate to Trust and Openness and Freedom in the work environment are climate-smart procedures.

Table 13.2   Ekvall's Climate Dimensions

Dimension	Definition	High	Low
Challenge (positive)	The emotional involvement of the members of the organization in its operations and goals.	People feel joy and meaningfulness in their job, and they are willing to invest energy in their work.	People feel alienated and are indifferent to their work; they are apathetic and disinterested in their job and the organization.
Freedom (positive)	The independence in behavior exerted by the people in the organization.	People make contact with others. They give and receive information and discuss problems and alternatives freely; they plan and take initiatives. They have choices and make decisions.	People are passive, rule-fixed, and anxious to stay inside established boundaries.
Idea Support (positive)	The way new ideas are treated.	Superiors and peers pay attention to ideas and suggestions. People listen to each other and encourage new initiatives. They create ways to test new ideas. The atmosphere is constructive and positive.	When Idea Support is low, there is an automatic "no" attitude. Suggestions are countered or discounted. People respond to ideas by finding what is wrong with them.
Trust and Openness (positive)	The emotional safety in relationships.	Everyone in the organization will offer ideas and opinions and take initiative without fear of reprisals or ridicule. It's okay to fail; communication is open and direct.	People are suspicious of each other and there will be a high price for mistakes. They are also afraid of being used or having their ideas stolen.

(Continued)

Table 13.2 (Continued)

Dimension	Definition	High	Low
Dynamism and Liveliness (positive)	The eventfulness in the life of the organization.	New things are constantly occurring; clashes between how people think and handle things often occur. There is a psychological turbulence and the pace is quick.	There are no new projects, no different plans. Everything goes its usual way and the pace is slow.
Playfulness and Humor (positive)	The spontaneity and ease that is displayed.	There is a relaxed atmosphere with jokes and laughter. There is room for the unexpected and people are flexible in responding to situations.	When playfulness is missing or limited, people have a grave and serious demeanor. The atmosphere is stiff, gloomy, and heavy. Jokes and laughter are not considered appropriate.
Debate (positive)	Encounters and clashes between viewpoints, ideas, and differing experiences and knowledge.	Many voices are heard and people are interested in putting forward their ideas.	People follow authoritarian patterns and don't question the status quo.
Risk Taking (positive)	The tolerance of uncertainty in the organization.	Decisions and actions occur quickly; people engage in new opportunities without hesitation. Action and effort are more important than detailed investigation and analysis.	There is a cautious, hesitant mentality. People try to do the safe thing. They decide to "to sleep on the matter." They set up committees and try to cover themselves before making a decision.

Dimension	Definition	High	Low
Idea Time (positive)	The amount of time people can use and do use for elaborating new ideas.	Suggestions that are not planned or included in the task assignments occur. It is possible to discuss and test impulses or fresh ideas. People tend to use all the possibilities around them.	Every minute is booked and accounted for. The time pressure makes thinking outside planned routines impossible.
Conflict (negative)	The presence of personal and emotional tensions (in contrast to the idea tensions in the debates dimension) in the organization.	People dislike or even hate each other; open hostility may occur. Plots and traps to set up others are typical. There is gossip and slander.	People behave in a more mature manner; they have psychological insight into their differences and control of their impulses.

SOURCE: Ekvall (1996).

Gore Rule # 2: Ranks, Titles, and Bosses Are Not Part of Gore's Vocabulary or System

At Gore, there are no standard job descriptions or categories. Instead, there are "associates" or "sponsors" who decide for themselves what commitments to assume. Committees evaluate these contributions and decide on rewards.

> **Climate Dimension Parallels:** Again, the Freedom to create and to move around within the organization without hierarchical constraints and the Trust or emotional safety it presupposes are easily recognized climate concepts.

Gore Rule # 3: Long-Term Thinking Is OK

At Gore, people are patient and willing to take years or even decades to develop revolutionary products and bring them to the market.

> **Climate Dimension Parallels:** Idea Time—that precious developmental gem—and Idea Support, the pillar that holds unique or different ideas up until they can be crafted into sellable products, are clearly creative climate assisters here.

Gore Rule # 4: Face-To-Face Communication Is Essential

At Gore, there is no hierarchy for communication. Anyone can talk to anyone else. Personal communication is preferred over e-mails and memos.

> **Climate Dimension Parallels:** The Freedom to share information easily and quickly and to engage in Debate early on in process are aspects of creative climate here. Also, it is more difficult to slip into the negative patterns of Conflict when communication is open.

Gore Rule # 5: Lead by Leading

At Gore, associates are expected to spend time (around 10%) pursuing new ideas. Anyone can launch a project or be a leader as long as he or she has passion and can attract followers.

> **Climate Dimension Parallels:** Idea Time is key here, but at Gore, you don't have to fight for it, you just have to do something with it. Challenge is also important to this Gore principle—emotional involvement and passion are directly connected to influencing others and making change.

Gore Rule # 6: Celebrate Failure

When a project doesn't work out at Gore, teams celebrate with a beer or champagne just as if it had been a success. They believe that failure and risk taking go hand in hand.

> **Climate Dimension Parallels:** Risk Taking and Idea Support—don't let negative or premature judgment strangle the life out of an idea before it gets a chance to be seen and heard—are inherent in this rule as well as the importance of playfulness/celebration.

More on Gore: Does This Climate Have an Impact on Product?

You can see the confluence of positive climate characteristics at Gore, but how do they impact the people and products in the organization? At Gore, leaders are "talent magnets" who feel free to pursue ideas independently, communicate with each other, and collaborate because they want to, not because they have to. Gore adheres to the idea of "natural leadership"—you get to be a leader by actually leading and then it's up to you to convince followers.

An example of how this works is the story of Dave Meyers, a Gore engineer who helped invent new kinds of plastic heart implants. Because Myers had 10% "tinkering" time, he was working on his mountain bike to try to make the gears shift more smoothly. In the process, he coated the gear cables with a thin layer of plastic similar to Gore-Tex, the well-known fabric created by the firm. This resulted in Gore's Ride-On line of bike cables. Inspired by this success, Meyers tried to improve the cables used for controlling oversized animated puppets at places such as Walt Disney World. Because the cables had small diameters, he tried taking guitar strings and coating them with a similar plastic. At that point in 1993, he made the connection to improving guitar strings. Because Myers wasn't a guitarist, he asked for help from a colleague, Chuck Hebestreit. Chuck was aware that musicians had problems with guitar strings because the natural oil on their fingers carried dust and skin, which contaminated the strings. For two years they experimented without success until John Spencer, another colleague at the same plant, heard about the project. Spencer, who had just finished working on the Glide dental floss project, thought the new project had possibilities and began to work on it in his spare time. This "natural" team approach paid off, and after three years of working entirely from their own motivation without asking for permission or being evaluated in any way, they were ready to take the project to the larger company to market the product. The marketing department at Gore, in turn, responded with a unique idea to get the more expensive guitar strings accepted in the marketplace by giving away 20,000 samples in the first year. The resulting innovation—Elixir guitar strings—now leads the market with a 35% share (Deutschman, 2004).

Clearly, the creative climate dimensions present at Gore had benefits to the bottom line. The relaxation of time and deadline constraints that Amabile noted in her creativity-in-the-wild research and Ekvall's creative climate concepts helped to produce profitable results.

❖ FINAL THOUGHTS FOR LEADERS

The climate metaphor, and the theory that supports it, rings true with most people's leadership experiences. In his book *The Way to Happiness*, author Felton J. Sheen (1997) used a climate metaphor when he commented that "each of us makes his own weather and determines the color of the skies in the emotional universe which he inhabits." The same is true of climate in organizations—you can impact it; you can mold it; you can have an influence on "the way things are done around here."

Yet understanding climate in general and developing a language to apply climate concepts in organizations are underutilized aspects in a leader's repertoire. Kotter (1996) maintained that

> Because we spend many of our waking hours at work, most of our development takes place—or doesn't take place—on the job. This simple fact has enormous implications. If our time at work encourages and helps us to develop leadership skills, we will eventually realize whatever potential we have. Conversely, if time at work does little or nothing to develop these skills, we will probably never live up to our potential. (pp. 165–166)

The connection of climate to the workplace and creative climate to meaningful, productive work in that environment is a critical aspect of a leader's success. Creative climate impacts the bottom line of organizations in quality, productivity, innovation, job satisfaction, well-being, and profit (Ekvall, 1996).

For leaders, practical work with creative climate begins with an awareness of concepts and then the use of these concepts as a basic language to help you recognize climate elements when you see or hear them. In workshops we often ask people to identify and describe their best and worst climate experiences, and they can invariably do this without hesitation. Similarly, in a synthesis of seven classroom studies that looked at the transfer and understanding of Ekvall's organizational "language" to educational settings (Peebles-Fish, 2003), teachers and students could identify Ekvall's climate dimensions and commensurate behaviors across a variety of content and grade ranges.

❖ APPLYING WHAT YOU'VE LEARNED

In this chapter, we have provided a research-based language that you can use to diagnose and act upon with climate-related challenges. Not all climates are as creative in so many aspects as the one at Gore, but as a leader, the more you are able to recognize climate cues and miscues in your organization, the more ideas and strategies you are likely to consider and implement that can change the day-to-day actions of the people who work there.

Here are a few exercises to help you integrate climate concepts into your leadership repertoire:

- Think of the workplace climate that stands out to you as the most negative, nonsupportive or nonproductive in which you have ever worked. Place the name of the workplace at the top of a sheet of paper, and list characteristics and factors that made it this way. Then do the same with the climate that stands out as the best in which you have ever worked. How do you recognize the characteristics of both? What behaviors exemplify each descriptor? Can you give specific examples? What was the leader's impact in these situations?

- Try using Ekvall's dimensions as a checklist to take the "temperature" of your immediate (team, building) or overall (division, organization) climate, rating the presence or absence of each dimension on a scale of 1–5 (1 = low; 5 = high; remember that conflict is a negative influence).

  – **Challenge** = the emotional involvement of members in the organization and its operations and goals

  – **Freedom** = the independence in behavior exerted by the people in the organization

  – **Idea Support** = the way new ideas are treated

  – **Trust/Openness** = emotional safety in relationships

  – **Dynamism/Liveliness** = the eventfulness in the life of an organization

  – **Playfulness/Humor** = the spontaneity and ease that is displayed

  – **Debate** = the occurrence of encounters and clashes between viewpoints ideas and differing experiences and knowledge

  – **Risk Taking** = the tolerance of uncertainty exposed in the organization

  – **Idea Time** = the amount of time people can and do use for elaborating new ideas

  – **Conflict** = the presence of personal and emotional tensions— in contrast to the idea tensions in the debate dimension

What were your results? What are the climate assisters and resisters that might be influencing the "weather" in your workplace? How might you use these results as starting points for discussion about behaviors or attitudes in your team or department or as short-term indicators of how to improve productivity of meetings? If needed, these same concepts can be used diagnostically to design training for areas that might be improved.

Conclusion

❖ DEVELOPING CREATIVITY FOR LEADERSHIP

Change. Leadership. Creativity. If you recall, we opened this book with those words and asked how much thought you had given to them. We invite you now to reconsider what you think about the relationship among these three concepts and to look again at the five supporting tenets on which this book was based:

1. Creativity is a process that leads to change; you don't get deliberate change without it.

2. Leaders help the individuals and organizations they influence to grow by deliberately facilitating productive change.

3. Because leaders bring about change, creativity is a core leadership competence.

4. An individual's ability to think creatively and to facilitate creative thinking in others can be enhanced.

5. As individuals develop their creative thinking and master those factors that promote creativity, they positively impact their leadership effectiveness.

These tenets and the skills that undergird them have never been more important. The world you live in now is changing with exponential speed. Try to imagine your life and the world around you in 10 years. It is not going to look the same as is does now. A recent special report in *Business Week* on the need for creativity noted,

Increasingly, the new core competency is creativity—the right-brained stuff that smart companies are now harnessing to generate top-line growth. The game is changing. It isn't just about math and

245

science anymore. It's about creativity, imagination, and above all, innovation. (Nussbaum et al., 2005)

Thomas L. Friedman (2004), in his best-selling book *The World Is Flat*, commented that to be successful in the flat-lined or globalized world of today, "we have to be the masters of our imaginations, not the prisoners" (p. 448). Choosing to lead and to make creativity a core competence in your life will require that you let go of old habits, and when you do, that choice can be life-changing. Kouzes and Posner (2002) commented

Leadership is not the private reserve of a few charismatic men and women. It is a process ordinary people use when they are bringing forth the best from themselves and others. What we've discovered is that people make extraordinary things happen by liberating the leader within everyone. (p. xxii)

We hope that the information in this book will help you find the leader inside yourself and develop the core competency of creativity to support you in both making and facing change.

Change. Leadership. Creativity. They are here to stay. But how can you develop each of them further? How can you go beyond the pages of this book and connect what you have learned to your own context? In the next section, we will present a model for developing creativity in leadership that can guide you to integrate your skills into your life and provide some resources and suggestions to help you stay connected to the field of creativity.

❖ WHERE TO BEGIN?

A friend of ours has observed, "Learning without application produces the same result as ignorance." Our experiences, both in classrooms and organizations, indicate that training in creativity principles and procedures can enhance people's leadership skills. We further contend that the principles and procedures described here can change the way leaders think and act. But how does this occur? Consider a well-known cartoon of a scientist filling a large chalkboard with equations, computations, and figures; he pauses in the middle of his frantic computations with no apparent answer and no idea of what comes next and writes, "And then a miracle happens." He then resumes writing equations and formulas. On the side, a colleague points to the miracle comment and says, "Could you be a bit more specific about that part there?"

Moving from tacit assumptions to using more deliberate applications of creative thinking is much like moving from "Then a miracle happens" to "Oh, so this is how I make something happen." By introducing the principles and procedures in this book, we hope that you can more easily integrate deliberate creativity into your repertoire of leadership skills. This takes time and practice. Mumford et al. (2000) observed that creative problem solving skills "develop rather slowly, emerging over a period of time as a function of certain abilities and experiences" (p. 24).

Becoming an effective leader is not a destination. It is a journey that involves continuous improvement, and the starting point for this journey will vary from person to person. Where do you think you are in your creative thinking skill development? How well do you use creative thinking and creative problem solving? How aware are you of the impact of psychological diversity on creativity? How in tune are you with the environmental factors that facilitate or inhibit creativity? Given where you are, what do you need to do to enhance your development?

❖ A MODEL FOR DEVELOPING CREATIVITY IN LEADERSHIP

To help support you in this transformational journey, we suggest that you engage in an organized learning process to develop your skills. Figure C.1 describes how we believe learning about CPS, cognitive style, and climate, as well as other general creativity principles and procedures, can enhance leadership skills. Think of the development in this model as being similar to learning a new language. At the beginning you are not aware of the vocabulary and structure of the language. Then something happens. As you are exposed to new words and interesting aspects of the language, it opens up for you, and you get excited about the possibility of learning more. It is this awareness and interest that moves you from initial development toward becoming a student of that language. As a student, you begin to see how much there is to learn. You struggle at first with the language, and through persistence and practice, you begin to develop competence. At this level of experience you can deliberately use the language, but you are not yet fully fluent. Fluency, the final level of development, occurs when you have fully internalized the language. At that point you no longer need to think through what you want to say or write; it just comes naturally.

Like making a new language second nature, our goal has been to help you to explicitly integrate creativity principles into your life. For some, this book will be the first step in the transition from a spectator to a creative change leader. For others, it will be a critical step in an ongoing evolution as a leader.

Borrowing from a well-known adult learning competency model (Gordon, 1976), the model in Figure C.1 has four levels of development. These levels range from "Spectator" to "Creative Change Leader." The model describes the growth people experience as they learn to incorporate creative thinking into their performance. On the left side of the model we have a description of *what you need* to move from one level of development to the next: awareness, proficiency, and integration. The right side describes *what you do* to move from level to level: begin learning about CPS, cognitive style, climate, and other aspects of creativity; practice what you are learning and apply it in your context; and internalize what you have learned—become a lifelong learner. The sections that follow describe each level in this model.

A Spectator: Unconsciously Unskilled

We call someone who is at the beginning level of development a **Spectator** because this person has not given much thought to the connection between creativity and leadership and does not yet realize that creative thinking plays a role in leadership effectiveness. A Spectator has little appreciation for how to foster others' creativity to move a team or organization forward. Like spectators at a sporting event,

Figure C.1   A Model for the Development of Creative Change Leaders

SOURCE: © 2005 Puccio, Murdock, and Mance. Reprinted with permission.

people at this level of development are not fully engaged in the process of influencing others through creative thinking; rather, they stand on the sidelines watching the process unfold. They do not actively attempt to direct their own creative thinking, much less that of others, toward the resolution of predicaments or the realization of new opportunities. People at this level of development are *unconsciously unskilled*. They don't know what they don't know, and therefore can't expect to be very good at it. By developing awareness of the pertinence of creativity to leadership effectiveness, they may then be motivated to learn more about it. Beginning to learn about CPS, cognitive style, climate, and other aspects of creativity is the first step in moving from *unconsciously unskilled* (Spectator) to *consciously unskilled* (Student of Creativity).

Student of Creativity: Consciously Unskilled

At the second level of development is the **Student of Creativity**. This is a person who is beginning to recognize the importance of creative thinking and how learning CPS, as well as adopting other creativity principles, can improve leadership skills. Students of creativity gather information about CPS and other creative thinking processes and begin to see connections from them to leadership. Like all beginning learners, people at this developmental level are aware of the subject matter, but need skill development. Do you remember when you first picked up a new hobby, sport, or activity? You might have had great enthusiasm, but you probably were not very proficient. At this developmental stage individuals are *consciously unskilled*; they know that they don't know very much about the topic. When Students of Creativity apply creative thinking strategies alone or in groups, as well as deliberately employ concepts such as cognitive style and climate, they begin to develop expertise that moves them toward the next level of development.

Effective Practitioner: Consciously Skilled

At this developmental stage a person may refine his or her skills by actively and deliberately applying creativity principles and procedures until he or she becomes an **Effective Practitioner**. Now there is a shift from the internal focus in the previous stage to a more external one, using creativity principles and procedures with others. Through practice, individuals develop competence and become *consciously skilled*. They participate in extensive formal practice, facilitating the CPS process with individuals and groups. They deliberately build climates that support creativity. They consciously and skillfully manage their own creativity style and consider others' styles.

At this stage the Effective Practitioner uses creativity well as a tool in specific situations and circumstances. If you need some creativity, you go to your toolbox and you know what tool to pick. If you need to build a team, you consider style factors. If you need to diagnose a problem situation, you use CPS tools from the Assessing the Situation stage. When you just need some ideas, you Brainstorm in a group. What has not occurred yet at this stage is the personal transformation that comes through internalizing creativity principles. You can use these creativity strategies as tools to assist you in leadership situations, but you have not transformed yourself yet as a leader. This internal shift to a leader who embodies the very nature of creativity in all that he or she does moves you from this stage to the fourth stage of development. Ongoing development can transform an Effective Practitioner into a person whose basic thoughts and actions in leadership embody the spirit of creativity.

Creative Change Leaders: Unconsciously Skilled

A person at this developmental level is called a **Creative Change Leader**. Recall in Chapter 1 that we made the case that not all change is creative. Some change simply refers to replacing or exchanging one thought or practice for an existing thought or practice. We refer to individuals at this level as Creative Change Leaders because they have internalized creativity principles and procedures to such a degree that the very essence of their leadership is defined by behaviors and attitudes aimed at pursuing, facilitating, and entertaining novel ideas that have a positive and profound influence in their context. These leaders actively seek to introduce or support creative change.

A key difference between a Practitioner and a Creative Change Leader is the difference between doing and being. For instance, a highly skilled Practitioner may be excellent at reinforcing how to defer judgment during a problem-solving session, but immediately afterwards he may prematurely criticize the first novel idea presented. If, however, this principle is internalized, deferring judgment becomes the primary way of thinking about options or situations. At the fourth level of development, CPS and other creativity principles are no longer seen as a set of tools that you use on a particular task and then put away when the job is done, but rather they become a set of active principles that transforms behavior and attitudes in all aspects of your life.

We believe that the greatest impact occurs at this level. When creativity has been internalized, a leader's behavior naturally begins to inspire creative change. Each and every interaction facilitates creative thinking in others. Promoting a climate for creativity just naturally occurs. Leadership becomes a creative process.

In Box C.1, Peter Pellegrino, a Technical Delivery Team Manager on the Change Management Process Team, describes his integration of creativity and CPS as a Change Leader in the Electronic Data System Corporation supporting Xerox.

Box C.1   Real-World Example

EDS Employee and Change Leader Describes Learning, Using, and Internalizing CPS

I remember with great clarity the first time that I participated in a brainstorming session. The entire CPS process was reviewed, and I felt an instant affinity to being able to solve problems and generate ideas in such a thoughtful and organized manner. The part of the process that really inspired me was using the tool Brainstorming. Freewheeling for ideas and generating as many thoughts as possible were new concepts for me. To me, deferring judgment was the critical component—it really allowed me to feel comfortable expressing everything that was on my mind.

Since that time, I have spent the past 18 years in various leadership positions within Information Technology (IT) at Xerox and EDS, and I have spent the last 12 years developing, implementing, and selling a process for managing change activities and implementations in complex, integrated IT environments. This process was developed using CPS principles. With each process upgrade, we ensure that the principles of CPS are used. I believe that the use of CPS creates a climate where creativity, nonjudgmental thought, and organized thinking become part of the organizational culture.

The key to being a successful manager is to tap the creativity that lies within each person. I feel that each individual has the potential to contribute new thoughts, new ideas, process improvements, and ways to do business better that provide more value for our clients.

Frequently we work as a team, and the concepts inherent to brainstorming, particularity striving for a great number of ideas and always deferring judgment, have become ingrained in our routine. We have effectively used CPS to develop a new service offering for our clients. Because our process had expanded to the point that we were reporting on over 1,000 change

(Continued)

(Continued)

activities per month, there was a burden on those responsible for reviewing this information for conflicts within their business area. We were able to re-engineer our process and develop an activity that offered customers a facilitated session and a reporting process that only showed change activities directly impacting their business area. We have since sold this on a number of occasions.

In my opinion, my career accomplishments, the success of our process, and the accomplishments of my team are all based on the integration of CPS into every aspect of my professional life.

SOURCE: Peter Pellegrino. Used with permission.

If you hold, as we do, that leadership is a process that addresses complex problems (i.e., open-ended, ill-defined, ambiguous situations), then for leaders to be successful, as Pellegrino noted, they must be effective creative thinkers. When the foundational principles of CPS—such as deferring judgment—are integrated into your everyday life, they become a natural part of your behavior. You no longer have to think about managing your judgment in both personal and professional tasks; it is second nature and therefore occurs almost automatically. A person who has internalized the concept of deferred judgment shifts immediately into divergent thinking when faced with a challenge and then uses convergent thinking to isolate the most promising alternatives without discarding novelty. This is also true of style and climate.

At this fourth level of development individuals have integrated principles such as deferred judgment into their way of being—they have become principles to live by. This integration is not limited to the basic principles; other CPS procedures can be internalized as well. For instance, phrases such as "How might we . . ." become a natural part of language as people think about challenges that impede progress.

In Box C.2, Tim Switalski, consultant from DARWIN Associates, describes his role in leading change in which the integration of skills for teams in a nuclear waste facility became a natural part of how the team behaved.

Box C.2 Real-World Example

Using CPS to Transform Thinking in an Organization

Imagine a highly secure and safety-conscious radioactive waste management facility employing many nuclear engineers and technicians operating under tightly controlled government regulations. Probably the last place you might expect to find a lot of creativity, right? Well, think again. Creative opportunity can emerge in very unlikely places, particularly when a more than 20-year-old organization now faces all the challenges associated with the process of decommissioning.

As part of my initial assessment of this organization and its objectives for an off-site senior staff annual meeting, I asked the leaders to characterize the current state of their organization. Their answer made it clear they were unprepared for the upcoming changes. The objectives we identified for the staff session were to (1) gain the senior staff's support for the new contract plan and (2) increase their individual and collective ability to manage complex change. During the session, we used the Pluses, Potentials, and Concerns tool (PPC°) to gain senior staff support. As a result, the staff also began to change its approach to problems in subtle but profound ways. They started to practice more affirmative judgment, examining the positive aspects of this new plan rather than criticizing its shortcomings. They noticed the ease with which they could make decisions that they could all support through this open, collective process. In the past, support for decisions had not always been evident, and subgroups often continued to discuss issues and make decisions on their own.

The success of the first meeting led to regular follow-up sessions, and staff managers further developed as a team while they learned more about CPS and began applying it to solve the difficult problems they were facing. Among these challenges was the downsizing of the workforce, which tested the staff's ability to tackle a difficult, emotional task and trust each other in the process. The use of CPS was useful in this case. They generated a lengthy list of criteria and converged on key ones for use in their own departments, along with those that were required by their existing policies. When the senior staff met to identify those employees who needed to be let go, they displayed each department's decisions on the walls of the conference room. Staff managers were then asked if they had an interest in any of the other department's targeted employees and several selections were made. Each department then had to choose who would remain, considering the new mix of employees. This resulted in a number of difficult choices that had to be made on the basis of benefit to the company, not just to their own department. The meeting was surprising to everyone because they anticipated an

(Continued)

(Continued)

emotionally draining experience that would run late into the evening. Instead, they made tough decisions collectively and openly that everyone could support and finished before the scheduled end time.

The ongoing process of team building and learning continued for over a year. Much work went into the development of a healthy, cohesive team. We focused systematically on building trust, managing conflict, making commitments, holding each other accountable, and focusing on collective results. The senior staff were highly committed to these concepts and practiced them until they were incorporated into everyone's daily behavior.

Another final aspect of this transformation process was the development of managers and supervisors throughout the organization. Using CPS, the senior staff generated criteria to identify and select 50 individuals to serve as a leadership coalition to work with the senior staff in leading and managing changes throughout the company. A training program called "Leading and Supporting Change" was offered to these coalition members. This gave people the information and skills needed to drive changes in the company's culture and to achieve the milestones included in the current contract. Developing the leadership coalition through CPS yielded several positive outcomes:

- Many more people feel that they are actively involved in the process of managing change;
- The senior staff and the middle management have developed a broader and deeper level of communication and can rely on a common language and process;
- Project teams are emerging to address operational problems in a proactive and creative manner; and
- Managers and senior staff alike have developed a keener sense of "bi-focal vision" that allows them to focus on both the day-to-day tactical concerns and the strategic priorities.

A key indicator of the degree to which CPS was internalized in this organization is illustrated by the phrase that now continually gets repeated: "How might we . . . ?"

SOURCE: Tim Switalski. Used with permission.

Switalski's experiences demonstrate how the language, tools, and general creative thinking process used initially in CPS training became integrated into leaders' thoughts and actions in a difficult situation. Such a change in thinking does not happen overnight. Continued development as a creative change leader comes through lifelong learning and practice, and yet as with Maslow's (1954) description of self-actualization, you never reach an end point. You can always improve. This book has been both about learning a process that leaders can deliberately apply in responding to predicaments or perceived opportunities (i.e., level three in Figure C.1), and about providing a process and set of principles that when integrated, changes how you lead (i.e., level four of the development model).

❖ WHERE DO YOU GO FROM HERE?

Below are some suggestions for things you can do to extend your general development in CPS, creativity, and leadership, and Box C.3 contains a few specific resources.

- Pursue more knowledge about creativity principles, procedures, models, and theories that can further reinforce your ongoing development—attend workshops, seminars, and lectures.
- Enroll in courses, attend conferences, read the journals, find some good books. Keep the learning going.
- Attend both creativity and leadership conferences; present at these conferences.
- Research and write about the connections between creativity and leadership that you see or have experienced.
- Network with people from the fields of creativity and leadership and exchange opinions and information.

Box C.3   Resources

A Few Sources to Get You Started

Conferences: The Creative Education Foundation (www.creativeeducation foundation.org) has hosted a creativity conference, called the Creative Problem Solving Institute, every June since 1954 (www.cpsiconference.com). The American Creativity Association (www.amcreativityassoc.org) offers an annual conference, typically in late winter or early spring. For more than a decade the Dow Creativity Center at Northwood University has offered a creativity conference targeted at college and university faculty members (www.northwood.edu). The Creativity Association of Europe holds an annual international conference in Italy (www.creaconference.com).

(Continued)

(Continued)

> **Journals:** Currently there are three English-language journals in the field of creativity: *The Journal of Creative Behavior* (www.creativeeducationfoun dation.org), the *Creativity Research Journal* (http://www.erlbaum.com/ journals.htm), and *Creativity and Innovation Management* (www.blackwell publishing.com). Creativity special editions of other journals can be found through traditional search engines.
>
> **Magazines:** There is currently one magazine for the field, although many disciplines may have a creativity angle. Go to www.amazon.com to find *Creative Pulse*. Creativity special editions of magazines can be found through traditional search engines.
>
> **Electronic Bibliographic Services:** General resources can be found in library databases, amazon.com, or barnesandnoble.com. An annotated periodical literature database (Creativity Based Information Resources—CBIR) is available at www.buffalostate.edu/orgs/cbir.
>
> **General Resources:** The International Center for Studies in Creativity (www.buffalostate.edu/centers/creativity), the Creative Studies Collection in E. H. Butler Library at Buffalo State (www.buffalostate.edu/library), the Center for Creative Leadership (www.ccl.org), Project Zero (www.pzweb.harvard. edu), the Innovation Network (www.thinksmart.com).

❖ SOME CLOSING THOUGHTS

Psychologist and early creativity researcher J. P. Guilford (1968) noted that "to live is to have problems and to solve problems is to grow creatively" (p. 12). As potential creative leaders, it will not be enough to rely solely on your own creativity; communities, teams, organizations, families, and societies depend on each member's ability to think creatively. Anthropologist Mary Catherine Bateson (2004) reminds us "that the best hope for our species lies in learning new patterns of attention to each other and to the biosphere, patterns that grow out of curiosity and respect and allow for wonder and learning" (p. 5). As current or potential leaders, you are in a critical position to either uplift the creative capacity of individuals and groups or to squelch it. You can model and facilitate the application of creative thinking to resolve complex problems, or you can ignore creative growth and limit its potential.

Given the complex issues that face people in both their personal and professional lives, the increased need for innovation in organizations, and the novel problems we face in our communities and around the world, there is clearly a need for creativity in leadership to draw out the talents of all people. Leadership can make a difference in people's lives, especially when creativity is brought to bear at all levels. If, as leaders, you can tap into this creative capital, collectively we will be in a better position to both address the difficult issues that hold us back as a society and to find unique and energizing actions that will propel us forward to new frontiers.

Management educator and writer Charles Handy once observed, "We cannot wait for great visions from great people, for they are in short supply. . . . It is up to us to light our own small fires in the darkness." We encourage you to use your creativity as a leader to light fires of influence and to make a difference in your world.

Case Studies

Becoming a Creative Change Leader[1]

❖ MANIFESTING A VISION: HOW
ONE PERSON BECAME A CREATIVE
CHANGE LEADER IN HER ORGANIZATION

The Challenge

How do you create for yourself a full-time position focused on innovation with a successful international company? To make the challenge even more difficult, you're currently not on the management fast track, there is a hiring freeze, and most people in your organization don't know you exist. Can it be done?

One person has shown us how she went from relative obscurity to prominent player in her organization's quest for continuous innovation with the help of CPS. This case will chronicle how Shari Rife found her vision, laid the groundwork for her new position, and followed through in a way that positively impacted the company and validated her role.

Initial Exposure to Creativity: Developing a New Career Vision

With an undergraduate degree in business, 15 years of experience as an administrative support person in the Information Technology division of her company, and three years of experience in Customer Service & Logistics, Shari Rife's career was alive but moving slowly. Though she consistently worked hard and pursued opportunities, she lacked a vision for her career.

Shari works for Rich Products Corporation, headquartered in Buffalo, New York. Rich's was founded in 1945 and is known around the world as an innovator and the founder of the non-dairy segment of the frozen food industry and a leading supplier and solutions provider to the food service, in-store, and retail marketplace. Rich Products has grown from a niche maker of soy-based whipped toppings and frozen desserts to a major U.S. frozen foods manufacturer. Since the 1960s, the company has developed products such as Coffee Rich (non-dairy coffee creamer) and expanded to include frozen bakery and pizza doughs and ingredients for the food service and in-store bakery markets, plus RICH-SEAPAK (seafood) and Byron's (barbecue). Rich Products markets more than 2,000 products in about 75 countries.

Approximately 18 years and two positions into her career at Rich, Rife received a surprising invitation to interview for participation in an intensive company-sponsored training program. The training focused on the Creative Problem Solving (CPS) process. Rife knew nothing about CPS but was willing to learn and was interviewed. Of the 50 people who were interviewed, Rife was one of the 15 selected to attend.

After 15 years of using outside creativity consultants to boost performance and innovation, Rich was sold on the value and principles of CPS. The CPS training program was designed to complement the external consultants with internal consultants skilled in CPS, thus building an internal base of expertise in creativity. To ensure employee follow-through, all participants attending the training were required to make a two-year commitment not only to learn but also to apply their CPS skills throughout the company. Specifically, this multinational company stipulated that employees involved in the CPS training would need to devote 25% of their time to applying what they learned to real business issues.

The training program began with a full week of intensive CPS instruction, followed by a second week of CPS facilitation skills training. Once the classroom training was complete, each participant was required to facilitate a set number of problem-solving sessions with coaching support. Monthly "lunch and learn" sessions took place over the first year to hone the participants' skills, and a call center was created to market and coordinate the utilization of the newly trained CPS facilitators.

Rife was very much taken by the training program. Struck by the usefulness of the CPS process, Rife gained self-confidence and the desire to apply the skills and principles on a much broader scale within the company. "At that point I knew what I wanted to do with my career," said Rife. She had found her vision and was now on a mission to make it a reality.

Laying the Groundwork for a Full-Time CPS Position

Rife was aggressive during her two-year commitment to apply CPS within Rich Products. Whenever a need arose, Rife would make herself available. She would take every opportunity offered to apply her new CPS skills while maintaining her other responsibilities. "I went from not being able to speak in front of groups to being in front of the room guiding teams through various problem-solving sessions," said Rife. These CPS experiences allowed her to begin internalizing the process and recognize how the principles and tools could be applied to a multitude of business problems. It became clear to Rife that her role could be much bigger within the company.

About one year into her CPS training program, Rife discovered and pursued a graduate degree specializing in the CPS process and creativity. Not only did this move demonstrate her commitment, it also helped facilitate the transition to her new career. During one class assignment, she was asked to state a goal and develop it using the convergent tool PPC^O (see Chapter 9). While Rife was clear about her vision—to become a full-time CPS facilitator in her company—she was uncertain how to make this a reality.

Her class assignment forced her to articulate and strengthen her career vision. More specifically, she listed pluses, potentials, and concerns of creating a full-time CPS/Innovation specialist position at Rich Products. She then generated ideas for overcoming the identified concerns, such as "How to not add to head count." The result of Rife's assignment was a recommendation to management outlining why they should hire her full-time to lead CPS and innovation initiatives (Table C.1 highlights excerpts from Rife's PPC^O work). Management reviewed Rife's recommendation and approved the new position based on the fact that they had experienced the value of CPS, had seen Rife in action, and were inspired by her commitment and vision.

Follow Through: Personal Growth and Impact Within the Organization

With her self-created position, Manager of Creative Process and Facilitation, Rife was given the freedom to define her duties and responsibilities. She described her role as an internal consultant and facilitator focused on bringing creativity, open-minded thinking, and planning to everyday meetings and processes. She was focused on encouraging all associates to display the principles of CPS every day, in every way. Now it was her time to prove herself and stimulate innovation.

During the early stages of her new role, most of Rife's time was spent providing CPS facilitation sessions. She would help groups have more productive problem-solving sessions and meetings. As her experience and reputation grew, she began receiving more requests from groups throughout her organization and discovered new areas in

PPC° Section of Recommendation

Pluses (Likes)	Potentials (Opportunities)
• Focused attention • Increased usage of CPS • Consistency in the process • Services offered to customers that no other manufacturer provides • Project tracking measurements, money saved and earned • Ability to see the process through to implementation • More implementation and success stories • Less money spent on outside consulting • More visibility throughout the company • Supports key initiatives • People dedicated to CPS will build credibility and further company reputation in the industry as a learning organization • Introduces more customers to company campus • Makes higher profile in the customer community (not selling them but partnering with them) • Enhanced/sharpened skills for dedicated CPS agents • Create a value-added, competitive advantage • Solidify customer relationships • Matches vision of company— brings it to life by actually solving problems and coming up with customer solutions	• More CPS-facilitated sessions conducted resulting in innovative ideas, savings, and earnings • Implementation • Big impact on Drive 2005 initiative • Could sell service/expertise to other companies • Increased business customer partnerships—care about helping their business grow, not just selling them
	Concerns
	• How to (H2) ensure the position is not eliminated in a year if budgets get tight • H2 prove this impacts the bottom line—it is a valuable business tool • H2 not add to head count • H2 convince management that a full-time position is required • H2 educate associates to ensure they know how to use the process when needed

Overcoming Key Concerns

H2 not add to head count

- Fill position with two existing associates and not replace their positions
- Replace an open position with this position
- Transfer associates from wholly-owned subsidiaries
- Have associates agree to work for nothing and get a percentage of everything impacted

H2 prove this impacts the bottom line/H2 ensure positions are not eliminated/H2 convince management a full-time position is required

- Document all success identifying money and time saved
- Show cost savings between internal full-time vs. paid outside consultant
- Start to educate non-managers about the power and impact of the process
- Introduce CPS to the entire corporate body—bottom up approach
- Introduce CPS service at trade shows to show customers this value-added service
- Offer off-site sessions for priority customers who attend trade shows we participate in
- Run problem-solving sessions with customers and get feedback on how it impacted their business

which she might apply her facilitation skills. Upper management also began asking Rife to work alongside outside consultants to learn their processes, such as strategic planning, and to be sure there was an effective interface between established internal processes, such as CPS, and the introduction of new processes.

Rife believes the principles and procedures of CPS have provided her with an ideal foundation for understanding and incorporating other group processes and credits CPS for much of her success: "Since my introduction to CPS, my career has blossomed—I travel worldwide, have speaking engagements for various organizations, train others, lead groups, and absolutely love what I do!" She consistently helps her organization innovate and succeed worldwide in different ways:

- *Facilitating Internal Ideation Sessions*—new product ideas, naming products, marketing opportunities, etc.
- *Leading Discovery Events*—focusing on finding out what consumers want and then figuring out how to solve the need
- *Facilitating Quarterly Leadership Meetings*—assisting in setting objectives and agenda, facilitating meetings, and driving efficient/effective meetings for the international division of her company
- *Leading Customer Innovation Events*—customer-specific meetings to develop strategies and/or signature products in a creative and collaborative way
- *Facilitating Strategic Planning*—international long-range planning for Brazil, Mexico, UK, and India
- *Redesigning Processes*—driving efficiency into processes by challenging the current design

- *Driving Efficiency in Meetings*—identifying clear objectives and agendas, facilitating teams and model behavior
- *Informal and Formal Coaching*—helping others drive innovation and internalize the CPS process
- *Coordinating Innovation Events*—a celebration and sharing of implemented ideas across the organization
- *Facilitating Governance Procedures*—implementing and facilitating a process for driving accountability and decision making for key corporate initiatives
- *Training*—delivering workshops on Facilitative Behaviors and Creative Leadership to drive foundational CPS and meeting management skills throughout the organization

Closing Thoughts

In only five years, Rife has transformed her career and now contributes significantly to the success of her company. She has clearly demonstrated her value and the value of CPS throughout Rich Products. She receives requests for her services from all levels of the company. Rife has also played a part in the creation of numerous new product concepts, process redesigns, and customer service innovations.

In the face of worldwide change and competition, Rich Products continues to lead its industry and is known for being innovative. When asked why the demand for CPS facilitation has increased, Rife simply states, "It has increased because it works."

As for the others who participated in the intensive CPS training, most have seen their careers advance. "CPS skills are critical management and leadership skills that can enhance a person's career," said Rife, whose overarching goal is to ensure everyone applies these skills "every day in every way." Shari Rife's story highlights both the personal transformation that can be realized through CPS and the positive organizational effects as it is applied in groups. Shari Rife epitomizes what it means to be a creative change leader.

Internalizing
Creativity in an Organization[1]

❖ A TURNAROUND STORY: HOW CPS AND CREATIVE
   LEADERSHIP REVIVED A THEATRE COMPANY

The Challenge

In 1972, two college theatre instructors with a passion for inspiring youth founded Theatre of Youth (TOY) in Buffalo, New York. Their mission was to create a company dedicated to meaningful theatre experiences for young people. TOY filled a need in the Buffalo community. Within four years, international guest directors, funding from a variety of sources, and a reputation for producing quality professional theatre combined to make TOY a significant arts organization. In 1976, TOY received the national Zeta Phi Eta–Winifred Outstanding Children's Theatre Award.

However, in 1992, the theatre was in trouble for a variety of reasons. TOY had begun producing plays for adult audiences and fewer productions for children (a project that eventually took over the company's resources and creative energies). A cycle of public funding cuts had begun. The company's artistic director abruptly resigned. The remaining staff was left to face growing financial obligations. TOY was disconnected from its true audience, and the public perception was that the company had compromised its artistic identity. It was failing fast. With only a few weeks before the beginning of the next theatre season, TOY was without an artistic director and a season of plays. The organization was in crisis. Would TOY close or find a way to rebuild?

Using CPS to Get TOY Back on Track

Meg Quinn had been a founding member of TOY and had returned to the organization for a few years as marketing director. However, by 1992 she had left the theatre again to complete a master's degree in creativity. As the crisis unfolded, Meg offered to assist the company as a CPS facilitator.

The situation was complex. The fundamental questions were whether the company could be saved and rebuilt and who would be willing to make the commitment. Quinn suggested that CPS was a productive way to understand and explore the situation. The Board of Directors, managing director, and staff were very supportive of a CPS initiative to analyze the company's challenges and opportunities, strengths and weaknesses.

Quinn involved two other facilitators from her class and they planned a series of three CPS sessions. The group involved TOY staff, community members, board members, and other people familiar with TOY (including the media).

The first session concentrated on the Clarification stage of CPS. Organizational strengths, weaknesses, and key challenges were identified. Community members were asked to describe their past and present perceptions of TOY. The theatre's founding mission and production history were reviewed. Opportunities and resources were listed. Energy and optimism were high after the first CPS session. As Quinn stated, "Using the CPS process gave people a sense that we weren't just spinning around in a storm. It was possible to get control of the situation."

Over the course of the three CPS sessions, it was clear that although the organization had drifted away from its original purpose, the staff and the community believed in the value of a children's theatre. Ultimately, there was a strong consensus that the theatre should reorganize and create an action plan for the future. The Board of Directors would focus on taking a stronger decision-making role.

Therefore, the last formal CPS session shifted to idea generation and action planning. Brainstorming and other idea generation techniques were used to explore solutions to a variety of challenges. According to Quinn, "CPS clarified how we were going to handle a complex task. We were able to use CPS to take hold of our problems, sort them out, and deal with them head-on in a constructive way." Because the CPS sessions were highly interactive and required everyone's input, there was a sense of ownership and accountability. Participants became vested in the change ahead and rallied around the refocused mission. The CPS sessions demonstrated to funders and the public that TOY was serious about getting back on track. CPS provided the road map that guided action steps.

Creative Leadership Promotes a Creative
Culture That Leads to Ongoing Success

The CPS sessions carried out by Quinn built confidence, support, and significant momentum, but this was only the beginning of the story. Shortly after the conclusion of these sessions, Quinn was asked to take on the role of artistic director. A business plan was in place but the company needed an artistic vision.

The CPS sessions helped to get TOY back on course, but it has been Quinn's ability to embody the principles of creativity in her leadership style as artistic director that transformed the culture at TOY. As a consequence, over the past 14 years TOY has achieved new heights artistically, culturally, and financially. When asked why TOY has been so successful, Quinn is quick to respond, "Because of the people who work there." Collaboration and teamwork are highly valued at TOY. People help and support one another. You won't hear people at TOY say "that's not my job." People are comfortable throwing out ideas and taking risks. They have learned that trusting each other, trying many ideas, and building off ideas is essential to ongoing success. Members of this organization constantly challenge accepted practice, searching for innovative ways to carry out business in terms of both play production and operations. According to Production Manager Chester Popiolkowski, "People from other theatre groups marvel at what we accomplish considering the financial resources we have." Through the years, the culture of TOY has come to embody the principles of creativity and CPS. Creativity principles have become so well entrenched that staff have developed hand signals to communicate things like "This is a just-off-the-top-of-my-head idea, so defer judgment!" or "Follow my thinking over here for a moment!" Problem solving can be a robust activity at TOY, so signals help everyone to keep track of active conversations.

The development of a creative culture is no accident. Quinn's ability to explicitly employ creativity principles and procedures on a regular basis has been infectious. Quinn values other people's ideas and input. She uses a facilitative style of leadership, embraces individual styles, and models creative behavior. These four intertwining leadership characteristics positively impact the organization artistically and administratively. As Ken Shaw, Head of Design at TOY, observed, "Meg is a strong facilitator who doesn't shut off ideas until they have a chance to be explored. This is one reason why she is a creative leader." When she assumed the role of artistic director of TOY, instead of taking the challenge head-on solo, she saw the value of many minds working together. She chose to use a process that tapped into people's imagination and involved them in the decision-making process. These early actions set the stage for a culture of creativity to bloom.

Quinn directs most of the plays that TOY produces. Her knowledge of creativity has had an impact on how she directs. "I think that I am able to get stronger performances from actors because I can recognize individual creative styles. I can better understand how each actor needs to work through the rehearsal process." A director guides a play toward a definite interpretation and vision. But at TOY, time is allowed for playing with ideas and risk taking. For instance, in *Alexander and the Terrible, Horrible, No Good, Very Bad Day* there is scene in which a large photocopy machine breaks down and rapidly ejects volumes of paper. Quinn decided to "build" the machine by having actors physicalize all of the moving parts. Chester Popiolkowski composed a soundtrack of electronic music that sounded like a machine that was working well and eventually overheated and exploded with paper. Quinn and the cast discussed the movable parts of a photocopy machine. Then, the cast began improvising a moving photocopier along to the recorded sound track. The rehearsal became a physical brainstorming session. One idea built on another idea, until the machine became an innovative interpretation of the script. Allowing each actor to contribute to staging the copier made the outcome far more energized and interesting than if it had been preconceived and directed into place.

Whether Quinn is directing a play or working on an everyday challenge, she keeps tuned into the creative needs of the organization and its employees. According to Quinn, actors are inspired by the creative climate at TOY and the opportunity to explore scripts in new ways.

Quinn's ability to lead creatively shows in the strong working relationships among the employees. Personal styles are embraced at TOY. People have gained an understanding of why people do what they do and how to best utilize each other's talents and habits. To leverage style differences even more, she had her entire team take FourSight. FourSight is a personal and group assessment instrument that identifies individual and team preferences within the creative process.

FourSight showed that every member of the team was a unique part of a balance of skills and competencies. The TOY team works because the range of individual preferences and strengths complement and support the whole group. The information gathered through this tool helped individuals to strengthen their own problem-solving abilities and to recognize how the diversity of preferences influenced communication and interpersonal relationships. As Quinn observed, "Theoretical and practical knowledge of different creativity styles saves wear and tear on relationships and helps to get the job done."

Operating a not-for-profit theatre requires inventive approaches to problem solving on many levels. Deliberate creativity was essential to helping TOY rediscover its mission, rebuild its reputation, and reinvent its business operation. Quinn's style of leadership, along with the creative imagination of a talented staff, resulted in new successes for TOY and the establishment of a secure theatre dedicated to children.

Results: What Does it all Mean?

Now located in Buffalo's historic, $3.5 million renovated Allendale Theatre, TOY is a viable theatre business. Since December, 1999, TOY has produced 34 shows, employed 300 actors, and welcomed over 300,000 children and adults to its performances. TOY has also carried out truly paradigm-breaking work, such as their recent venture with a major pharmaceutical company to develop and perform a play to help Buffalo public school children become more aware of the signs of a stroke. TOY receives many letters from students; foundation and corporate support is growing; and employees are delighted to be part of the organization.

The financial turnaround is even more impressive. Earned income accounts for 75% of TOY's operating budget. This is a complete turnaround from 15 years ago when less than 60% of total operating income was earned. Corporate sponsors such as Rite Aid, Wendy's, BlueCross BlueShield of WNY, and Fisher-Price help to make up the other portion of operating income.

What really drove this great turnaround story? Quinn firmly believes it stems from respecting the creative potential of each worker and creating an environment in which everyone is proud and happy to do his or her best work.

Creative Climate[1]

❖ WORK ENVIRONMENT ALLOWS IDEO
   TO DELIVER PROMISE OF INNOVATION

The Challenge

Pepsi, Nike, Prada, and other outstanding companies knock on your door when they are in need of an innovative product. Apple calls on you when they are stuck on a challenge and need a breakthrough. Your services promise the creation of breakthrough solutions, and your entire existence as a company rests on your ability to deliver innovation on demand. Are you up for the challenge and what it will take to succeed?

The Company

Who could meet the challenges above and how do they do it? IDEO, the now-famous design firm headquartered in Palo Alto, California, has created innovative products and solutions for over 20 years. Because he disliked corporate rules and was motivated to create a company that was fun to work for, David Kelley started what is now IDEO in 1978 under the name David Kelley Design. In 1991, Kelley's company was renamed IDEO, with a focus on industrial design. Today, IDEO helps companies design innovative products, services, and processes, employing approximately 350 people worldwide.

Since ABC's *Nightline* news show reported on IDEO's innovation process first-hand, the world has become familiar with their impressive achievements. *Fortune* magazine described their visit to IDEO as "a day at Innovation U" (Brown, 1999). The *Wall Street Journal* called IDEO "imagination's playground." There is consensus in the business/organizational world that IDEO is a leader in the area of innovation. What is it that enables them to consistently produce innovative solutions? Do they have more creative talent? Is it a charismatic leader? Do they have a secret formula?

Cultivating Creative Consistency

If you take a close look at IDEO and examine how they have consistently produced well-known innovations, such as Crest's Neat Squeeze

Are Ekvall's 10 dimensions of a creative climate present at IDEO?

At IDEO:

☑ **Challenge & Involvement**

- Brainstorming and other practices encourage all to participate
- Reputation & setting big goals challenges IDEOers
- Fun design challenges given by leadership

☑ **Freedom**

- Freedom to customize workspace with more than just pictures
- Freedom to select projects of most interest
- Freedom to have some downtime at work when needed

☑ **Idea Time**

- Brainstorming is considered almost a religion
- Movie and other types of excursions take place
- Workspace promotes spontaneous conversations

☑ **Idea Support**

- Constant encouragement/coaching by leadership
- Easy to get supplies for ideas/concepts
- Off-project ideas supported, e.g., Tech Cart

☑ **Trust & Openness**

- Lack of rules and procedures
- Peer evaluations a common practice
- Team members interview and help make hiring decisions

☑ **Playfulness & Humor**

- Practical jokes are common at IDEO
- Project teams often give out fun awards
- IDEOers are given the permission to play

☑ **Debates (Viewpoints and ideas are appropriately challenged.)**

- The Evaluate & Refine step of IDEO's Innovation process provides time for discussion of different viewpoints

☑ **Low Conflict (Little or no presence of interpersonal tension)**

- Strong efforts are made to blur the lines between management and workers
- Intensive interviewing occurs to find employees that best fit IDEO's culture

☑ **Risk Taking**

- "Fail often to succeed sooner" motto promoted by leadership
- Consistently try new things knowing some failures will occur

☑ **Dynamism**

- Past project prototypes appear throughout organization
- Flexible workspaces changing continuously with projects
- Regular guest speaker events

SOURCE: Creative climate dimensions based on Ekvall (1996).

stand-up toothpaste tube, you won't find any magic bullet. What you will find is a combination of effective leadership behaviors, creative work environment practices, and a variety of processes that work synergistically to produce a culture that exemplifies creativity.

Leadership

One of the first clients Kelley worked for was Steve Jobs of Apple. The lessons he learned from this experience were more valuable than the paycheck he earned from Apple. He was inspired by Apple's dynamic culture, and the atmosphere there reinforced his belief that having fun while working could be productive.

Although founder David Kelly is no longer involved with the day-to-day operations at IDEO, his early actions set the tone for creativity to flourish. Kelley frowned on rules. He participated in pranks and other fun antics, all of which made it clear that in his shop it was OK to be playful. Kelley's actions influenced the way new and upcoming leaders of IDEO would behave.

Leaders at IDEO have worked hard to eliminate the "us vs. them" mentality. Traditional indicators of hierarchy, such as plush corner offices and titles, are missing. Employee performance is more important than seniority, and the behavior of IDEO leadership consistently demonstrates that flexibility is "in" and rigid rules are "out."

Leaders understand that risk taking is essential and mistakes will occur. One way risk taking is encouraged and practiced is through in-house design challenges. Unlike a design challenge for paying customers, these in-house challenges typically have an open timeline and very few criteria. For example, a challenge was held to see who could design the best solution to a sun glare problem created by the office skylights. A simple and artistic solution using umbrellas dangling upside-down won the "people's choice" award.

Whether it's modeling the way, helping design the workspace, or supporting creative processes, IDEO leaders focus on inspiring employee imagination and innovation.

Work Environment

Because it understands the value of employees, IDEO pays a great deal of attention to the work environment, both physical and psychological (emotional). Nothing is out of bounds if it is for a good cause. One employee built a pulley system to suspend his bike in the air over his workspace to get it out of the way. It turned out to be such a hit that others followed his lead.

IDEO's offices look and feel like a cross between a college residence hall, a daycare playroom, and an art studio. Work areas are clustered together in different locations. Mind Maps and flipchart paper fill up walls. Old and new prototypes lie around or hang from the ceiling, providing fuel for new innovations. Magazines and unique gadgets are also in abundance throughout the workspace, providing even more fuel for ideas.

There is a method to their madness. IDEO has learned that having the right-size workspace makes a difference. Too much workspace decreases energy and slightly tight space generates energy. There are opportunities for spontaneous interactions among people. A studio system, similar to a movie studio, helps keep work groups small and flexible as the company grows. These studios are designed like little neighborhoods, having common areas where people can collaborate and private areas for solo time. They even have their own distinct personalities. Workspaces are modular and movable to accommodate changing projects, new teams, or any crazy needs that arise. Most importantly, employees have the freedom to customize their personal areas beyond simply bringing in family pictures.

When it comes to the human psyche, the environment at IDEO doesn't miss a beat. Their leadership practices reflect an environment where workers are energized, ideas flow, confidence is high, and imagination is plentiful. These practices include allowing employees to select projects of most interest to them, bringing guest speakers in regularly, providing generous amounts of food and drink for employees, and putting on interesting end-of-year work parties. There are fun project trips and spontaneous excursions to the movies. According to Scott Underwood of IDEO, such practices keep employees sharp and the environment buzzing with energy.

Another important aspect of IDEO's creative work environment is the presence of teams. According to General Manager Tom Kelley, "Teams are the heart of the IDEO method." With a strong belief against the "lone" inventor, IDEO establishes teams for all types of tasks and projects. By leveraging diverse knowledge bases, personalities, and experiences, IDEO teams generate countless breakthroughs. Teams provide the continuous, open exchange of information and ideas. In many cases employees work on multiple project teams at one time, which helps promote crossbreeding of ideas. It is also common and welcome for people outside a project team to spontaneously drop by and offer ideas during a brainstorming session.

Processes

Over the last 20 years, IDEO has developed a new five-step product development process that harnesses the collective imagination of project teams. Not only is the process repeatable, it also complements and strengthens their culture. The five-step process used during most new product development projects is **Understand, Observe, Visualize, Evaluate and Refine,** and **Implement.**

- **Understand.** When taking on a project, IDEO employees try to understand all of its aspects. This may include such things as the market, the client, and any possible constraints.
- **Observe.** IDEO invests much time and energy into understanding consumer needs and wants. Conducting real-world observations provides a great deal more insight beyond the typical interview process. For example, observing mountain bikers in action inspired a water bottle that keeps mud out of a rider's mouth.
- **Visualize.** This step is the most brainstorming-intensive. It includes the generation of many ideas or concepts, some rough prototyping, and, in some cases, even storyboard-illustrated scenarios.
- **Evaluate and Refine.** Supporting one of their company's mottoes, "Fail often to succeed sooner," this step is essential for developing well-thought-out innovations. Clients, consumers, and other IDEOers evaluate and refine some of the key prototyped concepts.
- **Implement.** Moving ideas from concept to commercialization is typically the longest step in the process. Implementation is one of the most rewarding steps for IDEO employees because it validates the whole process of turning ideas into reality and developing innovations.

Brainstorming is a mini-process with a significant influence on the IDEO culture. According to General Manager Tom Kelley, brainstorming is a crucial activity at IDEO. Although brainstorming sessions are loose, freewheeling thinking sessions at IDEO, they are also taken seriously. Rules are not just posted on the walls; they are painted on in big letters. Leaders sometimes join in and always support the brainstorming sessions with all types of resources. Because brainstorming is viewed as a skill, everyone works to continuously improve how well they do it.

Although brainstorming is most evident in the Visualize step of the IDEO innovation process, it has a ripple effect throughout the company. It encourages people to collaborate and share ideas even outside of sessions. Productive brainstorming sessions fire up teams with confidence, optimism, and energy, making it one of the engines behind IDEO's culture.

What Are the Results?

Having leaders who lead by example, a work environment that frees your mind, and flexible processes that guide you down a repeatable path have established a work culture at IDEO that produces exceptional results. With thousands of successful products over a 20-year history, it is easy to find examples of innovation. Although there is not one single factor that causes this innovation, it is clear that the blending of leadership that actively facilitates creative thinking, a work environment that supports employee imagination, and a product development process that is repeatable does much to ensure ongoing innovation.

How successful has IDEO been? Since the beginning, it has never had an unprofitable quarter. Potential clients are continuously knocking on their door and many are turned away for lack of time. The turnover ratio for key employees is less than 5%. IDEO has played key roles in the creation of many well-known innovations including the first consumer computer mouse, the Aerobe football, and the Palm V. Their products, such as the ForeRunner portable heart defibrillator, have saved lives.

As IDEO continues to be recognized for its accomplishments, winning awards, gracing the cover of popular magazines, and, of course, being featured on primetime television, its reputation and creative legacy grow. The creative climate and commensurate culture are powerful examples of the bottom-line effectiveness of creativity and leadership working together.

NOTE

1. Sources include: Ekvall, 1997; IDEO, n.d.; Kelley and Littman, 2001; Tom Peters Company, 2000, 2001; Scott Underwood, personal communication, August 5, 2004.

References

Alsop, R. (2001, April 30). The winner is . . . Dartmouth's Tuck School. *The Wall Street Journal*, pp. R4–R5.

Alsop, R. (2002, September 9). Still the one—Dartmouth's Tuck School once again won top honors in our survey. But it was the exception to this year's rule: The biggest did better. *The Wall Street Journal*, pp. R4–R5.

Alsop, R. (2003, September 17). A new winner—Wharton jumped to the top of our third annual survey of business schools, from fifth place last year. And that wasn't the only surprise. *The Wall Street Journal*, pp. R1, R4.

Amabile, T. M. (1987). The motivation to be creative. In S. G. Isaksen (Ed.), *Frontiers of creativity research: Beyond the basics* (pp. 223–254). Buffalo, NY: Bearly Limited.

Amabile, T. M., Burnside, R. M., & Gryskiewicz, S. S. (1999). *User's manual for KEYS: Assessing the climate for creativity.* Greensboro, NC: Center for Creative Leadership.

Amabile, T. M., Constance, N. H., & Steven, J. K. (2002). *Creativity under the gun.* Boulder, CO: Westview Press.

Amabile, T. M., & Conti, R. (1999). Changes in the work environment for creativity during downsizing. *Academy of Management Journal, 42,* 630–640.

Amabile, T. M., & Gryskiewicz, N. D. (1989). The creative environment scales: Work environment inventory. *Creativity Research Journal, 2,* 231–253.

Avolio, B. J. (1999). *Full leadership development: Building the vital forces in organizations.* Thousand Oaks, CA: Sage.

Barbero-Switalski, L. (2003). *Evaluating and organizing thinking tools in relationship to the CPS framework.* Unpublished master's project, State University of New York, Buffalo.

Barsade, S., & Gibson, D. E. (1998). Group emotion: A view from the top and bottom. In M. A. Neale, E. A. Mannix, & D. H. Gruenfeld (Eds.), *Research in managing groups and teams* (pp. 81–102). Greenwich, CT: JAI Press.

Bartel, C., & Saavedra, R. (2000). The collective construction of workgroup moods. *Administrative Science Quarterly, 45,* 187–231.

Basadur, M. (1994). *Simplex®: A flight to creativity.* Buffalo, NY: Creative Education Foundation.

Basadur, M., Graen, G. B., & Green, S. G. (1982). Training in creative problem solving: Effects on ideation and problem finding and solving in an industrial research organization. *Organizational Behavior and Human Performance, 30,* 41–70.

Basadur, M., Graen, G. B., & Scandura, T. A. (1986). Training effects on attitudes toward divergent thinking among manufacturing engineers. *Journal of Applied Psychology, 71,* 612–617.

Basadur M., Graen, G. B., & Wakayabashi, M. (1990). Identifying individual differences in creative problem solving style. *The Journal of Creative Behavior, 24,* 111–131.

Basadur, M., & Head, M. (2001). Team performance and satisfaction: A link to cognitive style within a process framework. *The Journal of Creative Behavior, 35,* 227–248.

Basadur, M., Pringle, P., & Kirkland, D. (2002). Crossing cultures: Training effects on the divergent thinking attitudes of Spanish-speaking South American managers. *Creativity Research Journal, 14,* 395–408.

Basadur, M., Pringle, P., Speranzini, G., & Bacot, M. (2000). Collaborative problem solving through creativity in problem definition: Expanding the pie. *Creativity and Innovation Management, 9,* 54–76.

Basadur, M., Wakabayashi, M., & Graen, G. B. (1990). Individual problem-solving styles and attitudes toward divergent thinking before and after training. *Creativity Research Journal, 3,* 22–32.

Basadur, M., Wakabayashi, M., & Takai, J. (1992). Training effects on the divergent thinking attitudes of Japanese managers. *International Journal of Intercultural Relations, 16,* 329–345.

Bass, B. M. (1985). *Leadership and performance beyond expectations.* New York: Free Press.

Bass, B. M. (1990). *Bass & Stogdill's handbook of leadership: Theory, research, and managerial application* (3rd ed.). New York: Free Press.

Bass, B. M. (1998). *Transformational leadership: Industrial, military, and educational impact.* Mahwah, NJ: Lawrence Erlbaum Associates.

Bastedo, M., & Davis, A. (1993, December). *God, what a blunder: The New Coke story.* Retrieved August 26, 2004, from http://members.lycos.co.uk/thomassheils/newcoke.htm

Bateson, M. C. (2004). *Willing to learn.* Hanover, NH: Steerforth.

BBC News. (2000, April 20). *Athens Olympics in jeopardy.* Retrieved October 31, 2004, from http://news.bbc.co.uk/1/hi/sport/720631.stm

BBC Sport. (2004, February 28). *Athens told to hurry up.* Retrieved October 31, 2004, from http://news.bbc.co.uk/sport1/low/olympics_2004/3495284.stm

Bennis, W., & Nanus, B. (1985). *Leaders: Strategies for taking charge.* New York: Harper & Row.

Block, P. (1987). *The empowered manager: Positive political skills at work.* San Francisco: Jossey-Bass.

Bloom, B. S., Englehart, M. D., Furst, E. J., Hill, W. H., & Krathwohl, D. R. (Eds.). (1956). *Taxonomy of educational objectives: The classification of educational goals. Handbook I: Cognitive domain.* New York: David McKay.

Bradley, J. (2003). *Flyboys: A true story of courage.* Boston: Little, Brown and Company.

Breen, B. (2004, December). The 6 myths of creativity. *Fast Company: The Creativity Issue,* 75–78.

Brown, E. (1999, April 12). A day at Innovation U. *Fortune, 139*(7), 163–165.

Burnside, R. M., Amabile, T. M., & Gryskiewicz, S. S. (1988). Assessing organizational climates for creativity and innovation: Methodological review of large company audits. In Y. Ijiri & R. L. Kuhn (Eds.), *New directions in creative and innovative management* (pp. 169–185). Cambridge, MA: Ballinger.

Butler, B. H. (2002, September). *Learning domains or Bloom's Taxonomy adapted for public garden educational programs. Starting right: Project planning and team building in informal learning.* AABGA professional development workshop.

Cambou, D. (Executive Producer), & Hill, B. (Writer, Producer). (2000). Drive-thru [Television series episode]. In B. Deitrich-Segarra (Executive Producer), *Modern marvels.* New York: The History Channel.

Camper, E. (1993, April 2). *The honey pot lesson in creativity and diversity.* Retrieved August 12, 2005, from http://www.insulators.com/articles/ppl.htm

Carnegie, A. (1905). *James Watt.* New York: Doubleday, Page & Company.

Carnevale, A. P., Gainer, L. J., & Meltzer, A. S. (1990). *Workplace basics: The essential skills employers want.* San Francisco: Jossey-Bass.

Cattell, J. M. (1906). A study of American men of science. II. The measurement of scientific merit. *Science, 24,* 699–707.

Chan, N. M. (2004). *An examination of the interplay of knowledge types, knowledge workers and knowledge creation in knowledge management.* Unpublished doctoral dissertation, University of Hong Kong, Hong Kong, China.

Cohen, J. (1971). *Thinking.* Chicago: Rand McNally.

Collins, J. (2001). *Good to great: Why some companies make the leap . . . and others don't.* New York: HarperBusiness.

Collins, J. C., & Porras, J. I. (1994). *Built to last: Successful habits of visionary companies.* New York: HarperBusiness.

Conner, D. R. (1992). *Managing at the speed of change: How resilient managers succeed and prosper where others fail.* New York: Villard Books.

Costa, A. L. (Ed.). (2001). *Developing minds: A resource book for teaching thinking.* Alexandria, VA: Association for Supervision and Curriculum Development.

Cox, C. M. (1926). *Genetic studies of genius, Volume II. The early mental traits of three hundred geniuses.* Stanford, CA: Stanford University Press.

Csikszentmihalyi, M. (2001). The context for creativity. In W. Bennis, G. M. Spreitzer, & T. G. Cummings (Eds.), *The future of leadership: Today's top leadership thinkers speak to tomorrow's leaders* (pp. 116–124). San Francisco: Jossey-Bass.

Csikszentmihalyi, M., & Getzels, J. W. (1971). Discovery-oriented behavior and the originality of creative production. *Journal of Personality and Social Psychology, 19,* 47–52.

Davis, G. A. (1986). *Creativity is forever* (2nd ed.). Dubuque, IA: Kendall-Hunt.

De Dreu, C. K. W., & West, M. A. (2001). Minority dissent and team innovation: The importance of participation in decision making. *Journal of Applied Psychology, 86,* 1191–1201.

De Pree, M. (1989). *Leadership is an art.* New York: Doubleday.

Deutschman, A. (2004, December). The fabric of creativity. *Fast Company: The Creativity Issue,* 55–62.

Dewey, J. (1933). *How we think: A restatement of the relation of reflective thinking to the education process.* Lexington, MA: Heath & Co.

Diehl, M., & Stroebe, W. (1987). Productivity loss in brainstorming groups: Toward the solution of a riddle. *Journal of Personality and Social Psychology, 53,* 497–509.

Diehl, M., & Stroebe, W. (1991). Productivity loss in idea-generating groups: Tracking down the blocking effect. *Journal of Personality and Social Psychology, 61,* 392–403.

Dillon, J. T. (1982). Problem finding and solving. *The Journal of Creative Behavior, 16,* 97–111.

Downton, J. V. (1973). *Rebel leadership: Commitment and charisma in a revolutionary process.* New York: Free Press.

Ekvall, G. (1983). *Climate, structure and innovativeness in organizations: A theoretical framework and an experiment.* Report 1. Stockholm: Faradet.

Ekvall, G. (1987). The climate metaphor in organizational theory. In B. M. Bass & P. J. Drenth (Eds.), *Advances in organizational psychology* (pp. 177–190). Newbury Park, CA: Sage.

Ekvall, G. (1991). The organizational culture of idea management: A creative climate for the management of ideas. In J. Henry & D. Walker (Eds.), *Managing innovation* (pp. 73–79). Newbury Park, CA: Sage.

Ekvall, G. (1996). Organizational climate for creativity and innovation. *European Journal of Work and Organizational Psychology, 5,* 105–123.

Ekvall, G. (1997). Innovations in organizations. *European Journal of Work and Organizational Psychology, 5*(1), 105–123.

Ekvall, G. (1999). Creative climate. In M. A. Runco & S. R. Pritzker (Eds.), *Encyclopedia of creativity* (Vol. I, pp. 403–412). San Diego, CA: Academic Press.

Ekvall, G., & Arvonen, J. (1984). *Leadership styles and organizational climate for creativity: Some findings in one company.* Stockholm: Faradet.

Ekvall, G., Arvonen, J., & Waldenstrom-Lindblad, I. (1983). *Creative organizational climate: Construction and validation of a measuring instrument.* Report 2. Stockholm: Faradet.

Ellis, H. (1904). *A study of British genius.* London: Hurst & Blackett.

Fagerhaug, T., & Anderson, B. (Eds.). (1999). *Root cause analysis: Simplified tools and techniques.* Milwaukee, WI: American Society for Quality Press.

Firestien, R. L. (1996). *Leading on the creative edge: Gaining competitive advantage through the power of creative problem solving.* Colorado Springs, CO: Pinon Press.

Firestien, R. L., & McCowan, R. J. (1988). Creative problem solving and communication behaviors in small groups. *Creativity Research Journal, 1,* 106–114.

Flavell, J. H. (1976). Metacognitive aspects of problem solving. In L. B. Resnick (Ed.), *The nature of intelligence* (pp. 231–296). Hillsdale, NJ: Erlbaum.

Florida, R. (2002). *The rise of the creative class . . . and how it's transforming work, leisure, community, & everyday life.* New York: Basic Books.

Flynn, J., Zellner, W., Light, L., & Weber, J. (1998, October 26). Then came Branson. *BusinessWeek Online.* Retrieved October 14, 2005, from http:www.businessweek.com/1998/43/b3601013.htm

Fontenot, N. A. (1993). Effects of training in creativity and creative problem finding upon business people. *Journal of Social Psychology, 133,* 11–22.

Forsha, H. I. (1995). *Show me: The complete guide to storyboarding and problem solving.* Milwaukee, WI: ASQC Quality Press.

Foxall, G. R., & Bhate, S. (1993). Cognitive styles and personal involvement of market initiators. *Journal of Economic Psychology, 14,* 33–56.

Friedman, T. L. (2004). *The world is flat: A brief history of the twenty-first century.* New York: Farrar, Stratus and Giroux.

Fritz, R. (1991). *Creating: A guide to the creative process.* New York: Fawcett Columbine.

Fullan, M. (2001). *Leading in a culture of change.* San Francisco: Jossey-Bass.

Galton, F. (1869). *Hereditary genius.* London: MacMillan.

Gardner, H. (1993). *Creating minds: An anatomy of creativity seen through the lives of Freud, Picasso, Stravinsky, Eliot, Graham, and Gandhi.* New York: BasicBooks.

Gardner, J. W. (1990). *On leadership.* New York: The Free Press.

Getzels, J. W. (1975). Problem finding and the inventiveness of solutions. *The Journal of Creative Behavior, 9,* 12–18.

Getzels, J. W., & Csikszentmihalyi, M. (1976). *The creative vision: A longitudinal study of problem finding in art.* New York: Wiley.

Goertz, J. (2000). Creativity: An essential component for effective leadership in today's schools. *Roeper Review, 22,* 158–162.

Goldenberg, J., & Mazursky, D. (2002). *Creativity in product innovation.* Cambridge, UK: Cambridge University Press.

Goldsmith, R. E. (1986). Personality and adaptive-innovative problem solving. *Journal of Personality and Social Behaviour, 1,* 95–106.

Goldsmith, R. E. (1994). Creative style and personality theory. In M. J. Kirton (Ed.), *Adaptors and innovators: Styles of creativity and problem solving* (Rev. ed.) (pp. 34–50). London: Routledge.

Goleman, D. (1998). *Working with emotional intelligence.* New York: Bantam.

Goleman, D. (2000, March-April). Leadership that gets results. *Harvard Business Review,* 78–90.

Goleman, D., Boyatzis, R., & McKee, A. (2002) *Primal leadership*. Boston: Harvard Business School Press.

González, D. W. (2002). *When we peek behind the curtain: Highlighting the essence of creativity methodologies*. Evanston, IL: THinc Communications.

González, M. (2003). *Implicit theories of creativity across cultures*. Unpublished master's thesis, State University of New York, Buffalo.

Goodwin, W. (2004, September 13). American seeks to weather airline dip [Radio broadcast]. *All things considered*. Washington, DC: National Public Radio.

Gordon, T. (1976). *Teacher effectiveness training instructor guide*. Solana Beach, CA: Gordon Training International.

Gordon, W. J. J. (1961). *Synectics*. New York: Harper & Row.

Gordon, W. J. J. (1980). *The new art of the possible: The basic course in Synectics*. Cambridge, MA: Porpoise Books.

The Great Idea Finder. (n.d.). *Fascinating facts about the invention of the microwave oven by Percy Spencer in 1945*. Retrieved July 13, 2004, from http://www.ideafinder.com/history/inventions/story068.htm

Guilford, J. P. (1968). Creativity, yesterday, today, and tomorrow. *The Journal of Creative Behavior, 1*, 3–14.

Guilford, J. P. (1977). *Way beyond the IQ: Guide to improving intelligence and creativity*. Buffalo, NY: Creative Education Foundation.

Guzzo, R., & Palmer, S. (1998, April). Group decision process and effectiveness in executive selection. Paper presented in J. J. Deal and V. I. Sessa's symposium *Choices at the Top: Learnings and Teachings on Selecting Executives*, at the thirteenth annual meeting of the Society of Industrial and Organizational Psychologists, Dallas, TX.

Hammerschmidt, P. K. (1996). The Kirton Adaption-Innovation Inventory and group problem solving success rates. *The Journal of Creative Behavior, 30*, 61–74.

Handy, C. (1993). *Understanding organizations: How the way organizations actually work can be used to manage them better*. New York: Oxford University Press.

Hayakawa, S. I. (1979). *Language in thought and action* (4th ed.). New York: Harcourt Brace Jovanovich.

Henry, J. (2001). *Creativity and perception in management*. London: Sage.

Hesselbein, F., Goldsmith, M., & Beckhard, R. (Eds.). (1996). *The leader of the future: New visions, strategies, and practices for the next era*. San Francisco: Jossey-Bass.

Higgins, J. (1994). *101 creative problem solving techniques*. Winter Park, FL: New Management.

Houtz, J. C., Selby, E., Esquivel, G. B., Okoye, R. A., Peters, K. M., & Treffinger, D. J. (2003). Comparison of two creativity style measures. *Perceptual & Motor Skills, 96*, 288–296.

IDEO. (n.d.). Retrieved September, 2004, from http://www.ideo.com

International LearningWorks. (1996). *High impact facilitation: Modeling videotape*. Durango, CO: Author.

Isaksen, S. G., Dorval, K. B., & Treffinger, D. J. (1994). *Creative approaches to problem solving*. Dubuque, IA: Kendall/Hunt.

Isaksen, S. G., Dorval, K. B., & Treffinger, D. J. (2000). *Creative problem solving: A framework for change* (2nd ed.). Dubuque, IA: Kendall-Hunt.

Isaksen, S. G., & Lauer, K. J. (2002). The climate for creativity and change in teams. *Creativity and Innovation Management, 11,* 74–86.

Isaksen, S. G., & Puccio, G. J. (1988). Adaption-innovation and the Torrance Tests of Creative Thinking: The level-style issue revisited. *Psychological Reports, 63,* 659–670.

Isaksen, S. G., & Treffinger, D. J. (1985). *Creative problem solving: The basic course.* Buffalo, NY: Bearly Limited.

Isaksen, S. G., & Treffinger, D. J. (2004). Celebrating 50 years of reflective practice: Versions of creative problem solving. *The Journal of Creative Behavior, 38,* 75–101.

Isen, A. M. (1999). Positive affect. In T. Dalgleish & M. J. Power (Eds.), *Handbook of cognition and emotion* (pp. 521–539). Chichester, UK: Wiley.

Ishikawa, K. (1985). *What is total quality control? The Japanese way* (D. Lu, Trans.). Englewood Cliffs, NJ: Prentice-Hall.

i Six Sigma. (n.d.). Retrieved January 17, 2006, from http://www.iSixSigma .com

Janszen, F. (2000). *The age of innovation: Making business creativity a competence, not a coincidence.* London: Prentice Hall.

Jardine, L. (1999). *Ingenious pursuits.* New York: Doubleday.

Jay, E., & Perkins, D. (1997). Problem finding: The search for mechanisms. In M. A. Runco (Ed.), *Creativity research handbook* (Vol. 1, pp. 257–293). Creskill, NJ: Hampton.

Jeffrey, L. R. (1989). Writing and rewriting poetry: William Wordsworth. In D. B. Wallace & H. E. Gruber (Eds.), *Creative people at work* (pp. 69–89). New York: Oxford University Press.

Johansson, F. (2004). *The Medici effect: Breakthrough insights at the intersection of ideas, concepts and cultures.* Boston, MA: Harvard Business Press.

Johnson, D. M., & Jennings, J. W. (1963). Serial analysis of three problem solving processes. *Journal of Psychology, 56,* 43–52.

Kabanoff, B., & Bottger, P. (1991). Effectiveness of creativity training and its relation to selected personality factors. *Journal of Organizational Behavior, 12,* 235–248.

Kahan, S. (2002, April). Visionary leadership. *Executive Update, 42,* 45–47.

Kaplan, P. J. (2002). *F'd companies: Spectacular dot-com flameouts.* New York: Simon & Schuster.

Karp, H. B. (1996). *The change leader: Using a gestalt approach with work groups.* San Diego, CA: Pfeiffer.

Kaufmann, G. (1988). Problem solving and creativity. In K. Grønhaug & G. Kaufmann (Eds.), *Innovation: A cross-disciplinary perspective* (pp. 87–137). Oslo, Norway: Norwegian University Press.

Kelley, T., & Littman, J. (2001). *The art of innovation: Lessons in creativity from IDEO, America's leading design firm.* New York: Currency.

Kelner, S. P., Rivers, C. A., & O'Connell, K. H. (1996). *Managerial style as a predictor of organizational climate.* Boston: McBer & Company.

King, B., & Schlicksupp, H. (1998). *The idea edge: Transforming creative thought into organizational excellence.* Methuen, MA: GOAL/QPC.

Kirton, M. J. (1961). *Management initiatives.* London: Acton Society Trust.

Kirton, M. J. (1976). Adaptors and innovators: A description and measure. *Journal of Applied Psychology, 61,* 622–629.

Kirton, M. J. (1994). *Adaptors and innovators: Styles of creativity and problem solving* (Rev. ed.). London: Routledge.

Kirton, M. J. (1999). *Kirton Adaption-Innovation Inventory Manual* (3rd ed.). Berkhamsted, UK: Occupational Research Centre.

Koestler, A. (1964). *The act of creation.* New York: Macmillan.

Korzybski, A. (1933). *Science of sanity: An introduction to non-Aristotelian systems and general semantics.* Lakeville, CT: International Non-Aristotelian Library.

Kotter, J. P. (1990). *A force for change: How leadership differs from management.* Boston: Harvard Business School Press.

Kotter, J. (1996). *Leading change.* Boston: Harvard Business School Press.

Kouzes, J. M., & Posner, B. Z. (1995). *The leadership challenge: How to keep getting extraordinary things done in organizations.* San Francisco: Jossey-Bass.

Kouzes, J. M., & Posner, B. Z. (2002). *The leadership challenge* (3rd ed.). San Francisco: Jossey-Bass.

Kramer, T. J., Fleming, G. P., & Mannis, S. M. (2001). Improving face-to-face brainstorming through modeling and facilitation. *Small Group Research, 32,* 533–557.

Krathwohl, D. R., Bloom, B. S., & Masia B. B. (1964). *Taxonomy of educational objectives: The classification of educational goals. Handbook II: Affective domain.* New York: David McKay Co., Inc.

Kubes, M., & Spillerová, D. (1992). The effects of personality characteristics on communication patterns in R&D teams. *Creativity and Innovation Management, 1,* 33–44.

Kuhn, R. L. (Ed.). (1988). *Handbook for creative and innovative managers.* New York: McGraw-Hill.

Lapierre, J., & Giroux, V. P. (2003). Creativity and work environment in a high-tech context. *Creativity and Innovation Management, 12,* 11–23.

Larkin, D. I. (1998). *John D. Larkin: A business pioneer.* Chelsea, MI: BookCrafters.

Lauer, K. J. (1994). *The assessment of creative climate: An investigation of the Ekvall Creative Climate Questionnaire.* Unpublished master's thesis, Buffalo State College, Buffalo, NY.

Loden, M., & Rosener, J. B. (1991). *Workforce America! Managing employee diversity as a vital resource.* New York: McGraw-Hill.

MacKinnon, D. W. (1978). *In search of human effectiveness.* Buffalo, NY: Creative Education Foundation.

Majaro, S. (1991). *The creative marketer.* Oxford: Butterworth-Heinemann.

Marzano, R. J., Brandt, R. S., Hughes, C. S., Jones, B. F., Presseisen, B. Z., Rankin, S. C., et al. (1988). *Dimensions of thinking: A framework for curriculum.* Alexandria, VA: Association for Supervision and Curriculum Development.

Maslow, A. H. (1954). *Motivation and personality.* New York: Harper & Row.

Mason, R. O., & Mitroff, I. L. (1981). *Challenging strategic planning assumptions: Theory, cases and techniques.* New York: Wiley.

Meadow, A., & Parnes, S. J. (1959). Evaluation of training in creative problem solving. *Journal of Applied Psychology, 43,* 189–194.

Meadow, A., Parnes, S. J., & Reese, H. W. (1959). Influence of brainstorming instructions and problem sequence on a creative problem-solving test. *Journal of Applied Psychology, 43,* 413–416.

Michalko, M. (1991). *Thinkertoys: A handbook of business creativity for the 90s.* Berkeley, CA: Ten Speed Press.

Miller, B., Vehar, J. R., & Firestien, R. L. (2001). *Creativity unbound* (3rd ed.). Evanston, IL: THinc Communications.

Mintzberg, H., Duru, R., & Theoret, A. (1976). The structure of unstructured decision processes. *Administrative Science Quarterly, 21,* 246–247.

Morrisey, G. L. (1996). *Morrisey on planning: A guide to strategic thinking.* San Francisco: Jossey-Bass.

Mullen, B., Johnson, C., & Salas, E. (1991). Productivity loss in brainstorming groups: A meta-analytic integration. *Basic and Applied Social Psychology, 12,* 3–23.

Mumford, M. D., Zaccaro, S. J., Harding, F. D., Jacobs, T. O., & Fleishman, E. A. (2000). Leadership skills for a changing world: Solving complex problems. *Leadership Quarterly, 11,* 11–35.

Munitz, B. (1988). Creative management demands creative leadership. In R. L. Kuhn (Ed.), *Handbook for creative and innovative managers* (pp. 487–493). New York: McGraw-Hill.

Murdock, M. C., Isaksen, S. G., & Lauer, K. J. (1993). Creativity training and the stability and internal consistency of the Kirton Adaption-Innovation Inventory. *Psychological Reports, 72,* 1123–1130.

Myers, I., McCaulley, M. H., Quenk, N. L., & Hammer, A. L. (2003). *Manual: A guide to the development and use of the Myers-Briggs Type Indicator* (3rd ed.). Palo Alto, CA: Consulting Psychologists Press.

Nelson, B. (2003, April 4). Tap into employees to get good ideas. *Managernewz.* Retrieved February 11, 2006, from http://www.managernewz.com/archive-21-200304.html

Nierenberg, G. I. (1996). *The art of creative thinking.* New York: Barnes & Noble Books.

Noller, R. B., & Parnes, S. J. (1972). Applied creativity: The creative studies project: Part III—The curriculum. *The Journal of Creative Behavior, 6,* 275–294.

Noller, R. B., Parnes, S. J., & Biondi, A. M. (1976). *Creative action book.* New York: Scribner's Sons.

Northouse, P. G. (2004). *Leadership: Theory and practice* (3rd ed.). Thousand Oaks, CA: Sage.

Nussbaum, B., Berner, B., & Brady, D. (2005, August 1). Get creative. *Business Week.* Retrieved February 7, 2006, from http://www.businessweek.com/magazine/content/05_31/b3945401.htm

Offner, A. K., Kramer, T. J., & Winter, J. P. (1996). The effects of facilitation, recording and pauses upon group brainstorming. *Small Group Research, 27,* 283–298.

Oldach, M. (1995). *Creativity for graphic designers.* Cincinnati, OH: North Light Books.

Osborn, A. F. (1953). *Applied imagination: Principles and procedures of creative problem-solving.* New York: Scribner.

Osborn, A. F. (1957). *Applied imagination: Principles and procedures of creative problem-solving* (2nd ed.). New York: Scribner.

Osborn, A. F. (1963). *Applied imagination: Principles and procedures of creative problem-solving* (3rd ed.). New York: Scribner.

Oxley, N. L., Dzindolet, M. T., & Paulus, P. B. (1996). The effects of facilitators on the performance of brainstorming groups. *Journal of Social Behavior and Personality, 11,* 663–646.

Palus, C. J., & Horth, D. M. (2002). *The leader's edge: Six creative competencies for navigating complex challenges.* San Francisco: Jossey-Bass & Center for Creative Leadership.

Parnes, S. J. (1961). Effects of extended effort in creative problem solving. *Journal of Educational Psychology, 52,* 117–122.

Parnes, S. J. (1967). *Guidebook to creative behavior.* New York: Charles Scribner.

Parnes, S. J. (1981). *The magic of your mind.* Buffalo, NY: The Creative Education Foundation.

Parnes, S. J. (1987). The creative studies project. In S. G. Isaksen (Ed.), *Frontiers of creativity: Beyond the basics* (pp. 156–188). Buffalo, NY: Bearly Limited.

Parnes, S. J. (2004). *Visionizing: Innovating your opportunities* (2nd ed.). Amherst, MA: Creative Education Foundation.

Parnes, S. J., & Meadow, A. (1959). Effects of brainstorming instruction on creative problem solving by trained and untrained subjects. *Journal of Educational Psychology, 50,* 171–176.

Parnes, S. J., & Meadow, A. (1960). Evaluation of persistence of effects produced by a creative problem solving course. *Psychological Reports, 7,* 357–361.

Parnes, S. J., & Noller, R. B. (1972a). Applied creativity: The creative studies project: Part I—The Development. *The Journal of Creative Behavior, 6,* 11–22.

Parnes, S. J., & Noller, R. B. (1972b). Applied creativity: The creative studies project: Part II—Results of the two-year program. *The Journal of Creative Behavior, 6,* 164–186.

Parnes, S. J., & Noller, R. B. (1973). Applied creativity: The creative studies project: Part IV–Personality findings and conclusions. *The Journal of Creative Behavior, 7,* 15–36.

PBS. (n.d.). *American experience: D-Day.* Retrieved November 5, 2004, from http://www.pbs.org/wgbh/amex/dday/sfeature/sf_info.html

Peebles-Fish, L. (2003). *Creating an educational vocabulary to observe creative classroom climates.* Unpublished master's project, Buffalo State College, Buffalo, NY.

Pinker, K. D. (2002). *The effects of a master of science in creative studies on graduates.* Unpublished master's thesis, Buffalo State College, Buffalo, NY.

Powell, A., & Koon, J. (n.d.). *United States laws.* Retrieved January 24, 2002, from http://www.dumblaws.com

Prato Previde, G., & Carli, M. (1987). Adaption-innovation typology and right-left hemispheric preferences. *Journal of Personality and Individual Differences, 8,* 681–686.

Presseisen, B. Z. (2001). Thinking skills: Meanings and models revisited. In A. L. Costa (Ed.), *Developing minds: A resource book for teaching thinking* (pp. 47–57). Alexandria, VA: Association for Supervision and Curriculum Development.

Puccio, G. J. (1990a). [Person-environment fit interview data]. Unpublished raw data.

Puccio, G. J. (1990b). *Person-environment fit and its effect on creative performance, job satisfaction, and stress.* Unpublished doctoral dissertation, University of Manchester, Manchester, UK.

Puccio, G. J. (1999). Creative problem solving preferences: Their identification and implications. *Creativity and Innovation Management, 8,* 171–178.

Puccio, G. J. (2002). *FourSight: The breakthrough thinking profile—Presenter's guide and technical manual.* Evanston, IL: THinc Communications (available at www.foursightonline.com).

Puccio, G. J., & Chimento, M. (2001). Implicit theories of creativity: Laypersons' perceptions of the creativity of adaptors and innovators. *Perceptual and Motor Skills, 92,* 675–681.

Puccio, G. J., Firestien, R. L., Coyle, C., & Masucci, C. (2006). A review of the effectiveness of Creative Problem Solving training: A focus on workplace issues. *Creativity and Innovation Management, 15,* 19–33.

Puccio, G. J., Joniak, A. J., & Talbot, R. (1995). Person-environment fit: Examining the use of commensurate scales. *Psychological Reports, 76,* 457–468.

Puccio, G. J., & Murdock, M. C. (2001). Creative thinking: An essential life skill. In A. Costa (Ed.), *Developing minds: A source book for teaching thinking* (pp. 67–71). Alexandria, VA: ASCD.

Puccio, G. J., Murdock, M. C., & Mance, M. (2005). Current developments in creative problem solving for organizations: A focus on thinking skills and styles. *The Korean Journal of Thinking & Problem Solving, 15,* 43–76.

Puccio, G. J., Talbot, R. J., & Joniak, A. J. (2000). Examining creative performance in the workplace through a person-environment fit model. *The Journal of Creative Behavior, 34,* 227–247.

Puccio, G. J., Treffinger, D. J., & Talbot, R. J. (1995). Exploratory examination of relationships between creativity styles and creative products. *Creativity Research Journal, 8,* 25–40.

Puccio, G. J., Wheeler, R. A., & Cassandro, V. J. (2004). Reactions to creative problem solving training: Does cognitive style make a difference? *The Journal of Creative Behavior, 38,* 192–216.

Ramos, S. (2005). *Cross-cultural studies of implicit theories of creativity: A comparative analysis between the United States and the main ethnic groups in Singapore.* Unpublished master's thesis, State University of New York, Buffalo, NY.

Reese, H. W., Parnes, S. J., Treffinger, D. J., & Kaltsounis, G. (1976). Effects of a creative studies program on structure-of-the-intellect factors. *Journal of Educational Psychology, 68,* 401–410.

Rhodes, M. (1961). An analysis of creativity. *Phi Delta Kappan, 42,* 305–310.

Rickards, T., & Bessant, J. (1980). The creativity audit: Introduction of a new research measure during programmes for facilitating organizational change. *R&D Management, 10,* 67–75.

Rife, S. L. (2001). *Exploring the personality composition of the four preferences measured by the Buffalo Creative Process Inventory.* Unpublished master's thesis, State University of New York, Buffalo, NY.

Rose, L. H., & Lin, H. T. (1984). A meta-analysis of long-term creativity training programs. *The Journal of Creative Behavior, 18,* 11–22.

Ruggiero, V. R. (1998). *The art of thinking: A guide to critical and creative thought* (5th ed.). New York: Longman.

Runco, M. A. (Ed.). (1994a). *Problem finding, problem solving, and creativity.* Norwood, NJ: Ablex.

Runco, M. A. (1994b). Conclusions concerning problem finding, problem solving, and creativity. In M. A. Runco (Ed.), *Problem finding, problem solving, and creativity* (pp. 271–290). Norwood, NJ: Ablex.

Runco, M. A., & Dow, G. (1999). Problem finding. In M. A. Runco & S. R. Pritzker (Eds.), *Encyclopedia of creativity* (Vol. 2, pp. 433–435). New York: Academic Press.

Schein, E. H. (1985). *Organizational culture and leadership.* San Francisco: Jossey-Bass.

Schneider, B. (1990). *Organizational climate and culture.* San Francisco: Jossey-Bass.

Schroder, H. M. (1994). Managerial competence and style. In M. J. Kirton (Ed.), *Adaptors and innovators: Styles of creativity and problem solving* (Rev. ed.). London: Routledge.

Schwarz, R. M. (1994). *The skilled facilitator: Practical wisdom for developing effective groups.* San Francisco: Jossey-Bass.

Scott, G. M., Leritz, L. E., & Mumford, M. D. (2004a). The effectiveness of creativity training: A meta-analysis. *Creativity Research Journal, 16,* 361–388.

Scott, G. M., Leritz, L. E., & Mumford, M. D. (2004b). Types of creativity training: Approaches and their effectiveness. *The Journal of Creative Behavior, 38,* 149–179.

Senge, P. M., Kleiner, A., Roberts, C., Ross, R., Roth, G., & Smith, B. (1999). *The dance of change: The challenge of stustaining momentum in learning organizations.* New York: Doubleday.

Sheen, F. J. (1997). *The way to happiness*. Edinburgh, Scotland: Alba House.

Siegel, S. M., & Kaemmerer, W. F. (1978). Measuring the perceived support for innovation in organizations. *Journal of Applied Psychology, 63*, 553–562.

Simon, H. A. (1965). *The shape of automation*. New York: Harper & Row.

Simon, H. A. (1977). *The new science of management decisions*. Englewood Cliffs, NJ: Prentice-Hall.

Simonton, D. K. (1977). Creative productivity, age, and stress: A biographical time-series analysis of 10 classical composers. *Journal of Personality and Social Psychology, 35*, 791–804.

Simonton, D. K. (1984). *Genius, creativity and leadership*. Cambridge, MA: Harvard University Press.

Simonton, D. K. (1985). Quality, quantity, and age: The careers of 10 distinguished psychologists. *International Journal of Aging and Human Development, 21*, 241–254.

Simonton, D. K. (1987). Genius: The lessons from historiometry. In S. G. Isaksen (Ed.), *Frontiers of creativity research: Beyond the basics* (pp. 66–87). Buffalo, NY: Bearly Limited.

Simonton, D. K. (1997). Creative productivity: A predictive and explanatory model of career trajectories and landmarks. *Psychological Review, 104*, 66–89.

Simonton, D. K. (1998). Donald Campbell's model of the creative process: Creativity as bland variations and selective retention. *The Journal of Creative Behavior, 32*, 153–158.

Simonton, D. K. (1999). William Shakespeare (1564–1616): English dramatist, poet, and actor. In M. A. Runco & S. R. Pritzker (Eds.), *Encyclopedia of creativity* (Vol. 2, pp. 559–563). New York: Academic Press.

Smith, S. M., & Dodds, R. A. (1999). Incubation. In M. A. Runco & S. R. Pritzker (Eds.), *Encyclopedia of creativity* (Vol. 1, pp. 39–43). San Diego, CA: Academic Press.

Soo, C., Devinney, T., Midgley, D., & Deering, A. (2002). Knowledge management: Philosophy, processes, and pitfalls. *California Management Review, 44*, 129–150.

Sorensen, D. P. (1997). *Innovations: Key to business success*. Menlo Park, CA: Crisp Publications.

Stein, M. I. (1968). Creativity. In E. F. Boragatta & W. W. Lambert (Eds.), *Handbook of personality theory and research* (pp. 900–942). Chicago: Rand McNally.

Stein, M. I. (1974). *Stimulating creativity: Volume 1—Individual procedures*. New York: Academic Press.

Stein, M. I. (1975). *Stimulating creativity: Volume 2—Group procedures*. New York: Academic Press.

Sternberg, R. J. (1985). *Beyond IQ: A triarchic theory of human intelligence*. New York: Cambridge University Press.

Sternberg, R. J. (Ed.). (1999). *Handbook of creativity*. Cambridge, UK: Cambridge University Press.

Sternberg, R. J. (2002). Successful intelligence: A new approach to leadership. In R. E. Riggio, S. E. Murphy, & F. J. Pirozzolo (Eds.), *Multiple intelligences and leadership* (pp. 9–28). Mahwah, NJ: Lawrence Erlbaum.

Sternberg, R. J., Kaufman, J. C., & Pretz, J. E. (2004). A propulsion model of creative leadership. *Creativity and Innovation Management, 13,* 145–153.

Sternberg, R. J., & Lubart, T. I. (1992). Buy low and sell high: An investment approach to creativity. *Current Directions in Psychological Science, 1,* 1–5.

Sternberg, R. J., & Lubart, T. I. (1999). The concept of creativity: Prospects and paradigms. In R. J. Sternberg (Ed.), *Handbook of creativity* (pp. 3–15). Cambridge, UK: Cambridge University Press.

Stevens, G. A., & Burley, J. (1997, May–June). 3,000 raw ideas = 1 commercial success! *Research & Technology Management,* 16–27.

Stogdill, R. M. (1948). Personal factors associated with leadership: A survey of the literature. *Journal of Psychology, 25,* 35–71.

Sullivan, A. (2001, February). E-com's biggest mistakes. *Network World.* Retrieved July 29, 2004, from http://www.nwfusion.com/ecomm2001/mistakes/mistakes.html

Sutton, R. I. (2002). *Weird ideas that work: 11½ practices for promoting, managing, and sustaining innovation.* New York: The Free Press.

Sutton, R. I., & Hargadon, A. (1996). Brainstorming groups in context: Effectiveness in a product design firm. *Administrative Science Quarterly, 41,* 685–718.

Swartz, R. J. (1987). Teaching for thinking: A developmental model for the infusion of thinking skills into mainstream instruction. In J. B. Baron & R. J. Sternberg (Eds.), *Teaching thinking skills: Theory and practice* (pp. 107–126). New York: Freeman & Company.

Swartz, R. J. (2001). Thinking about decisions. In A. L. Costa (Ed.), *Developing minds: A resource book for teaching thinking* (3rd ed., pp. 58–66). Alexandria, VA: Association for Supervision and Curriculum Development.

Talbot, R. J. (1997). Taking style on board. *Creativity and Innovation Management, 6,* 177–184.

Tichy, N. M., & DeVanna, M. A. (1990). *The transformational leader* (2nd ed.). New York: Wiley.

Tom Peters Company. (2000). *David Kelley* [Interview]. Retrieved June 6, 2004, from www.tompeters.com/cool_friends/friends.php

Tom Peters Company. (2001). *Tom Kelley* [Interview]. Retrieved June 6, 2004, from www.tompeters.com/cool_friends/friends.php

Torrance, E. P. (1971). The courage to be creative. *Retail Credit Company Inspection News. 56*(4), 8–11.

Torrance, E. P. (1972). Can we teach children to think creatively? *The Journal of Creative Behavior, 6,* 114–143.

Torrance, E. P. (1979). *The search for satori and creativity.* Buffalo, NY: Creative Education Foundation.

Torrance, E. P. (1983). The importance of falling in love with something. *Creative Child and Adult Quarterly, 8,* 72–78.

Torrance, E. P. (1987). A climate for inventing. *Creative Child and Adult Quarterly, 12,* 230–236.

Torrance, E. P. (2004). Predicting the creativity of elementary school children (1958–80)—and the teacher who "made a difference." In D. J. Treffinger (Ed.), *Creativity and giftedness* (pp. 35–49). Thousand Oaks, CA: Corwin Press.

Torrance, E. P., & Presbury, J. (1984). The criteria of success used in 242 recent experimental studies of creativity. *The Creative Child and Adult Quarterly, 9,* 238–243.

Totterdell, P. (2000). Catching moods and hitting runs: Moods linkage and subjective performance in professional sports teams. *Journal of Applied Psychology, 85,* 848–859.

Totterdell, P., Kellett, S., Teuchmann, K., & Briner, R. B. (1998). Nurses and accountants tracking moods. *Journal of Personality and Social Psychology, 74,* 1504–1515.

Treffinger, D. J. (1992). Searching for success zones. *International Creativity Network, 2,* pp. 1–2, 7.

Treffinger, D. J., Isaksen, S. G., & Firestien, R. L. (1982). *Handbook of creative learning, Volume 1.* Williamsville, NY: Center for Creative Learning.

Turnipseed, D. (1994). The relationship between the social environment of organizations and the climate for innovation and creativity. *Creativity and Innovation Management, 3,* 184–195.

Van Gundy, A. (1987). Organizational creativity and innovation. In S. G. Isaksen (Ed.), *Frontiers of creativity research: Beyond the basics* (pp. 358–379). Buffalo, NY: Bearly Limited.

Van Gundy, A. (1992). *Idea power: Techniques & resources to unleash the creativity in your organization.* New York: AMACOM.

Vaux, N. (2002, August). *Norman Rockwell: American illustrator and painter.* Retrieved February 21, 2003, from http://www.lucidcafe.com/library/96feb/rockwell.html

von Oech, R. (1998). *A whack on the side of the head: How you can be more creative.* New York: Time Warner.

Wallas, G. (1926). *The art of thought.* New York: Franklin Watts.

Walters, J. S. (2002). Why dotcoms failed (and what you can learn from them). *The CEO Refresher . . . Brain Food for Businesses!* Retrieved February 12, 2006, from http://www.refresher.com/!jswdotcom.html

Wang, C. W., & Horng, R. Y. (2002). The effects of creative problem solving on creativity, cognitive type and R&D performance. *R&D Management, 32,* 35–45.

Wang, C. W., Horng, R. Y., Hung, S. C., & Huang, Y. C. (2004). The effects of creative problem solving on cognitive processes in managerial problem solving. *Problems and Perspectives in Management, 1,* 101–114.

Wang, C. W., Wu, J. J., & Horng, R. Y. (1999). Creative thinking ability, cognitive type and R&D performance. *R&D Management, 29,* 247–254.

Weisberg, R. W. (1999). Creativity and knowledge: A challenge to theories. In R. J. Sternberg (Ed.), *Handbook of creativity* (pp. 226–250). Cambridge, UK: Cambridge University Press.

Wertheimer, M. (1945). *Productive thinking*. New York: Harper & Brothers.

West, M. A. (1997). *Developing creativity in organizations*. Leicester, UK: British Psychological Society.

West, M. A. (2002). Ideas are ten a penny: It's team implementation not idea generation that counts. *Applied Psychology: An International Review, 51*(3), 411–424.

West, M. A., & Wallace, M. (1991). Innovation in health care teams. *European Journal of Social Psychology, 21*, 303–315.

Wheatley, M. J. (1999). *Leadership and the new science: Discovering order in a chaotic world* (2nd ed.). San Francisco: Berrett-Koehler.

Yammarino, F. J. (1993). Transforming leadership studies: Bernard Bass' leadership and performance beyond expectations. *Leadership Quarterly, 4*, 379–382.

Yoon, L. (2003, April 28). Former CFO now CEO at American Airlines. *CFO .com*. Retrieved October 15, 2004, from www.cfo.com/article.cfm/3009134/c_2984789?f=archives&origin=archive

Zaccaro, S. J., Mumford, M. D., Connelly, M. S., Marks, M. A., & Gilbert, J. A. (2000). Assessment of leader problem-solving capabilities. *Leadership Quarterly, 11*, 37–64.

Zaleznik, A. (1977). Managers and leaders: Are they different? *Harvard Business Review, 55*, 67–78.

Zaleznik, A. (1998). Managers and leaders: Are they different? *Harvard Business Review on Leadership* (pp. 61–88). Boston, MA: Harvard Business Review Press.

Author Index

Subject Index

About the Authors

Gerard J. Puccio is Professor and Chair of the International Center for Studies in Creativity at Buffalo State College, a unique academic department founded in 1967 that offers a master's of science degree in creativity and a graduate certificate in creativity and change leadership. He has published more than 40 scholarly works and delivered more than 40 presentations at conferences and research meetings. As an internationally recognized creativity researcher, he has presented his work in England, Italy, the Netherlands, Canada, France, Singapore, India, and Hong Kong. Recently he was one of the featured speakers in a panel discussion on creativity and intelligence at an international conference sponsored by the French Federation of Psychology to celebrate the 100th anniversary of Binet's work. In recognition of his scholarly efforts, he received the State University of New York award for exemplary contributions to research.

In addition to his scholarly work, he has delivered workshops and consulting services to numerous organizations, including Procter & Gamble, Kraft, Nabisco, 3M, IBM, Fisher-Price Brands, and Rich Products. He has delivered creativity training programs and courses in a number of countries, including Spain, Ireland, Brazil, England, and Tanzania.

He received his doctoral degree in organizational psychology from the University of Manchester, England.

Mary C. Murdock is Associate Professor and a graduate faculty member at the International Center for Studies in Creativity, Buffalo State College, where she teaches graduate courses and supervises master's work. She has international teaching experience as a guest lecturer on qualitative research in the Cognitive Psychology Unit of the University of Bergen and in teaching Creative Problem Solving courses at international schools in five countries (Colombia, Dominican Republic, Tanzania, China, Malaysia).

She is an Advisory Board member of the American Creativity Association (ACA) and founder of the Buffalo–Niagara ACA chapter, a Colleague of the Creative Education Foundation, and past editor of *Celebrate Creativity*, the National Association for Gifted Children's Creativity Division newsletter.

Her publications include two texts: *Creative Problem Solving and Role Playing*, co-authored with E. Paul Torrance, and *Creativity Assessment: Readings and Resources* with Gerard Puccio. She was also a co-editor, along with Center colleagues, of *Understanding and Recognizing Creativity: The Emergence of a Discipline*.

She holds a B.A. in English from the University of North Carolina at Greensboro, an M.Ed. in gifted education, and a doctorate in educational psychology from the University of Georgia.

Marie Mance is Director of Leadership Development at Buffalo State College and an adjunct faculty member at the International Center for Studies in Creativity, teaching in the undergraduate and graduate programs. She holds an M.S. in creativity and M.Ed. in counseling/student personnel. She has traveled internationally to present creativity and creative problem-solving courses and workshops in Nigeria, Singapore, and South Africa. She has also designed and delivered workshops in creativity, strategic planning, and other change initiatives for a number of organizations in the public and private sector. Currently she is developing and presenting leadership programs for faculty, staff, and students at Buffalo State with creativity as a core component. She also coaches in the leadership program and has completed training at the Coaches Training Institute. She is pursuing certification to become a Certified Professional Co-Active Coach. She is President of the Niagara Frontier chapter of ASTD (American Society for Training and Development) and a Colleague of the Creative Education Foundation.